The author of this book suggests that Old Testament scholars should strengthen their growing links with neighbouring disciplines and encourage a plurality of interpretative interests within biblical studies. Given such a pluralist context, Dr Brett's contention is that the new 'canonical' approach to Old Testament study will have a distinctive contribution to make to the discipline without necessarily displacing, as many scholars have assumed, other traditions of historical, social scientific and literary inquiry. The book offers a comprehensive critique of the canonical approach as developed by Brevard Childs, and places this in the setting of recent discussions in literary theory and 'postmodern' theology.

BIBLICAL CRITICISM IN CRISIS?

BIBLICAL CRITICISM
IN CRISIS?

*The impact of the canonical approach on
Old Testament studies*

MARK G. BRETT

*Lecturer in Old Testament,
Lincoln Theological College*

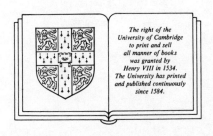

The right of the
University of Cambridge
to print and sell
all manner of books
was granted by
Henry VIII in 1534.
The University has printed
and published continuously
since 1584.

CAMBRIDGE UNIVERSITY PRESS

*Cambridge
New York   Port Chester
Melbourne   Sydney*

Published by the Press Syndicate of the University of Cambridge
The Pitt Building, Trumpington Street, Cambridge CB2 1RP
40 West 20th Street, New York, NY 10011, USA
10 Stamford Road, Oakleigh, Melbourne 3166, Australia

First published 1991

Printed in Great Britain at the University Press, Cambridge

British Library cataloguing in publication data
Brett, Mark G. (Mark Gregory) 1958–
Biblical criticism in crisis?
1. Bible. O.T. Criticism
1. Title
221.6

Library of Congress cataloguing in publication data
Brett, Mark G.
Biblical criticism in crisis?: the impact of the canonical
approach on Old Testament studies / Mark G. Brett.
p.   cm.
Based on the author's thesis (doctoral) – University of Sheffield.
Includes bibliographical references and index.
ISBN 0 521 40119 4
1. Bible. O.T. – Criticism, interpretation, etc. – History – 20th century.
2. Childs, Brevard S. 1. Title. 11. Title: Canonical approach on Old Testament
studies.
BS1160.B68 1991
221.6'01 – dc20   90-40830 CIP

ISBN 0 521 40119 4 hardback

To
May Beatrice Brett
and
Edward Charles Brett

Contents

Acknowledgements

This book is based on doctoral research which was undertaken at the University of Sheffield in the Department of Biblical Studies. I gratefully acknowledge the funding that I received during that period from the University of Queensland, Princeton Theological Seminary, and the British Committee of Vice-Chancellors and Principals. I am also deeply indebted to my wife Susan who supported my study both at Princeton and at the University of Tübingen.

A number of people have made helpful comments on the manuscript in various stages of its production, and I would particularly like to thank Gerald West, John Barton and Louise Foster. Nigel Gotteri kindly offered bibliographical assistance in the area of linguistics. John Rogerson has been a constant source of encouragement, both as a supervisor and since. I would also like to thank Stephen Fowl and Alan Winton for their critical solidarity and for the innumerable edifying conversations over the past six years which have no doubt shaped the following pages in ways that will not be evident from end-notes.

The book is dedicated to my first teachers.

Abbreviations

Am. Anthrop.	American Anthropologist
Am. Hist. Rev.	American Historical Review
Am. J. Theol.	American Journal of Theology
Am. Soc. Rev.	American Sociological Review
Ann. Rev. Anthrop.	Annual Review of Anthropology
BASOR	Bulletin of the American Schools of Oriental Research
BETL	Bibliotheca Ephemeridum Theologicarum Lovaniensium
BZAW	Beihefte zur Zeitschrift für die alttestamentliche Wissenschaft
CBQ	Catholic Biblical Quarterly
Crit. Inqu.	Critical Inquiry
Cult. Herm.	Cultural Hermeneutics
Curr. Anthrop.	Current Anthropology
DVLG	Deutsche Vierteljahrschrift für Literaturwissenschaft und Geistesgeschichte
Ev. Th.	Evangelische Theologie
Expos. T.	Expository Times
Gesch. & Gesell.	Geschichte und Gesellschaft
HBT	Horizons of Biblical Theology
Hist. & Th.	History and Theory
Hist. Zeit.	Historische Zeitschrift
HTR	Harvard Theological Review
IDB Sup.	Interpreters Dictionary of the Bible, Supplementary Volume
IEJ	Israel Exploration Journal
Interp.	Interpretation

JAAC	*Journal of Aesthetics and Art Criticism*
JAAR	*Journal of the American Academy of Religion*
J. Anthrop. Res.	*Journal of Anthropological Research*
JBL	*Journal of Biblical Literature*
JBT	*Jahrbuch für Biblische Theologie*
J. Hist. Ideas	*Journal of the History of Ideas*
J. Ling.	*Journal of Linguistics*
JR	*Journal of Religion*
JSNT	*Journal for the Study of the New Testament*
JSOT	*Journal for the Study of the Old Testament*
JSS	*Journal of Semitic Studies*
JTC	*Journal for Theology and the Church*
JTS	*Journal of Theological Studies*
MLN	*Modern Language Notes*
NLH	*New Literary History*
NTS	*New Testament Studies*
PAS	*Proceedings of the Aristotelian Society*
Philos. & Phenom. Res.	*Philosophy and Phenomenological Research*
Philos. Quart.	*Philosophical Quarterly*
Philos. Rev.	*Philosophical Review*
PMLA	*Proceedings of the Modern Language Association*
PP	*Past and Present*
Relig. Stud.	*Religious Studies*
Relig. Stud. Rev.	*Religious Studies Review*
SJT	*Scottish Journal of Theology*
Sth. J. Anthrop.	*Southwestern Journal of Anthropology*
Stud. Theol.	*Studia Theologica*
SVT	*Supplements to Vetus Testamentum*
TT	*Theology Today*
USQR	*Union Seminary Quarterly Review*
VT	*Vetus Testamentum*
ZAW	*Zeitschrift für die alttestamentliche Wissenschaft*

Introduction: setting the scene

The 1960s was a troubled decade for biblical critics who harboured theological interests. These critics witnessed the decline of an influential school of thought which, especially in the non-fundamentalist circles of North America, Britain and Germany, had promised to bridge the gap between academic studies and the use of the Bible in the churches. During the 1950s and early 1960s, the members of this so-called Biblical Theology Movement argued that theology needed to be governed by biblical categories – or more specifically by 'Hebrew thought' – and that these distinctive categories could be discovered through the critical study of individual Hebrew words and their etymologies. Indeed, even the Greek New Testament was thought to breathe the same Hebraic spirit. At the same time, this movement stressed that the God of the Bible was a God who acted in *history*, and that historical criticism was therefore the most appropriate method of biblical study. Rigorous study of the Bible in its ancient Near Eastern context would serve only to clarify the distinctiveness of the biblical traditions. In short, for the Biblical Theology Movement, the historical and critical study both of the Hebrew language and of Israelite history was of decisive theological significance.

Beginning in 1961, the foundations of this movement were undermined from several directions at once. First, James Barr formulated a detailed and devastating critique of its characteristic linguistic methods. In *The Semantics of Biblical Language*, he demonstrated that both the relevance of etymologies, and the conflation of 'biblical concepts' with particular Hebrew words, were highly problematic issues. Also in 1961, the theologian Langdon Gilkey published an essay[1] showing that several works of Biblical Theology had unwittingly smuggled in decidedly modern philosophical ideas even where they claimed to be thinking only with the categories of Hebraic thought. He also argued that the stress on God's action in history actually masked highly sceptical, although properly critical, conclusions about what actually happened in the decisive acts of God in Israelite history. Two years later Barr pushed this latter problem even further by rejecting the idea that revelation in history was at all central to the Old Testament.[2] Subsequent scholarship seemed only to confirm that the apparently distinctive ideas of the Old Testament were not as distinctive as the Biblical Theology Movement had claimed.

These were the issues that lay behind the publication, in 1970, of Brevard Childs's book *Biblical Theology in Crisis*. In this work, Childs collected the previous criticisms of the Biblical Theology Movement and added many of his own. He also made some programmatic suggestions about how biblical criticism could both move forward from this crisis and remain relevant to the needs of the churches. One of the clearest points to emerge from his writing at this stage (and one which had already emerged in his earlier, more technical monographs) was that biblical theology needed to give up its 'scientific' interest in the historicity of biblical material; he argued that we have no access to historical facts except through the lenses that biblical traditions provide. The attempt to reconstruct critically what actually happened in Israelite history was both doomed to failure on critical grounds and, in any case, theologically uninteresting. What was needed, he suggested, was a biblical theology that explored all the scriptural traditions of the entire Christian canon, comparing and contrasting them without reference to the hypotheses of modern historians of Israel. Moreover, the basic unit of investigation was to be the individual text, not the individual word. Philology was merely the servant of exegesis, and biblical theology (now in the more general sense) was to be primarily an exegetical enterprise.

The question that immediately arose, however, was what *kind* of exegesis? The dominant exegetical disciplines in biblical criticism had laid great stress on the origins and development of the biblical traditions before they came to be arranged in the present form of our received texts. Whether these earlier forms of the material were thought of as literary sources or oral traditions, the effect had been the same: attention had been drawn away from the 'final' or present form of the canonical literature. Exegetical hypotheses were almost invariably focused on the previous life of textual units before they came to be arranged and edited into their present contexts. Although Childs was already a recognized master of these critical historical disciplines, he quickly began to argue that the gap that they created between professional scholarship and the churches' use of the Bible was unbridgeable. Both church and synagogue had always used the canonical literature in its present form, and it is unlikely that they will ever do otherwise. Childs argued, therefore, that the rich resources of critical scholarship should be turned to focus on the biblical literature in its canonical shape and context.

An additional implication of these arguments was drawn out in Childs's commentary, *Exodus*, published in 1974. The historical critical disciplines that dealt with source documents and oral traditions could only provide the *preliminary* basis for what must be the central concern of exegesis – the final form of biblical texts. Many scholars took this concern to be simply a variant of a more recent historical discipline, redaction criticism, that focused on the final editing of the biblical manuscripts. But this was not the case. Childs was not primarily concerned with the intentions or historical settings of these final editors; he was concerned with the meaning of the texts as such, irrespective of what any author or editor might have intended at some particular stage in a text's development.

Childs's methodological statements were often not, however, as clear as one would wish. Moreover, the relationship between his canonical approach and the historical or 'diachronic' disciplines which he continued to use was ambiguous. The diachronic questions of literary sources and oral traditions were treated in the *Exodus* commentary in separate sections from his discussions of the final form. At points, he characterized these discussions of the final form as 'synchronic' to distinguish them from the diachronic exegesis he also provided. In short, there seemed to be an unresolved tension between two different approaches which were being held together in the same commentary.

With the publication of his magnum opus in 1979, *Introduction to the Old Testament as Scripture*, this uneasy tension had turned into an outright polemic against diachronic approaches. He repeatedly argued that his own 'canonical approach' (again, at times characterized as synchronic) resolved a long list of impasses into which historical criticism of the Bible had led us. Moreover, the focus on biblical authors and editors in their historical contexts was misplaced, he suggested, since these authors and editors had deliberately obscured their own merely individual contributions so that successive biblical communities could focus on the text itself. For Childs, the meaning of a biblical text was not simply identical with the historically reconstructed *intentions* of any particular author or editor.

II

I have, so far, outlined the development of Childs's work in terms which are internal to the discipline of biblical studies (although modern theology has been hovering in the wings). But having described the canonical approach in its mature formulation, it now becomes interesting to locate it within the wider context of the philosophy of interpretation. For example, Childs's argument that the meaning of a biblical text is not simply identical with its author's intention has a great deal in common with the literary movement known as New Criticism, a movement which was widely influential during the middle decades of this century. The New Critics also developed a 'formalist' approach to literary texts which set out to read them quite independently of such extrinsic information as the biography or intentions of an author. A poem, for example, was held to be a successful piece of work only if it conveyed its own meaning on its own intrinsic merits. An author, by this view, became simply one other reader once a poem was created.

The connections between New Criticism and Childs's canonical approach were recognized by John Barton in his lucid work on the variety of methods in recent biblical studies, *Reading the Old Testament* (1984). Barton's argument, in summary, is that Childs's approach is 'a natural successor to redaction criticism within a literary climate permeated by New Criticism',[3] although he is careful to point out that this is not Childs's own understanding of the matter. Barton's balanced account of the canonical approach is worthy of careful consideration. However, in the discussion that follows, I hope to show that there is a much wider range of literary theories that might be fruitfully compared with the canonical approach (and literary critics might be relieved to hear this since New Criticism was well past its heyday by the time Childs published his commentary on *Exodus*). Our discussion, as with Barton's, is not simply an account of Childs's scholarly intentions. Nor is it an attempt to evaluate a biblical scholar by 'external' criteria provided by the philosophy of interpretation. Rather, there are certain weaknesses in Childs's methodological reflections which can be *charitably reconstructed* by comparisons with the influential works of Hans-Robert Jauss, Karl Popper and Hans-Georg Gadamer.[4] Childs has received some unjustified criticisms, and I aim to show how the canonical approach can become a coherent mode of biblical interpretation.

The argument of this book will be unfolded in several stages, each addressing the central methodological problems of the canonical approach. First, Childs has sometimes appeared methodologically totalitarian: it seems as if he wants to overwhelm the entire discipline and press everyone into his service. In his better moments, however, even he has expressed more pluralist sentiments. My own argument is that the canonical approach, suitably clarified, should become *one* approach to the Bible among others. Accordingly, my 'pluralist' account of biblical studies, expounded in the first chapter, provides the wider disciplinary context for the canonical approach. In this situation of pluralism we should take care not to conflate interpretative interests that are logically separable. The concern, for example, with an author's intention is one among several interests scholars may legitimately pursue. The newer literary concern with texts as such represents another set of interests. Many of our recent methodological disputes in biblical studies have been confused since we have failed to recognize that the discipline encompasses different kinds of interpretative tasks.[5] Scholars need to be persuaded that no one method, however rigorous, will answer all the questions that may be brought to a text. Thus, the answer to the first problem with the canonical approach, its totalitarian tendency, is to place it in a pluralist context.

After a detailed analysis of Childs's work in chapters 2 and 3, the second major problem emerges: the canonical approach plays down the significance of historical background in the interpretation of ancient texts. In chapter 4 I analyse this issue of historical background and discover two quite separate problems, one of which relates to the interpretation of any culture (not just the biblical ones) and one which is peculiarly theological. Some of Childs's arguments about the irrelevance of historical background are here defended, and others rejected. In the long run it seems fruitless to prohibit scholarly interests in biblical authors and their historical contexts; these are perfectly coherent interests to pursue, even if the results of historical reconstruction are 'merely' hypothetical.

In chapter 5 I argue that Childs's theoretical weaknesses might best be remedied by drawing on Gadamer's philosophical discussion of 'the classic'. Gadamer argues, for example, that what makes a text classic is precisely its influence upon generations later than its author. Neither the author nor the original audience can appreciate a text *as a classic*; its future reception cannot be foreseen. I argue that the interpretation of biblical texts as *canonical* is analogous. If this analogy is accepted, then certain objections to the canonical approach can be refuted. For example, James Barr's insistence that there was no canon in the biblical period becomes an irrelevant criticism of Childs's work.[6] I also argue in chapter 5 that Gadamer's account of the classic, along with Popper's view of objective knowledge, can provide some justification for the low profile in

the canonical approach of both authorial intention and historical background. There is a surprising convergence of these two
philosophers on one point: some texts can and do 'speak for
themselves'.

In some respects, this shift of focus from authorial intention
and historical background brings the canonical approach more
into line with the stress in some schools of literary theory on the
role of the reader. My argument requires, however, that the
canonical approach be distinguished from attempts to write the
history of biblical exegesis. It is, no doubt, continual exegesis
and commentary which preserves a text and gives it the status of
a classic in the first place. However, for a text to *remain* classical it
must engender new and different readings. Although Childs has
been in constant conversation with the interpreters of past ages –
a feature of his writing which distinguishes him from most
Whiggish modern critics – he has always been providing us with
fresh interpretations. His interest in the history of exegesis has
never been simply antiquarian. Indeed, I argue that the history
of interpretation represents a logically separable interest from
contemporary exegesis, no matter how much we may engage in
conversation with great interpreters from the past. Separating
the canonical approach from 'reception history' (a discipline of
literary criticism associated especially with Hans-Robert Jauss)
is important, since although Childs has strongly emphasized the
history of exegesis, the distinctiveness of his approach does not
actually lie in this area. What is distinctive about the canonical
approach is that it provides fresh interpretations of the final
form of scripture, interpretations that are relatively independent of any author, editor or reader in any past situation.

III

Finally, I address Childs's theological interests. None of the
preceding reconstruction of the canonical approach is directly
dependent upon theology, and as a pluralist I would not like to
develop a general theory about exactly what kinds of biblical
interpretation will be useful for the modern church. Nevertheless, in recognition of Childs's emphasis on the theological value
of the canonical approach, this book goes one step further. It

examines the points of contact between Childs's work and a
major school of modern theology (or to use a more technical
term 'postmodern' theology) which has been developed especially by Childs's colleagues at Yale University, Hans Frei and
George Lindbeck. This school has been at the forefront of recent
hermeneutical debates, especially in North America, and Great
Britain. Lindbeck characterizes this theology as 'intratextual', a
somewhat complex notion which at this stage can only be
introduced in barest outline.[7] My argument, however, will be
that the canonical approach can make an important contribution to discussions about intratextuality, and indeed, if it is to
enter into modern theological conversations then it needs to
enter through the door that Lindbeck, among others, has
opened. Biblical scholars cannot go on assuming the normative
value of the Bible in Christianity without actually conversing
with modern *theologians* about the nature of biblical authority.[8]

The notion of intratextuality begins from the now familiar
theory,[9] that a community's perception of reality is decisively
shaped by its cultural tradition, its symbolic framework, and in
some sense by its language. There are different views about how
this lens for viewing reality should be conceived, but a wide
range of social theorists and philosophers suggest that individuals do not have any access to reality except through a socially
constructed interpretative framework that is constituted by
webs of culture, symbol and language. On the basis of this
theory, Lindbeck has constructed what he calls a cultural-
linguistic model of religion, that is, of all religions.

He has also, however, gone one controversial step further. He
has argued that, especially in Christianity, canonical *scripture*
provides the basic material for this cultural-linguistic framework. He makes scripture intratextual in two respects: first,
following Hans Frei, he suggests that it is the figural or
typological reading of scripture that provides the analogical
links between the diverse elements of the canon. Second, it is the
figural reading *of the world* that makes the world intelligible
within the cultural-linguistic framework of Christianity. That is,
scripture itself becomes the interpretative framework through
which individuals and events – both in the biblical period and in

the present – are to be understood. No individual or event referred to in scripture should be reinterpreted independently of this framework; although it may be possible to redescribe historical phenomena by means of non-biblical categories, such modern redescriptions cannot be said to belong to the same tradition of religious belief and practice (or, at the very least, one should say that if biblical conceptualities are to be displaced, then the burden of proof lies with those whose fundamental categories of thought are non-biblical). On this view, critical reconstructions of Israelite history which attempt to go behind scripture, and even critical interpretations of *contemporary* events which are formulated without the aid of scripture, lead to difficulties. In both cases, alternative interpretative frameworks are being conflated with the framework provided by the biblical canon.

This is, as already noted, only a preliminary outline of Lindbeck's views, and it will be filled out in the more extended discussion below. In chapter 6 I will argue that Lindbeck's ideas and those of Childs resemble each other in a number of ways, but one important point needs to be noted at this stage. The idea of intratextuality seems to be not unrelated to the attempt of the Biblical Theology Movement to think with 'biblical categories'. The rather naive theological and linguistic methods of the earlier movement have been replaced with much more subtle arguments, but the overall effect seems to be the same.

Let us not, however, underestimate the differences. First, intratextual theology has no interest in the critical reconstruction of events in the biblical period. This has been given up as an impossible exercise, or at least, an exercise that can never hope to secure public agreement. In line with Karl Barth's theology, intratextual theologians eschew all apologetic strategies of justifying Christian beliefs. Both the public realm and the academy, they argue, are far too fragmented for such strategies to be successful. They characterize themselves as postmodern since they have given up the Enlightenment optimism that all rational agents can come to the same conclusions.[10] This has also been Childs's position for many years.

Second, intratextual theologians are not concerned to recover the intentions or thought-world of biblical times. On the contrary, it is precisely the biblical *texts* which are thought to shape the interpretative framework of Christianity. The new Yale theologians are not dependent on the old etymological approach to biblical concepts; rather, they speak more often of *narratives* as the basic unit of theological significance. Especially Hans Frei has argued that biblical scholars of the nineteenth century lost a hermeneutical opportunity when they ignored the realistic novels written by their contemporaries. Frei has introduced the notion that biblical narrative is more often 'history-like' than it is 'historical'. The meaning of a biblical text, for Frei, is to be located in the realistic narrative itself and not in any supposed historical referents to which the texts apparently point. The critical pursuit of these referents has been the undoing of biblical scholarship.

Frei's argument, in *The Eclipse of Biblical Narrative* (1974), has been influential in recent biblical scholarship, and Childs himself has cited it favourably. I would suggest, however, that in a context of hermeneutical pluralism the question of reference need not be disposed of as quickly as some might wish. Indeed, some have argued that precisely on theological grounds we should be interested in what lies 'behind' the text. For example, what if the biblical canon has, for ideological reasons, seriously misrepresented the events to which it bears witness? The historical detail of what lies behind the text may then become a matter of pressing theological relevance, and this is one of the reasons why the critique of ideology has been much emphasized in recent hermeneutical discussions. I will return to this thorny issue, and to the problem that it represents for intratextual theology, as the details of my argument unfold.

We need to begin by placing the canonical approach within a pluralist understanding of contemporary biblical studies.

CHAPTER I

Distinguishing interpretative interests

CHILDS VERSUS GOTTWALD

The first problem with the canonical approach is its totalitarian tendency; Childs has sometimes argued as if everyone should become interpreters after his own image. At other times he envisions a more pluralist situation for biblical studies. The argument of this chapter is that the second Childs is to be preferred. Our discipline now includes a whole range of interpretative interests which are logically distinct, and it is indeed questionable whether biblical studies should be thought of as a single discipline at all. Some might feel that this diversity of interests amounts to a crisis in biblical studies[1] that will resolve itself in one direction or another. But it seems more likely that our different interpretative goals will turn out to be permanently incommensurable. It is clear, however, that a number of our current methodological disputes are confused by a failure to recognize our plurality, and this especially applies to the work of Childs. First, he has attacked some positions which he need not have, and second, he has tried to include too many different tasks under the label of the canonical approach.

As an example of a confused attack, consider his recent comments on materialist approaches to the Hebrew Bible – those which place biblical texts against a reconstructed background of environment, technology, economy, and sociology. Childs argues, for example, that the work of Norman Gottwald 'destroys the need for closely hearing the text on its verbal level' (1985: 25).* Gottwald has responded, almost predictably, by

---

* All references to Childs's works are keyed to the section on Childs following the main bibliography.

saying that Childs fails to account for the sociological matrices within which all texts are shaped.[2] Taken at face value both these arguments border on being tautologies; what we have here is first and foremost a conflict of interpretative interests and not a substantive conflict about method at all. To put the point another way, the statement of an interpretative goal logically precedes any question of method.[3] Only where a dispute centres on a single, clearly defined goal does it become *purely* methodological. Otherwise the situation is more complicated: we disagree about what constitutes an appropriate interpretative interest, or about the priority of different interests.

At the deeper level, then, the dispute between Childs and Gottwald turns on the appropriateness of their respective interpretative interests. Childs thinks that 'hearing the text on its verbal level' is a superior goal to placing it in a reconstructed social or material environment. Why does he think this? I suggest that the crux of the matter is for him theological: he thinks that any scientific attempt to go 'behind' the text compromises the theological value of the Bible (and in this view he seems to be following the theology of Karl Barth).[4] We should be grateful to Gottwald, Childs suggests, for making this theological issue clear. Gottwald's cultural materialism is simply a more radical and consistent version of any attempt to gain a privileged scientific access to the forces at work behind the biblical text (1985: 24–5). Childs, on the other hand, stands within the circle of canonical tradition and

rejects a method which is unaware of its own time-conditioned quality and which is confident in its ability to stand outside, above and over against the received tradition in adjudicating the truth or lack of truth of the biblical material according to its own criteria. (1985: 12)

He regards any such attempt as merely speculative, its historical contingency being all too quickly unmasked by subsequent interpreters. Moreover, he often seems to be critical of any kind of objective description of biblical texts which fails to account for the normative role of the biblical literature (1974a: xiii).

James Barr has suggested that there is a spirit of anti-objectivism in Childs's work that has contributed in some measure to the popularity of the canonical approach.[5] He also thinks that there is a middle ground, neglected by Childs, between self-confident objective certainty and outright anti-objectivism. Barr is clearly right on this point, and a defence of such a middle ground will be provided below. This issue of objectivity, however, is focused only on the kind of epistemological self-consciousness that biblical critics ought to have. There is another important difference between Childs and Gottwald which, as has already been indicated, has more to do with interpretative interests than with epistemology. I will argue that between these two scholars there is another option on the 'methodological spectrum'; there is another style of social science with a different kind of interpretative interest. A clear grasp of this non-materialist *via media* will also help to clarify the distinctiveness of the canonical approach.

The main point here is that the canonical approach should not be tied to any attacks on critical, historical reconstruction. It is not always necessary to overwhelm alternative interests, and this is a case in point. It would be far better simply to articulate the distinctive goal of the canonical approach and allow other interpreters to pursue their own interests in relative isolation. The results of these independent research programmes may well turn out to have wider implications, but we should not expect all biblical research to be commensurable in the way that historical-critical methods (meaning here source, form and redaction criticism) ought to be. If Childs's critique of scientific objectivity is one of his strategies in cutting off alternative approaches to the Bible, then a methodological pluralism will need a balanced account of objectivity.

OBJECTIVITY AS TIME-CONDITIONED

According to Childs, all attempts to go behind the biblical tradition in order to reconstruct scientifically the real truth of the matter are doomed to failure; they reflect an unawareness of their 'time-conditioned quality' (1985: 12). This argument raises at least two questions: (a) if the force of Childs's argument rests on a contrast, then what kind of interpretation is *not* time-conditioned? and (b) would an *awareness* of the time-conditioned nature of one's historical reconstruction make any substantive difference to one's hypotheses?

In answer to the first question, Childs seems to have no account of biblical interpretation that would resist the eroding power of time. On the contrary, he has himself argued that there is no such thing as a timeless interpretation, but the inference he draws from this view is purely theological: 'The challenge to hear the Old Testament as God's word in a concrete definite form for one's own age carries with it the corollary that it will be soon antiquated' (1974a: 438; cf. xvi). The only contrast that we are left with here is one between canonical interpretation and scientific interpretation; he recognizes that both are time-conditioned.

One would need to conclude, then, that it is an *unawareness* of the time-conditioned nature of historical reconstruction that is the real problem with scientific approaches like Gottwald's. But this second implication of Childs's argument is just implausible. One would be hard-pressed to find anyone who thought that the value of science lay in its capacity to provide results that will stand forever. Even if one restricted one's attention to only anti-relativist philosophies of science, one would be driven to the same conclusion.

Consider the work of an exemplary anti-relativist, Karl Popper. Popper has repeatedly argued that we can never claim to have demonstrated the truth of a theory with absolute finality. Before Einstein's innovations appeared, for example, Newton's work on gravity seemed incontrovertible. Yet, Popper suggests, it is unlikely that there ever will be a theory so well established as Newton's. Even a relatively secure view can tell us nothing about the degree of corroboration it is likely to enjoy in the future. All scientific results are 'relative' to the state of critical discussion thus far. Even the most widely held view which has survived over the longest period is not immune.

To put it in a nutshell: we can never rationally justify a theory – that is, claim to know its truth – but we can, if we are lucky, rationally justify a preference for one theory out of a set of competing theories, for the time being; that is, with respect to the present state of the discussion.[6]

In short, 'we must regard all laws or theories as hypothetical or conjectural'.[7] Science is not rendered invalid by its 'time-conditioned quality' nor by its lack of absolute certainty.

If Popper can say this about the so-called hard sciences, the paradigm of sound knowledge, then any criticism of historical reconstruction as 'merely hypothetical' needs to be severely qualified. I would suggest, in line with Popper, that we can and should distinguish between better and worse hypotheses about ancient Israel, but we cannot dispose of all such hypotheses *simply because they are hypotheses*. If this, as it appears, is what Childs is doing then we should part company with him. It would be more responsible simply to articulate the distinctive interest of the canonical approach and allow historians to get on with their own chosen tasks. As we shall see, even amongst sociological historians these tasks are not all of a piece. There is an important *via media* between Childs and Gottwald.

EMICS AND ETICS: NATIVE TALK AND TALK ABOUT NATIVES

We have already seen that, according to Childs, a materialist approach to the Bible 'destroys the need for closely hearing the text on its verbal level'. Behind this rhetorical formulation lies an important grain of truth, and it will be instructive at this point to examine another very similar, but much clearer, criticism of Gottwald's work.

J. W. Rogerson has recently examined Gottwald's *Tribes of Yahweh* in the light of some methodological distinctions developed by W. G. Runciman. Runciman argues that there is no special problem of 'explanation' in the human sciences, but there is a special problem of 'description'. That is to say, models of explanation developed in the natural sciences can, according to Runciman, be easily transferred to sociology, anthropology and history, but there is a special problem in these latter disciplines of *describing the actors' point of view*. Historians and social scientists have two logically separable tasks: in addition to explaining an event or process, they can also attempt 'to describe what it was like for those involved in it'.[8] Rogerson criticizes Gottwald for obscuring just this distinction. It is one thing to *explain* Israelite faith in socio-economic and techno-environmental terms, it is quite another to *describe* that faith as a native Israelite would have understood it. Rogerson thinks that materialist sociology belongs to the category of explanation and biblical theology to the category of description; Gottwald has unnecessarily 'demythologized' the latter into the former.[9]

It is certainly true that Gottwald's overall emphasis is on explanation, indeed, on *law-governed* explanation (i.e., historical explanation which accounts for events and processes by applying general, probabilistic laws). This is because he regards law-governed explanations to be the most scientific way of dealing with history, and on this point even some non-Marxists would agree.[10] But it is not simply that he has confused two separate tasks. It is rather that the results of the one task have become the object of the other: the beliefs of ancient Israelites are one part of a variety of historical materials that need to be explained. Gottwald is quite clear on the conceptual distinction, although he uses a different vocabulary. He characterizes cultural materialism as 'etic' and the description of Israelite beliefs and practices as 'emic'. These terms were developed by social theorists on analogy with the distinction between phonemics (which describes the significant differences between the sounds of speech as perceived by native speakers in their own linguistic system) and phonetics (which describes scientifically all the sounds of human speech irrespective of whether particular native speakers would describe their language in these technical terms):

The terms 'emic' and 'etic' in ethnological theory were coined by the linguist Kenneth Pike on analogy with phon*emic* and phon*etic*. *Emics* refers to cultural explanations that draw their criteria from the consciousness of the people in the culture being explained . . . *Etics* refers to cultural explanations whose criteria derive from a body of theory and method shared in a community of scientific observers . . . Etic statements cannot be verified or falsified by what cultural actors think is true, but only by their predictive success or failure . . . etics makes room for emics insofar as what cultural actors think about their action is part of the data to be accounted for in developing a corpus of predictions about lawful social behaviour.[11]

Thus, Gottwald recognizes that there are actually two separate interests here, but if we paraphrase his view in the Runciman/Rogerson vocabulary, the results of the descriptive interest should become data for the explanatory interest.

One does not have to be a materialist to see the methodological force of this argument. It is only a contingent fact about the development of social science that, in Gottwald's view, the best etic approach so far happens to be cultural materialism. There are, indeed, other kinds of scientific or 'non-native' explanation, but the validity of etics as a general methodological category seems irrefutable. Just as specialists in phonetics use scientific terms like 'labial' or 'dental' so historians will often need a metalanguage (i.e., an analytical vocabulary of which ordinary language users need never be aware). For example, we may possess information about ancient economic processes which was unavailable to the biblical authors, and we are quite justified in using it in historical explanation. If it seems that ancient societies lacked the concept of an economy it by no means follows that they were never influenced by economic forces, just as if they lacked the concept of malaria it by no means follows that they could never have died from it. Such modern conceptions only become anachronistic where the goal of inquiry is a *descriptive* or *emic* one.[12]

There are, however, social scientists who regard the pursuit of law-governed explanations as a distraction, and for them the descriptive task is the most important. The anthropologist Clifford Geertz has been a highly influential spokesperson for this non-materialist tradition, and the following passage from his *Interpretation of Cultures* is characteristic;

It is this maneuver, usually too casually referred to as 'seeing things from the actor's point of view', too bookishly as 'the *verstehen* approach', or too technically as 'emic analysis', that so often leads to the notion that anthropology is a variety of either long-distance mind reading or cannibal-isle fantasizing, and which, for someone anxious to navigate past the wrecks of a dozen sunken philosophies, must therefore be executed with a great deal of care. Nothing is more necessary to comprehending what anthropological interpretation is, and the degree to which it *is* interpretation, than an exact understanding of what it means – and what it does not mean – to say that our formulations of other people's symbol systems must be actor-oriented.[13]

Geertz speaks for many in the so-called interpretative (or as North Americans prefer 'interpretive') tradition of social science who have reacted against the law-governed explanatory strategies of earlier anthropologists and sociologists.

This interpretative tradition will be examined further in chapter 4 below, but my argument for the moment is this: it is a mistake to attempt to resolve the conflict between emic and etic social science since these actually represent separate interests. The first, emics, is concerned with describing events, meanings, symbols or processes from the native's point of view. Etics is concerned with providing scientific accounts of these things, whether the natives could accept these accounts or not. Not all etic accounts are as materialist, or as law-governed, as the social theory of Gottwald and Harris; an etic *methodology* does not necessarily undermine the possibility that human beliefs and actions can be significant causes in history and not just the epiphenomena of material conditions. The methodological distinction turns on the final court of appeal – the native communities or the scientific communities. As long as the reference groups are clear, one could abandon the technical terms and speak of native 'explanation' or scientific 'description'. In the present context, however, it will be simpler to retain these technical terms.

It should be clear, then, that emic or interpretative social science provides a middle way between Gottwald and Childs. 'Hearing the text on its verbal level', as Childs puts it, is an ambiguous metaphor that could mean at least two things: (a) hearing the text as an expression of an ancient Israelite point of view, and (b) hearing the *text itself* in a way that is relatively independent of the ancient Israelites who produced it. Childs's canonical approach is more a matter of 'hearing' the *text itself*, but this point has sometimes been confused with descriptive or emic historical interests both by others who call themselves canonical critics and by Childs himself.

CANONICAL CRITICISM VERSUS THE CANONICAL APPROACH

At one point in his *Introduction to the Old Testament as Scripture* Childs tells us that he wants to describe 'the features of this peculiar set of religious texts in relation to their usage within the historical community of ancient Israel' (1979: 73). This misleading statement, and others like it, have given rise to a number of misunderstandings. First, it is manifestly the case that ancient Israel did not use *the final form* of the Hebrew text since this was not stabilized, according to Childs himself, until the end of the first century CE (1979: 97). Moreover, he argues that we do not have enough evidence to reconstruct historically the formation of the canonical literature. The debate about canonization, he suggests, is just one more example of the impasses into which historical methods have led us (1979: 68). This sceptical view clearly separates him from 'canonical critics' like J. A. Sanders who have provided us with just such reconstructions of the biblical canon in the making. It is a misunderstanding to assume, as many have done, that the canonical approach rests on early dates for the formation of the Hebrew Bible. In addition, Childs places no great stress on the order of the canonical books or their precise number (cf. 1970a: 99).[14] His preference for the *Hebrew* text rather than the Greek Bible rests, as we shall see, more on theological considerations than on historical ones.

It follows from all this that exegesis focused on the final form of the Hebrew text cannot simply be identified with a description of the texts used by actual communities during the biblical period, and still less with a description of those communities themselves. Childs's references to the function of scripture in communities of faith are misleading in this respect. J. A. Sanders has correctly grasped this point and concluded that Childs effectively denies the importance of those very communities who preserved the text during the biblical period.[15] Canonical criticism, as practised by Sanders and others, is held to be superior in overcoming this problem.

I would prefer to say that Sanders and Childs have different interests, and Childs has therefore been right to resist the label of canonical criticism for his own work. Although many biblical scholars do not distinguish between 'canonical criticism' and the 'canonical approach', this distinction is crucial if we are to attain any clarity on the issues at stake. Sanders cannot be refuted by claiming that his reconstructions of the canonical process are merely hypothetical. All historical works are hypothetical, but that does not stop us from distinguishing between better and worse ones. Childs, on the other hand, is trying to provide us with fresh interpretations of the final form of *scripture itself*, interpretations which are relatively independent of any particular editor or community which has preserved it.

Such a formalist characterization of Childs's work should not, however, overlook the fact that his exegetical interest is actually founded on an account of editorial motives. He argues that even *before* the stabilization of scripture 'the tradents consistently sought to hide their own footprints in order to focus attention on the canonical text' (1977: 68). The canon is a literary collection from all the biblical generations, and it preserves a long historical process of critical theological reflection. The final form 'alone bears witness to the full history of revelation' (1979: 76). In reading the final form of the text itself we therefore, according to Childs, preserve the 'intentions' of its editors.

There are two different arguments here that require separate attention. First, the canon does indeed include the literary traces of a long historical conversation. Whether we should call this a 'full history of revelation', however, begs a number of important questions which we shall leave to one side for the time being. The complexity of traditions that are preserved in the Hebrew canon reflects a feature of most literate cultures and not just of the Israelite one. All living cultures are in a state of continual evaluation and adjustment, but in literate cultures we would expect to find textual traces of *earlier* evaluations and adjustments while in oral cultures these are more likely to be forgotten over the course of time. Consider the following passage from the anthropologist Jack Goody. Literate tradition, he writes,

grows continually, and in so far as it effects any particular individual he becomes a palimpsest composed of layers of belief and attitudes belonging to different stages in historical time . . . From the standpoint of the individual intellectual, of the literate specialist, the vista of endless choices and discoveries offered by so extensive a past can be a source of great stimulation and interest; but when we consider the social effects of such an orientation, it becomes apparent that the situation fosters . . . alienation . . . Such coherence as a person achieves is very largely the result of his personal selection, adjustment and elimination of items from a highly differentiated cultural repertoire.[16]

Historical critics, and also canonical critics like Sanders, are intellectuals who find the complexity of the Hebrew canon a source of stimulation and interest; they want to identify the origins of all its cultural traditions and reconstruct the details and order of their synthesis. The canonical approach, on the other hand, accepts the selections and adjustments that have been made and pays attention to the final result – the Hebrew canon of the first century CE.

TRADITIONS, 'INTENTIONS' AND TEXTS

To say that the canonical approach is focused on the final literary deposit of the Hebrew Bible raises a number of conceptual problems which shall be dealt with in due course. But to mention perhaps the most obvious one, can we really make sense of a *text in itself* in relative isolation of the agents who produced it? In chapter 5, I shall use a combination of arguments from Popper and Gadamer to say that we can, but some preliminary distinctions need to be made at this stage that will clear the ground for this later argument.

First, Old Testament scholars have long recognized, at least in discussions of 'traditional material', that a biblical text sometimes preserves a kind of meaning that is relatively independent of the *individual* agents who produced it. This is quite clearly the case, for example, in Hermann Gunkel's classic work on Gen. 1 in *Schöpfung und Chaos*. In this study, Gunkel argued that Gen. 1 preserves a large number of traces of earlier mythological material, and moreover, that the early life of these traces was unknown to the Priestly writer of Gen. 1. The first chapter of Genesis is, on Gunkel's influential view, a 'deposit of tradition' and not the free construction of the Priestly author.[17]

Similarly, in his classic *History of Pentateuchal Traditions*, Martin Noth distinguished the various 'themes' of the traditional narratives and associated these with sites or areas of Israelite tribal territory. He was not able, however, to reconstruct from this material any specific intention of a particular narrator, the specific occasion of a performance, an audience or a time. In spite of its impressive scope, Noth's study amounts to an investigation of *collective* meanings, meanings that were common to a great number of narrators, occasions and audiences. He writes:

> Owing to the lack of concrete knowledge of details such as names, places, circumstances, times, and the like, one must say a great deal impersonally and passively about origin and growth, about the transmission and elaboration of traditions . . . And yet in all of this we are never dealing with impersonal and passive processes but with highly personal and dynamic actions. The only thing is that we have no adequate way to describe these actions since knowledge of the acting subjects is lacking.[18]

In the course of oral transmission 'the individual signature is always getting rubbed out'.[19]

This kind of argument has been taken by Childs to its extreme. He has no wish to deny that the biblical materials were produced by acting subjects, it is just that the historical reconstruction of these acting subjects is for him inevitably speculative. Even given Noth's modesty, *A History of Pentateuchal Traditions* says more than the evidence allows. In line with Noth, Childs suggests that the Bible has been constructed by many unseen hands, and its texts preserve only collective meanings that are available for interpretation. But unlike Noth, the canonical approach does not pursue the earlier life of collective meanings before they were arranged and edited into their present contexts.[20]

Childs, however, has also argued that the tradents of the biblical tradition deliberately obscured their individual contributions to the text in order that later generations should focus on the text itself. He suggests that in reading the final form we preserve the self-effacing 'intentions' of its editors to address future readers. I shall argue below that the canonical approach should not be founded on this dubious premise, but a preliminary discussion is in order at this stage. Let us imagine for a moment that Childs was correct in his view that the biblical editors deliberately sought to obscure their own historical situations and their own merely individual contributions. This kind of view would seem to require a distinction between communicative 'intentions' which are embodied in the text and prior 'intentions' which are not. The distinction is a simple one, but it needs more discussion than Childs actually devotes to it.

The word 'intentions' is in scare quotes in the previous paragraph because it trades on an ambiguity. Not all authorial (or editorial) intentions are *communicative intentions*. Very often an author has *motives* that for one reason or another do not come to expression. The clearest case of this is lying, as E. D. Hirsch points out in *Validity in Interpretation*:

If part of the verbal meaning of a lie were that it is false, then there would be no point in telling a lie . . . We do not say that someone has misunderstood a lie when he is taken in by it. He has understood it only too well; the liar's verbal meaning has been successfully communicated.[21]

Hirsch concludes that authorial intention – in the sense relevant to exegesis – is not identical with all the intentions and motives of an 'actual historical person', but only with that part of the author 'which specifies or determines verbal meaning'. Discovering that a piece of communication is a lie is, to use Hirsch's terminology, a matter of 'significance' and not verbal meaning, a matter of placing that verbal meaning within a larger context.

Lying is, then, a clear case where the motives of an author are not explicitly embodied in the text. One can easily think of other authorial motives which may be equally irrelevant to verbal meaning, e.g., the motives of making money, gaining prestige, reinforcing one's power, establishing social identity, and so on. An author's *communicative intention* can, according to Hirsch, be understood without a reader knowing all aspects of the 'intentions' that lie behind the text. But Hirsch has gone one step further even than this.

At the time of writing *Validity in Interpretation* Hirsch was still anxious to defend the role of the author, 'the actual historical person', in determining the verbal meaning of a text; he was simply concerned in his argument about lying to clarify imprecise references to an author's intention that could be easily rejected as semantically irrelevant. In more recent work, however, he has begun to consider an issue that is relevant to Childs's view of the biblical editors: what about the 'intention' of authors to address *future* readers? Does this have any bearing on what would count as verbal meaning?

The new Hirsch has been persuaded by Saul Kripke that we 'typically intend to speak truly and to fix a reference to some sort of human or natural reality'[22] (lying would be the exception that proves the general rule). Since we generally speak 'provisionally and under correction', reference can be 'adjusted' to suit new circumstances. In Hirsch's view, the intention to address future readers is characteristic of literature, law, and religion, although it is also nascent in face-to-face communication; speakers and writers generally intend their statements to have future, if not foreseeable, relevance.[23] Language in general is 'designed for broad and continuing application'. We recognize that we are limited human beings and actually intend our verbal meanings 'to transcend our momentary limitations of attention and knowledge':

Thus, while it is true that later aspects of verbal meaning *are* fixed by its originating moment in time, that moment has fixed only the *principles* of further extrapolation, and these will not cover with full determinacy all unforeseen possibilities.[24]

This is a most remarkable concession to make for a literary critic who not long ago upheld the rights of authorial intention against the leading exponents of 'autonomous', textual meaning, T. S. Eliot, the New Critics and, in a different critical tradition, H. G. Gadamer. Hirsch is now prepared to accept that texts can in themselves bear meaning that was never part of the original author's consciousness. He used to insist that 'there was no magic land of meanings outside human consciousness', but he is now ready to say that there *is* a land of meanings beyond consciousness, 'the land of the future'. These future meanings of a text are not, however, radically indeterminate, as some would have it; rather, these future meanings are not *exhaustively* determined by the original author's consciousness. But as two critics of the new Hirsch have rightly pointed out:

> the intention to communicate with future readers is so general and so different from the matter of *what* is to be communicated (the particular meaning or intention to be embodied) that for purposes of understanding a text's meaning we need to separate the two kinds of intention.[25]

If there is such a general 'intention' of addressing future readers and situations, it is surely not an integral part of communicative intention in the strictest sense. It is, indeed, quite common to find that in the light of a new situation, or new evidence and arguments, authors may discover fresh implications in their texts. But why should these new reflections and fresh implications justify a new understanding of their *original* meaning?[26] Are not these fresh implications a matter of Hirschian 'significance' generated more by the text itself than the original intention? It would seem much more coherent to conclude that the 'intention to address future readers' has the logical status of a *motive*, rather than of a communicative intention. As already mentioned, motives are not in themselves a part of verbal meaning.

It is not necessary at this point for us to examine all the implications of Hirsch's new position. Some of the issues will be taken further in chapter 5, but a few observations are immediately relevant. In a similar way to the new Hirsch, Childs believes that the Hebrew canon is the literary deposit of a long critical process in which authors and editors spoke 'under correction' in their constant strivings for truthfulness before God; they intended the texts to have 'broad and continuing future application', and for this reason, their own conscious intentions do not cover 'with full determinacy' the unforeseen possibilities of textual meaning. Accordingly, the canonical approach focuses on the text itself rather than authorial or editorial consciousness. But in spite of these affinities between Childs and the new Hirsch, I will argue that the canonical approach cannot rest upon a theory of 'intentions to address future readers' that are not actually embodied in the text itself.

On the contrary, it needs a theory of relatively autonomous texts. Fresh readings of a classical text may draw implications that can find no justification in the intentions of its authors or editors. This view would be in line with a more formalist Childs who sometimes discovers canonical meanings 'irrespective of intentionality' (1979: 79, 259, 661; 1985: 49). But my theoretical defence of the canonical approach will first need a more detailed account of Childs's exegetical practice.

At this point we need to draw together the conclusions of this chapter. I have argued that the canonical approach has a distinctive interpretative interest which should be distinguished both from etic approaches like Gottwald's as well as from emic approaches that attempt to reconstruct historically the beliefs and practices of ancient Israel as native Israelites would have seen things. Childs stands much closer to emic attempts to 'hear the text on its verbal level', but his attention is focused on the final form of the text itself.

CHAPTER 2

The development of canonical exegesis

THEORY AND PRACTICE

I have so far characterized the canonical approach in the following terms: it may be understood as a new type of interpretative interest (most closely related to, but distinguishable from, emic description) which, for theological reasons, seeks to interpret biblical texts in their final form. In reaching this formulation I have drawn from the work of Childs in a highly selective way, and this *ad hoc* method of reconstruction finds its justification in the fact that Childs himself has failed to provide a coherent exegetical theory. That is to say, he has not yet provided a sufficiently clear and explicit discussion of the interpretative interests and concepts that shape the canonical approach. This lack of coherent theory has turned out to be one of the major obstacles to a balanced appreciation of his work.[1] Nevertheless, a reconstruction of the canonical approach cannot be undertaken simply on the theoretical level; it also requires a patient account of Childs's actual exegetical practice. To rephrase a famous philosophical attack on metaphysics: practice without theory is blind, theory without practice is empty.

Discussions of Childs have tended to focus on his publications since *Biblical Theology in Crisis* (1970). It would certainly be a mistake to assume that, given a sufficiently sensitive reader, an author's work (in this case extending over thirty years) can always be knitted together into a seamless whole. Nevertheless, I would suggest that there are certain elements in Childs's work which have been present ever since his early studies on myth, published in 1960. Since this time he has consistently

27

advocated 'emic' goals for Old Testament studies, although he has never used the technical term itself. In his earlier work he employed phenomenological, form-critical and traditio-historical methods, always with an emphasis on 'the native point of view'. Before discussing the mature formulations of the canonical approach it will therefore be of some interest to look at Childs's early monographs *Myth and Reality in the Old Testament* (1960), *Memory and Tradition in Israel* (1962) and *Isaiah and the Assyrian Crisis* (1967). It is possible to find in these works Childs's early attempts to use emic methods in formulating the task of biblical theology.

CHILDS'S EARLY MONOGRAPHS

Although my discussion of Childs's work will follow a roughly chronological order, a strictly chronological discussion would be too limited for the purposes at hand. There is no necessary path of development from the early monographs to the later work, rather, it is only in the light of the later work that certain lines of continuity may be discerned retrospectively. The analysis of this chapter will therefore by guided by the 'mature' statements of the canonical approach without thereby suggesting that Childs's later work can be read anachronistically into his publications during the 1960s. I would suggest that there are at least four principles of biblical interpretation at work in the early monographs which reappear in different ways in Childs's later studies. These principles are: (a) the progressive refinement of biblical tradition; (b) the privilege of 'theological reference'; (c) the need for theologically 'constructive' as well as descriptive exegesis; and (d) a formalist tendency in treating ambiguous historical reference.

The progressive refinement of biblical tradition

Childs has never defended a doctrine of 'progressive revelation' (cf. Childs, 1974a: 495). Such a doctrine would always give a higher normative value to the New Testament. Rather, he has insisted that *Christians* should read the Old and New Testaments in the light of each other, not that the New Testament has a heavier deposit of pure revelation. There is, nevertheless, an implicit doctrine of 'the progressive theological refinement of biblical tradition' in Childs's work. This is quite clearly reflected in his later idea that the prehistory of the biblical text is always subordinate, both exegetically and theologically, to the final form. Although Childs's emphasis upon the final form did not emerge with any clarity until the 1970s, the idea of progressive refinement was already present in his early work on myth.

In *Myth and Reality in the Old Testament* Childs examined the extent to which mythological ideas have found their way into the Old Testament. The main texts at issue in this monograph are Gen. 1: 1–2, 3: 1–5, 6: 1–4, Exod. 4: 24–26, Isa. 11: 6–9, 14: 12–21. In each case it is argued that foreign material has been assimilated only after a long period of theological struggle, only after the myth has been 'broken'.

In the case of Gen. 1 Childs accepts Gunkel's view, argued in *Schöpfung und Chaos* (1895), that there was an infiltration of Babylonian myth early in Israel's history. The assimilation of this material, however, was not achieved without signs of struggle and tension. For example, Childs finds (following Gunkel) Old Testament texts in which the anarthrous word *tᵉhôm* 'points to' an original proper name, the Hebrew equivalent of Tiamat, and to a primeval battle which initiates creation. Isa. 51: 9–10 is cited as an example of this usage (1960: 37),[2] although Childs later blurs the issue by speaking of this text as a 'similar tradition of chaos in an earlier stage of demythologizing' (1960: 42). This statement makes it unclear whether Isa. 51: 9–10 should be thought of as part of an independent though 'similar' tradition, or rather – as Gunkel thought – as a link in the chain of a *single* creation tradition.[3] In any case, Childs argues that the Priestly writer of Gen. 1 stands at the end of a process of assimilation which slowly destroyed the original Babylonian myth, transforming it into a new theological framework. Thus, for example, although the anarthrous word *tᵉhôm* ('deep') has been retained in Gen. 1: 2 it is taken to be a vestige without significance. The independent life once in the word has been 'demythologized' to such an extent that without the parallels from comparative religion, its mythical origin would have passed unnoticed . . . It is evident that such a tremendous change did not come about without a long history of struggle. (1960: 42)[4]

Childs's solution to the problems of Gen. 1: 2 is in effect a synthesis of the opposing approaches earlier taken by Gunkel and Wellhausen. Childs seems to agree with Wellhausen that the long prehistory of the creation myth constructed by Gunkel is largely irrelevant to the exegesis of Gen. 1; the vestiges of this prehistory are 'without significance'. But the reasons why the mythical prehistory is subordinate to the priestly intention are not simply bound up with Wellhausen's source-critical method of exegesis. Childs is quite willing to see a long prehistory behind Gen. 1 but he draws his own peculiar inference from its reconstruction: it is to be seen as a long process of *critical theological reflection* in which the tradition is progressively refined. He is therefore anxious to recover the theological integrity of biblical authors. The priestly writer, for example, was 'far too precise' to retain any 'half-digested' mythical fragments without good reason. Hence, Childs sees the chaos motif as being intentionally retained by P in order to bear witness to a 'threatening possibility', the 'negative' side of creation (1960: 43; cf. 50, 56, 58, 72, 96).

Wherever Gunkel finds a 'treasury of mythical vestiges', Childs finds skilled theological assimilation, particularly in Gen. 1 : 2 and 3 : 1–5. In other texts where an original myth is not so well appropriated (this is conceded in the treatments of Gen. 6 : 1–4 and Exod. 4 : 24–26) Childs is careful to stress 'the decisive points at which the demythologizing process had set in' (1960: 96). What is at stake for Childs is a struggle between two different 'concepts of reality', the mythical and the biblical (1960: 39). This opposition is developed especially in his fourth chapter where 'mythical' categories of space and time are contrasted with 'biblical' categories of space and time. This chapter contains a number of ideas belonging to the Biblical Theology Movement which Childs later came to criticize in *Biblical Theology in Crisis* (1970).

Whatever the continuing validity of Childs's bold hypotheses concerning mythical and biblical minds, it is interesting to note that he advocates a kind of emic approach both to the study of myth as well as to the Bible. He stresses that his monograph sets out to avoid 'foreign categories' and 'Western presuppositions' (1960: 8). His treatment of myth therefore rests on *phenomenological* description, and it resists 'philosophical,[5] historical, form-critical, or aesthetic' categories (1960: 16). In other words, he is – at least ostensibly – trying to understand both biblical and mythical categories on their own terms. Thus he cites approvingly Malinowski's account of myth as not simply a fiction, but 'a living reality, believed to have once happened in primeval times' (cited in Childs, 1960: 19).

Childs's attempt to provide an emic account of both mythical and biblical categories is associated with some notable theological conclusions about the nature of reference. These theological conclusions introduce a series of tensions into his work which, unfortunately, he has never analysed in any detail.

The privilege of theological reference

As early as *Myth and Reality in the Old Testament* Childs had developed a notion of 'divine' or 'theological' reality which was explicitly *not* identified with historical reality as reconstructed by modern sciences.[6] The early Childs could argue, for example, that the Old Testament constituted a unified witness to the reality of a New Israel (1960: 97–8). He is careful to stress that this witness was formed within historical Israel, within the development of her institutions and traditions. Foreign myths which opposed this vision of reality had to be 'broken' in the process of their assimilation. But Childs adds a significant qualification to the idea that the witness to this new reality was formed within historical Israel:

Biblical reality is not found in some external divine action. There are no 'objective events' which can be divorced from the particular colouring of Israel. We cannot penetrate 'behind' Israel to find reality. Only as it is reflected in the experience of this people do we have access to it. (1960: 99)

N.b. biblical privilege

This is an early formulation of an idea that Childs would reiterate in several different ways in his later work, and with reference to several different philosophical and theological authorities.[7] The basic position which he has consistently maintained is that 'biblical' or 'theological' reality cannot be scientifically demonstrated. Whatever truth our historians recover, it is not a theological truth if it is arrived at independently of the received biblical traditions. Israelite tradition is, according to Childs, the exclusive 'witness' to theological reality; it is the privileged means of referring to this reality. This claim naturally led Childs into conflict with those scholars of the Biblical Theology Movement who stressed the theological relevance of archaeology (e.g. 1962: 85; 1970a: 49; 1974a: 204).

From his earliest work onwards Childs has, in effect, attempted to hold together two different theories of reference. He has spoken of theological reference in terms of 'witnessing' or 'pointing' to divine reality. The second theory of reference is more straightforwardly connected with the historical background of biblical texts. He has, for example, consistently refused to allow historicity to become a criterion of theological reality. Such a criterion would be etic, and for him 'an extrinsic norm of historicity makes neither literary nor theological sense' (1979: 62; cf. 1967a: 124; 1974a: 229). Especially in his later work one finds many critical remarks on 'referential readings' which are concerned only with historical realities. Indeed, in the later work, it is only the received biblical tradition of the final form, refined by a long critical theological discussion, which is seen as possessing referential privilege. In *Memory and Tradition* he argued that although successive generations of Israelites had reinterpreted the same events the later layers of tradition were on the same level as the first in terms of their theological value (1962: 89).

This is not to say that the Old Testament contains no history writing.[8] Rather, Childs is concerned simply to focus on the content of biblical tradition, whether modern historians support its historicity or not. This view was already formulated in *Myth and Reality*:

Can the reality of which the Old Testament speaks be restricted to 'objective history'? Is this an attempt to penetrate behind Israel's formulation of her experience to the 'real events'? Does not this approach allow historical criticism to restrict the realm into which reality can appear? . . . By rejecting modern categories in a search to find reality, we are made receptive to Israel's own categories by which she expressed her existence. In saga, in legend, the broken myth, through these unhistorical vehicles as well as through the historical, Israel articulated her understanding . . . reality is tied to every part of her total life, not just to events possessing confirmed historicity. (1960: 102–3; cf. 1979: 158)

Descriptive and constructive exegesis

Given that Childs has constructed, at least implicitly, two different theories of reference, an important question now arises: exactly what role does historical criticism have in discerning 'theological reality'? Can it refer to, or speak about, this reality at all? Childs begins to answer this question by saying that

Historical criticism . . . determines the historicity of events recorded, and classifies the material into its various literary forms . . . In other words, historical criticism is a descriptive science. With its tools it cannot pass a value judgement on the reality to which the Bible addresses itself. (1960: 104)

The opposition here between historical 'facts' and theological 'values' is, however, somewhat misleading. It becomes clear that the basic issue at stake has as much to do with theological truth claims as it does with value judgments. But having restricted the access of historical criticism to the domain of historical realities he must introduce the notion of a 'constructive' or 'confessional' exegesis. In *Myth and Reality* Childs introduces his confessional stance in the most uncompromising way. He does not even entertain the idea that the Hebrew scriptures may have a theological validity of their own. The final criterion for theological reality is simply a Christian confession of faith; the Old Testament is even said to be 'theologically meaningless' apart from the New Testament (1960: 98, 105).

By the time Childs came to speak of a 'canonical approach' to the Old Testament his view had thankfully become much more subtle. The path toward this more subtle view was, however, paved with misunderstandings. In his article 'Interpretation in Faith', he called for a theological exegesis with an 'explicit framework of faith' which included consideration of the New Testament (1964: 436, 438, 440). This unfortunately created the impression that genuine 'theological' exegesis was necessarily Christian, an implication which Childs attempted to dispel in the conclusion of *Isaiah and the Assyrian Crisis*:

such a confessional stance does not necessarily claim to be the only context from which the Old Testament can be read . . . However, the claim is being made that the *theological* norms of *Christian* theology can only emerge from the context of Christian Scripture, that is, Old and New Testaments together. (1967a: 127)

It should be clear from this quotation that Childs's confessional stance has not claimed *a priori* privilege (cf. 1970a: 99, 112–13). Theological norms can, according to Childs, be developed from within *different* theological traditions, but these traditions will move beyond the limits of the Hebrew scriptures in themselves. 'Constructive' or 'theological' exegesis operates within the context of these larger traditions:

For Judaism it was the oral and written tradition of the Synagogue Fathers; for Christianity it was the apostolic witness to Jesus Christ. (1967a: 127)

Childs seems to be saying that when it comes to the constructive task, both Judaism and Christianity are equally justified in using a larger theological 'context'.[9] These larger contexts imply a movement beyond purely descriptive exegesis of Hebrew scripture in itself, without arriving at 'arbitrary dogmatism' (1967a: 126).

There is more to be said about the relationship between descriptive and 'constructive' exegesis, but we will defer further discussion until we consider Childs's later work. For the present we may observe that for the early Childs the subject matter of descriptive exegesis (meaning here historical criticism) seems to be historical realities, while the ultimate subject matter of constructive exegesis is 'theological' reality. These two domains of reality are neither identified nor entirely separated; they remain in tension.

historical crit + Theology

The preceding discussion has, however, traded on an ambiguity in the term 'historical criticism'. The quest for historicity is not the only kind of historical interest pursued by historical critics. One thinks, for example, of the study of literary genres as well as of the reconstruction of Israelite tradition. Both of these tasks can be seen as purely descriptive, rather than 'constructive', and they are both represented in Childs's early work. However, in carrying out these predominantly emic tasks he developed some distinctive views on the problem of historical reference, an issue to which we now return. I will argue that even in his early work Childs often tended to adopt a New Critical formalism in his approach to historical reference. In order to appreciate this tendency, and to clarify my claim, we need first to look at a clearer case of formalism in the *Introduction*.

Formalism and ambiguous historical reference

One of the most controversial issues taken up by reviewers of Childs's *Introduction to the Old Testament as Scripture* was the treatment of Second Isaiah. Childs pointed out that, unlike the Book of Amos, Isa. 40–55 is almost devoid of specific historical references; it contains at best scattered vestiges of its original setting. The reference to the Persian king Cyrus functions more as a 'theological projection' which blurs into the description of Abraham' in 41: 8ff. The oracles which originally functioned in a specific context in the sixth century have, in the course of their 'canonical shaping', been detached from this historical situation:

In their collected form as sacred writings the oracles did not serve primarily as historical records of a prophet's lifework, but as a continuing message of God's plan for his people in all ages. (1979: 327)

To make exegesis dependent on a reconstruction of Second Isaiah's original historical references would be, according to Childs, to misconstrue the theology of the final form.[10] Thus, the ambiguity or vagueness of any historical reference in Isa. 40–55 (including references to the enigmatic 'servant') is not to be sharpened by reconstructing the original background of the text. Just as Gunkel found mythical vestiges in Gen. 1 so Childs finds

historical vestiges in Second Isaiah. One methodological principle of the canonical approach is that such vestiges of textual
prehistory, including original historical references, are of minimal significance for exegesis of the final form.[11] Already in the
earlier work of Childs we find some similar views.

In his study on the motif of 'the enemy from the north' in
biblical tradition, he discusses a number of prophetic texts
which provide no direct evidence of the actual identity of the
enemy. He emphasizes this opacity even with respect to certain
texts in Isaiah where the evidence points more clearly to Assyria
as the referent in mind. After conceding this point, Childs goes
on to insist that 'there remains a certain element of indetermin-
ation' in Isaiah's description (1959: 191). He also explicitly
criticizes those who have treated the subject as primarily a
problem of historical reference, suggesting that 'the development of the enemy motif within Israel's *tradition* has not been
adequately treated' (1959: 187).[12] This kind of opposition
between tradition and historical reference also underlies his
later monograph *Isaiah and the Assyrian Crisis*.

Childs begins this monograph on the Assyrian crisis by raising
the question of how the message of Isaiah relates to the actual
invasion of 701. He shows how the conflict of source material,
both inside and outside the Bible, had led to an 'impasse' in
historical study. In particular, he criticizes John Bright for a
tendency to treat 'all the biblical passages on a similar plane of
historical verisimilitude' (1967a: 18; cf. 119). In the light of this
impasse, Childs undertakes a form-critical analysis of the
relevant traditions:

> Even if the historical problem proves in the end again to be insoluble in
> the light of the evidence, this does not preclude an understanding of
> how Israel's traditions regarding the events developed . . . The
> problem in the history of tradition is distinct from the problem of
> determining historicity. (1967a: 19)

Indeed, Childs ends up concluding that his study intensifies the
historical problems rather than alleviating them; the biblical
texts are judged to be 'inarticulate for the particular concerns of
the modern historian' (1967a: 118). But these historical problems in no way restrain Childs's *exegetical* confidence.

His treatment of Isa. 22: 1–14 provides a notable example. In this case the typical form of an 'invective-threat' has been 'fractured by means of a dominant historical reference'. Nevertheless,

It is a false move to attempt to correlate the text with some historical event and on the basis of this alleged relationship to interpret the text. Equally misleading is the attempt to reconstruct an event which harmonizes with the accounts in 2 Kings 18–19. Such techniques usually result in supplying the crucial links and in blurring the actual witness of the text which is being examined. Isa. 22 simply does not provide the necessary information which would allow it to be related directly to a known historical event. (1967a: 26)

Childs is reluctant to concede that historical reconstruction may have exegetical relevance, even where that reconstruction is based on other biblical texts (cf. 1967a: 120). Indeed, he holds that questions asked by modern historians have 'obscured the understanding of the manner in which the texts themselves really function'. Israelite reflection upon the Assyrian crisis forms a complex web of tradition which provides no direct access to the historical facts. 'In principle', he concludes, 'most portions of the Bible are involved to some degree with a similar exegetical issue' (1967a: 121–3).

Already at this point in the development of Childs's exegetical practice his own version of form and tradition criticism had led him to embrace, at least implicitly, a key doctrine of New Critical formalism: 'external' evidence is not to be used in making the supposed referents of a text more precise. It is interesting to note that in their classic essay on New Critical methodology Wimsatt and Beardsley saw external evidence as actually

private or idiosyncratic; not part of the work as a linguistic fact: it consists of revelations (in journals, for example, or letters or reported conversations) about how or why the poet wrote the poem – to what lady, while sitting on what lawn, or at the death of what friend or brother.[13]

From a formalist perspective, the *specific* referent of the text – the person or event which a poet or prophet 'had in mind' – cannot be used as evidence for interpreting the text unless the text itself provides this warrant.

The early Childs implicitly held a similar view when he tied exegesis to Israelite tradition rather than to historical referents as reconstructed by 'external' evidence (including, as we have seen, even referents reconstructed from other biblical texts). The later Childs was to come even closer to formalism by suggesting that *even if* we could be certain, on traditio-historical grounds, that a sixth-century prophet had a specific referent 'in mind', this referent is not relevant to the exegesis of that prophet's words as they stand in scripture. Even where specific historical reference cannot be denied, as Childs concedes with respect to the Book of Amos, he holds that it is the text which interprets history and not history which interprets the text. This is, however, to anticipate one of the arguments of the *Introduction*. Having retrospectively perceived these anticipations of the canonical approach in Childs's early work, we can now move on to examine his mature statements on the disciplines of commentary, 'introduction' and Old Testament theology.

EXODUS: A 'CANONICAL' COMMENTARY

Childs's commentary, *Exodus* (1974), may be considered a mature statement of the canonical approach. The idea of a 'confessional' biblical theology of both Testaments had been expressed already in his earliest work, but it took some years for a distinctive canonical approach to emerge. He quickly recognized that the brief article 'Interpretation in Faith' (1964) was inadequate and that his ideas would require elaboration in another monograph (1967a: 127). His next major study in this area was *Biblical Theology in Crisis* (1970), but this book was much clearer in expressing Childs's view of previous biblical theology than it was in formulating his own approach. *Biblical Theology* still did not have any clear advocacy of final form study. There is evidence in the work of a growing interest in 'synchronic' interpretation (1970a: 46, 98, 109), but Childs does not endorse interpretation that is 'text-bound in the sense that the text has authority separated from the reality of which it speaks' (1970a: 103). The clear stress on final form study emerged only in his unpublished Sprunt Lectures of 1972 (cf.

Childs 1973: 90) and became 'the heart' of the *Exodus* commentary (1974a: xiv).

The commentary is organized into a standard format of six sections: (1) translation, textual and philological notes; (2) literary, form-critical and tradio-historical issues; (3) Old Testament context; (4) New Testament context; (5) history of exegesis and (6) theological reflection in the context of the whole Christian canon. In each chapter of the commentary, the focus of section (3), 'Old Testament context', is on the final form of the text. But the heading is somewhat misleading. 'Exodus context' might have been more accurate since many of the references to other books in the Old Testament are simply comparative in nature, and they have no direct bearing on the final form interpretation. Others are form critical and could just as easily have been placed in section (2). In fact, the main focus seems to be on the *immediate* context of the text in Exodus. The wider context of the whole Old Testament canon is more often considered within the framework of section (6), 'Theological Reflection'.

Let us consider, however, two examples where Childs *does* go beyond the text of Exodus and refer to another biblical book in order to interpret the final form. In his reading of Exod. 1, he suggests that the thrust of the story is this:

The sons of Jacob increase miraculously in accordance with the divine promise (Gen. 12) . . . The tradition marks the transition from being members of a large family to the emergence of a nation in the period of Egyptian slavery. (1974a: 14–15)

Notice, however, that Exod. 1 does not actually speak of a 'nation' as does Gen. 12: 2, and indeed the promise to Abraham of miraculous increase is not really made specific in Gen. 12 but rather in Gen. 13, 15 and 17. One would expect a section on 'Old Testament context' to mention at least Gen. 15: 13–14 where the promise to Abraham seems to include a reference to slavery in Egypt (cf. 1985: 218). In his discussion of the history of exegesis, Childs mentions that pre-modern commentators had related Exod. 1 to Gen. 1: 28, and indeed the Hebrew vocabulary of Gen. 1: 28 matches the vocabulary of Exod. 1: 7 much better than the vocabulary of Gen. 12; in being 'fruitful',

'multiplying' and 'filling' the land the Israelites were fulfilling
the divine command of Gen. 1: 28. Yet, surprisingly, Gen. 1: 28
does not rate a mention in Childs's own final form reading of
Exod. 1. What could account for these oversights?

In spite of the 'synchronic' emphasis of the final form reading
it seems that Childs may have kept one eye on the results of
diachronic reconstruction. His discussion of the 'Old Testament
context' of Exod. 1 refers only to Gen. 12, a text commonly taken
to be the *earliest* (i.e. Yahwist) account of the divine promises to
Abraham. Since the bulk of 1: 8 – 2: 10 is assigned to the earliest
sources, either the Jahwist or Elohist documents, Childs appears
unwilling to make connections with material in Genesis that is
considered later than these sources. The pre-modern connection
between Exod. 1: 7 and Gen. 1: 28 is accounted for by source
critics by assigning both to the later work of P, and accordingly
the relevance of Gen. 1: 28 for the final form reading is passed
over in silence. Similarly, Gen. 15: 13–14 is often taken to be a
later addition and this too is overlooked. In short, Childs's
reference to Gen. 12 could have been defended on purely source-
critical grounds; he seems reluctant to point out connections
that might run against the chronological grain. The sense in
which this is 'synchronic' interpretation of the 'Old Testament
context' is not at all clear.

A similar point could be made with respect to Childs's final
form reading of the renewed call of Moses in Exod. 6: 2–13. Here
he remarks that 'The reference to God's revelation of himself as
El Shaddai immediately calls to mind Gen. 17: 1 ff. and the
covenant between Abraham and God' (1974a: 115). Again
there is nothing new here; both texts are commonly understood
as Priestly. Most of the observations in Childs's final form
reading of Exod. 6: 2 – 7: 7 could have been found in an
historical-critical commentary.

The point of these examples is to show that there is a
considerable overlap between the material contained in sections
(2) and (3) of the commentary; many of the final form
observations could have been included under the heading of
'Literary, Form-Critical and Tradio-Historical Problems'. In
this respect Childs is justified in describing section (3) of the
standard format in the following way:

This section attempts to deal seriously with the text in its final form, which is its canonical shape, while at the same time recognizing and profiting by the variety of historical forces which were at work in producing it . . . the study of the prehistory has its proper function within exegesis only in illuminating the final text. (1974a: xiv)

It may be true that in practice Childs is drawing on the results of historical research to produce his final form readings, but the pressing question here is this: can the canonical approach give rise to a *distinctive* style of research while it remains so heavily dependent on historical results? In what sense would it differ, for example, from redaction criticism (which also attempts to read the final form while preserving chronological scruples)?

There is, indeed, an ambivalence to historical study in the *Exodus* commentary that has led to conceptual problems. When, for example, Childs argues that the prehistory of the text is at times relevant to understanding 'the synchronistic dimension' of the final form (1974a: xiv), then I would argue that the distinctiveness of his approach has become clouded by unclear thinking. I do not, however, think that these problems are insoluble. The next section seeks to show that an awareness of methodological pluralism would clarify things a great deal.

Pluralism and monism in hermeneutics

There seem to be two competing attitudes toward historical study in the *Exodus* commentary, and I would argue that one of these is much more coherent than the other. The coherent attitude I shall characterize as hermeneutical 'pluralism', and the incoherent one, hermeneutical 'monism'. The pluralist attitude would suggest that there are different types of exegesis, depending, for example, on whether one has diachronic or 'synchronic' interpretative goals.[14] On the pluralist view, synchronic interpretation of the final form can be performed without chronological scruples; it could make use of connections made by historical critics as well as connections prohibited by them. Hermeneutical monism, on the other hand, would suggest that all biblical interpreters are doing basically the same kind of thing only with different emphases; all results should be commensurable in the end. On the monistic view, final form readings cannot conflict with the findings of historical critics, and conversely, historical critics cannot transgress the findings of final form critics.

Here are two examples of a pluralist tendency. (1) In his discussion of the redaction of the plague narratives in Exod. 7: 8 – 11: 10 Childs argues that 'Often the synthetic approach has been used apologetically against source criticism with little understanding of the different levels of the text which are being discussed . . . However, to show a larger pattern which cuts across the sources does not disprove their existence' (1974a: 149–50). (2) In his discussion of the passover narrative Childs addresses the problem of relating Exod. 12: 1–20 and 12: 21–8 in a similar way: 'The controversy between the positions of Cassuto and Bacon lies in failure to clarify properly the context from which one is speaking. If one is addressing the historical issue of the development of passover, it is essential with Bacon to see the diachronistic dimension of the various texts in ch. 12 . . . Nevertheless, Cassuto is correct in defending the coherence of the text when read from a synchronistic perspective' (1974a: 199; cf. also 366, 372).

Unfortunately, Childs is more often a hermeneutical monist. For example: 'Ultimately the use of source and form criticism is exegetically deficient if these tools do not illuminate the canonical text' (1974a: 149). Similarly, in his introductory statement on final form interpretation, he argues that 'the study of the prehistory has its proper function within exegesis only in illuminating the final text' (1974a: xv). This suggests that in the last analysis all exegesis aims to interpret the final form.

There is a sense in which this is uncontroversially true: historical-critical exegesis begins with the final form and then proceeds to provide diachronic solutions to the puzzles which the text contains. But such diachronic hypotheses are not synchronistic readings of the final form as such, rather, they are concerned with the history of the text's development. Childs seems to appreciate this point in his more 'pluralist' moments, but the monistic final form critic is often responsible for some confused arguments. It will be instructive at this point to examine some of these less happy examples of the canonical approach in practice.

Textual prehistory and final form

Childs points out in his traditio-historical discussion of Exod. 6: 3 that the names of God in this verse, notably El Shaddai, have provoked much discussion regarding the form of patriarchal religion. But he concludes that 'the historical question in its modern form is obviously foreign to the perspective of the biblical author' (1974a: 114). Childs then goes on to talk about the passage in its canonical shape without attempting any penetration into Israel's history of religion: the renewed call of Moses in Exod. 6 should be viewed as 'a sequel, not a parallel to the call in Midian'. It now serves as a confirmation of Exod. 3.1ff. The hermeneutical pluralist could agree with all this and then go on to argue that the diachronic questions are still as pressing as ever. Where did the divine name El Shaddai come from? Is this not a puzzle that historical hypotheses, however conjectural, might illuminate? Whether the redactor knew of this prehistory could well be irrelevant; Exod. 6 is not the only source of evidence relevant to the traditio-historical question.

We find another kind of monism in Childs's reading of the call narrative in Exod. 3: 1 – 4: 17. In his form-critical and traditio-historical analysis he focuses in particular on the problem in 3: 12 where God replies to Moses' protestations in the following way:

I will be with you, and this will be the sign for you that I have sent you: when you have brought forth the Israelites out of Egypt, you shall worship God on this mountain.

To what does the demonstrative pronoun 'this' (*zeh*) refer? The most obvious grammatical solution is reflected in the translation: the reference is to the worship of Yahweh on Mount Horeb after the liberation from Egypt. But what kind of 'sign' comes only after the event?

In order to solve this problem Childs undertakes a form-critical study of 'signs' in the Old Testament. He finds two types of sign: (a) an historical event that precedes, and has some affinities with, a future event which is threatened or promised; (b) an extraordinary event that confirms the appointment to an office. Exod. 3 does not, however, fit either of these patterns, but

Childs develops an elaborate theory that utilizes his form-critical hypothesis. First, he draws on Gressmann's suggestion that the burning bush originally belonged to a local etiology which legitimized a holy place. Then he argues that the adaptation of this etiology to the biblical call narrative had, unfortunately, to place the 'sign' before Moses' objection. Given these two premises the form-critical analysis then comes into play: the present call narrative participates in both types of sign. The burning bush both confirms Moses' appointment (type b) and, in the light of subsequent events after the liberation, prefigures 'the devouring fire at Sinai' (type a). Childs concludes that 'Once this has been seen, the final form of the text becomes transparent' (1974a: 59–60).

Whatever one might think of this hypothesis, its role in section (2) of the commentary is methodologically quite proper. However, it reappears again in section (3), the final form reading. A theoretical basis for 'synchronistic' reading is here reiterated with admirable clarity: understanding the earlier traditions cannot be substituted for a reading of the interplay of elements which are fused in the present text as a result of 'skillful design' (1974a: 72). But then Childs goes on to say of 3: 12 that it needs to be understood in the light of its 'historical dimension'; the verse refers to the burning bush, which itself confirms Moses' prophetic commission and participates in the future of a redeemed people (1974a: 74). The connection with Sinai is not defended by means of a close reading of the Sinai narratives but by means of a traditio-historical hypothesis. Childs had earlier argued concerning 3: 12 that 'to refer the demonstrative to the burning bush runs into a . . . difficulty grammatically' (1974a: 56). In other words, if the final form of the text is referring to the burning bush then this cannot be defended as 'skillful design'. The final form has become 'transparent' by means of a strategy quite familiar to historical critics; the text contains puzzles which are solved by recourse to diachronic reconstruction.

It is possible that the final form of 3: 12 is in the last analysis grammatically opaque, or, as Noth suggests, that the 'sign' here has somehow fallen out of the text. But it would be methodologically quite responsible simply to accept that we have here a

form-critical anomaly and read Exod. 3: 12 as it stands: the sign
is a future confirmation that Moses' call is authentic. We should
remember that from the perspective of the final form this sign is
framed by the extraordinary event of the burning bush, and the
other miraculous signs mentioned in 4: 1–7. The evidence of
Yahweh's power and will is not restricted to a future event.

In spite of Childs's theoretical disposition towards hermeneutical monism, we would argue that he provides no
persuasive examples of traditio-historical results clarifying a
synchronic reading. The very idea seems conceptually confused.
He is much more coherent in his pluralist moments. Nevertheless, it may be argued that there is a class of texts which may be
fruitfully read 'synchronically' *precisely because* their prehistory is
impossibly complex. This point has been made especially by
structuralists with reference to traditional, orally transmitted
texts such as myths, legends and folktales.[15] Since the individual
signature is always being rubbed out in the process of oral
transmission, anthropologists and folklorists have thought it
worthwhile to pay attention to narrative *structures* as well as to
the individual intentions of story-tellers on particular occasions.
Childs has formulated at least one final form interpretation that
reveals a similar strategy.

In his analysis of Exod. 16, the provision of manna and quails
in the desert, he concludes that all attempts 'to find in the
present order an intentional purpose of an author' have failed
(1974a: 278). His own solution moves in another direction: the
order of Exod. 16: 1–12 reflects a *traditional* pattern in the
Priestly source, parallels of which may be found in Num. 14 and
16. This traditional pattern, he suggests, 'explains to a large
measure the lack of logical sequence within Exod. 16: 1–12'.
Behind the literary sources of Exod. 16 lies 'an oral stage which
did much to shape the tradition' (1974a: 279–80). This thesis
reappears in his final form reading of the same text: the present
sequence 'belongs to a traditional pattern for the disputation
between the murmurers and the covenant officers to precede the
theophany' (1974a: 287). However, the textual prehistory of
Exod. 16 involves some other problematic elements as well, and
Childs goes on to conclude that 'The abrupt handling of the quail

[in 16: 13–21] leaves the narrative in somewhat an unresolved tension which reflects the complex history of tradition behind the story'.

In the light of this example we might be able to arrive at the following methodological conclusion: synchronic final form readings cannot use diachronic reconstructions without lapsing into confusion. Nevertheless, a final form interpretation may be more tolerant of logical tensions if there is evidence of historical 'development' behind the text, development which may be postulated on the basis of narrative roughness or reconstructed 'traditional patterns'. (At the same time, we should remember that even individual authors, ancient or modern, can frequently be shown to be opaque, inconsistent or stylistically rough.) In other words, the canonical approach may leave behind some residual opacities in biblical texts.

One more example of confusing 'final form' with 'textual prehistory' may be useful at this point. In his exegesis of the second commandment in Exod. 20: 4–6 Childs finds that the 'historical dimension' of this text is a necessary part of his final form interpretation (1974a: 406): first, the syntactical difficulties in v. 4 reveal a secondary expansion of a short prohibition, possibly in response to renewed challenges from Canaanite religion; second, there has been a redactional enclosing of the second commandment within the first. As if conscious of the difficulty in using diachronic reconstruction in his final form reading, Childs concedes that 'one must be cautious not to overstate the certainty with which the different levels of tradition can be distinguished' (1974a: 406–7). I would argue that epistemological certainty is in this context entirely beside the point. The real problem here is that Childs has not given a final form reading of the second commandment at all. He has allowed the evidence of prehistory to defuse a synchronic reading – precisely the problem he attributes to historical critics.

It may well be the case that, due to the constraints of the method, properly synchronic readings will leave a number of textual puzzles unsolved. We will return to this issue below, but one further point about hermeneutical pluralism is relevant at this stage. I have suggested that historical-critical method cannot be brought in the back door *of the canonical approach* to solve the puzzles left over after a synchronic reading. This does not, however, imply that diachronic and synchronic methods cannot mutually influence one another. Diachronic studies obviously do make connections that can also be relevant to a final form reading; the *Exodus* commentary provides numerous examples of this. But close, final form readings are also likely to raise fresh questions for traditio-historical research. Childs touches on this point only once (1974a: 339), without providing examples, and he seems more anxious to defend the rights of historical criticism against the inroads of synchronic methods (e.g. 1974a: 149–50, 199, 276). In the next section, however, I shall try to provide an example of a final form reading that might contribute to the discussion of historical questions.

Rereading Exodus 4: 24–6

Consider the notorious problems of Exod. 4: 24–6. The final form gives no explanation for the fact that Yahweh suddenly attempts to kill one of the male travellers on the way back to Egypt – just which male traveller is not at all clear. The event seems highly ironical since Yahweh had just instructed Moses in 4: 19 to 'Go back to Egypt, for all the men who wanted to kill you are dead'. In any case, Zipporah is the protagonist, and Childs translates vs. 25–6 as follows:

[25]Then Zipporah took a piece of flint, and cut off her son's foreskin and touched his feet with it, saying. 'You are a blood-bridegroom to me!' [26]So he let him alone. At that time she said 'blood-bridegroom' in reference to the circumcision.

Childs claims that the dominant critical concern with the 'original' meaning of this passage has obscured the redactor's intention (1974a: 98). But even this redactional intention proves elusive, for he concludes that

the effect of this redaction is at least to *imply* that it was the failure of Moses to have the child circumcised which evoked the attack. Otherwise why would the circumcision of the child have spared his life? In sum, the traditional interpretation of the 'pre-critical' period reflects, to a large extent, the redactor's perspective. (1974a: 101, italics added)

Previously he had noted that modern critics rejected this solution in part because the circumcision command of Gen. 17 is commonly dated as post-exilic (1974a: 96), but now he suggests that Exod. 4: 24–6 reveals that circumcision was already important 'at this early date'. (We are left wondering why God was more lenient on the uncircumcised generation of the wilderness wanderings mentioned in Jos. 5.)

There is, however, another way of reading the final form. After setting the scene in Exod. 1 the narratives in chapters 2–4 are full of anticipations of things to come. First, the birth story, with its ironic twists, implies that Yahweh has a special interest in this particular Levite child. Then comes the failed attempts of Moses to act justly on behalf of his people (2: 11–15). But he is not long a failed administrator of justice: he 'saves' (2: 17) and 'rescues' (2: 19) Reuel's daughters after his flight to Midian. The Hebrew words used here are to become key terms in the subsequent narrative. Then Moses receives a divine call, and readers are introduced to the remarkable 'rod of God' which is to reappear many times. After being sent back to Egypt with the miraculous rod (4: 20) we have a speech from Yahweh that anticipates the final plague. Moses is given a message from Pharaoh: if Israel – the firstborn of God – is not released, then Pharaoh's firstborn son will be killed (4: 22–3).

Yahweh's attack on the male traveller follows immediately on this message for Pharaoh, but the blood of the circumcision averts the threat. Surely this text, like the bulk of Exod. 2–4, is anticipatory: it brings to mind the passover blood which similarly averts a divine threat.[16] There is certainly no suggestion in the text that Moses had disobediently neglected a prescribed age of circumcision for his son or sons (4: 20 suggests that Moses was travelling with his wife and sons, yet vs. 24–6 mention only one son[17]).

A number of factors need to be considered here. In spite of the grammatical difficulties, the immediate context of Exod. 4: 24–6 suggests a play on the word 'firstborn'; Israel is the firstborn of Yahweh; the firstborn of Pharaoh is threatened, and by implication we might infer that the firstborn of Moses and Zipporah is also proleptically threatened. This would make

Gershom the target of Yahweh's attack. Indeed, the feminine pronoun in v. 25, '*her* son', would seem unnatural if Moses was under attack; '*his* son' would have connected Zipporah's action with an attack on Moses more clearly. Childs subscribes to the popular view that Moses was the target of the attack, and then remarks: 'One could wonder why the child is designated *her* son' (1974a: 103). This particular problem disappears if it was not Moses who was under attack.

There is another clue in the verb 'touched' that connects this passage with the passover event and the killing of the Egyptian firstborn sons: the verb in its hiph'il form, as it occurs here, reappears only once more in the Book of Exodus, in the command of Moses to 'touch' or 'smear' the blood of the passover lamb on the Israelite lintels and doorposts (12: 22).[18] Moreover, the passover regulation which follows immediately after the narrative of the passover event deals with the law of circumcision as a precondition of celebrating the feast (12: 43–9).

I am suggesting, then, that Exod. 4: 24–6 anticipates the passover. But the objection will be raised immediately that this reading has not dealt with all the puzzles in the text; we have not accounted for the old crux 'blood-bridegroom'. Childs suggests that the sentence in 4: 26, 'At that time she said "blood-bridegroom" in reference to the circumcision', is redactional. Moreover, he concludes that the redactor seems not to have understood what the phrase *ḥᵃtan damîm* meant (1974a: 100, 104). The redaction is explanatory in a very limited sense: it neither clarifies the phrase *ḥᵃtan damîm*, nor who is being addressed. It simply stresses that the key feature of the event was circumcision. This leads Childs to his conclusion that the text simply dramatizes this key feature; Moses has been held culpable for not circumcizing his son.

This conclusion, however, underestimates the active role given to Zipporah and neglects the problematic *ḥᵃtan damîm* altogether. Whatever the difficulties of this phrase, one may plausibly infer that it has something to do with kinship, and more specifically, that it has something to do with relation by *marriage*.[19] The focus of this phrase would seem therefore to be on

Zipporah's relationship with her husband rather than with her son. Perhaps we can go further than to suggest that the obscure actions of Zipporah serve to stress the full allegiance of this Midianite wife to Moses and to his religious practices. Through circumcising *her* son the foreigner expresses solidarity with Moses and at the same time anticipates the subsequent events of the first passover.

It is interesting to note that the passover regulations of Exod. 12: 42–9, inserted immediately after the passover event, prescribe the circumcision of *foreigners* as a precondition for their participation in the feast. The name 'Gershom' is also pertinent to the foreigner theme since Moses named the child with the explanation 'I was a stranger in a foreign land' (2: 22). Although Childs recognizes this explanation as 'traditional' (cf. Exod. 22: 21, 23: 9; Deut. 23: 7–8, which all refer to Egypt as the 'foreign land' where the Israelites lived in the past), he follows the majority of commentators in assuming that the 'foreign land' is Midian and translates the explanation in a more ambiguous perfect tense: 'I have been a stranger in a foreign land'. But this naming of Gershom seems doubly poignant in Exod. 2: 22 if we take it to be referring to Moses' experience in Egypt. At this early point in the narrative Moses had not only become alienated from his Egyptian guardians but also from his own people. This double poignancy is lost if we simply assume that the referent of 'foreign land' in 2: 22 is Midian rather than Egypt. But whatever one concludes about this particular issue, it is clear that both Zipporah and Gershom point to the issue of 'foreignness' in Exod. 4: 24–6.

We are now in a position to return to the question which motivated my rereading of the passage: can a final form interpretation contribute to the historical-critical discussion of Exod. 4: 24–6, or has the reading above made historical-critical study redundant? I would suggest that it is still possible to raise a number of historical questions. Even if it is true, for example, that the redactors and users of the text of Exodus did not understanding the 'original' meaning of the term *ḥᵃtan damîm*, there is nothing to prevent hypotheses concerning its meaning in the context of Semitic rites of circumcision. Childs has persuasively argued that the text in its present form is not an etiology, but to use one of his own pluralist arguments, this does not exclude the possibility that similar etiological stories were known to, and adapted by, the original biblical author.

Two further hypotheses might be based on my reading: (a) Childs accepts the idea that this pericope may be assigned an 'early date' (1974a: 101). But what if the connection between passover and the 'firstborn' was also early? In his traditio-historical discussion of passover and exodus, Childs draws attention to the arguments of those scholars who suggest, against Martin Noth, that one cannot derive the apotropaic protection of the passover from the tradition concerning the firstborn (1974a: 190). This was an important link in Noth's reconstruction of the exodus traditions which several scholars have sought to break. Would my own final form reading support Noth's position? In the long run it may not, but there is at least the *possibility* that a final form reading might well contribute to the reopening of traditio-historical questions. In my view, there are good reasons to think that Exod. 4: 24–6 provides a connection between firstborn and passover.[20]

(b) If my stress on Zipporah's allegiance to Moses and to his religious practices is justified, could there be any implications here for earlier social functions of this story? One possibility invites itself. Num. 12 suggests that Moses' authority was questioned by Miriam and Aaron; they drew attention to his Cushite/Midianite wife. We also seem to have an anti-Midianite text in Num. 25 where Phinehas, the grandson of Aaron, stops a plague amongst the Israelites by killing a Midianite woman. This story might be construed as legitimizing the Aaronid priestly line over against the Mosaic (Gershomite) priestly line connected with the tribe of Dan (Jud. 18: 30). If this line of interpretation has any validity, then Num. 12 and Exod. 4: 24–6 could be understood together as stories which *reinforce* the authority of Moses (and thereby of Gershomite priests): he could not be impugned by drawing attention to his foreign wife since this foreign woman, by circumcising *her* son Gershom, had clearly demonstrated allegiance to Israelite religious practices. This kind of story could well have been useful in any conflict between Aaronid and Mosaic/Gershomite priests. Both these possibilities – the connection between passover and firstborn, as well as the suggested social function of the story – hopefully serve to illustrate the general point that a final form reading might well turn out to have significance for historical reconstruction.

To summarize my overall argument on the relation between diachronic and synchronic interpretation in the *Exodus* commentary: Childs's actual exegetical practice is at times marred by conceptual confusion, but he does occasionally reveal a healthy sense of hermeneutical pluralism. A pluralist view would suggest that the goal of final form interpretation is not to be confused with the various goals of historical criticism. Historical interpretation might, however, contribute relevant information for final form readings (as long as that 'information' is not used to provide an inherently diachronic solution to a problem in the received text), and *vice versa*. The final form focus of the canonical approach might well bring to light textual details of interest to historical critics.

This is not to suggest that finally everyone should have the same interpretative interest. On the contrary, a clear consciousness of the *different* interpretative interests at work in biblical criticism will probably do more to encourage mutual exchange than the prior assumption of commonality. If we recognize at the outset the different goals being pursued, then we may be able to avoid fruitless arguments like 'final form critics fail to take account of textual prehistory' or 'final form critics fail to account for sociological background' or 'sociological critics fail to pay close attention to the text'. Such arguments come close to being tautologies. Genuine disagreements only arise when we start to question *why* the various goals of criticism should be pursued, and *how* they should be related. This point is especially significant when it comes to Childs's work on the history of exegesis.

History of exegesis and the New Testament

There are two sections in the standard format of the *Exodus* commentary which have proved especially controversial – those which deal with the history of exegesis and the New Testament. Sean McEvenue, among others, has been particularly critical of these sections:

> The New Testament authors and subsequent Christian and Jewish theologians were not trying to illuminate the past. Rather, they were writing a theology, each for his own community and time, and they were using Exodus freely to suit their own purposes . . . Why should one expect the writers of the New Testament to illuminate the Book of Exodus? Childs appears to expect them to do this, and it is this expectation which has led him astray.[21]

There are at least two issues here which need to be separated. Would the pre-modern Jewish and Christian exegetes acknowledge that they were 'using Exodus freely to suit their own purposes'? Would they have seen a significant (emic) contrast between exegesis and theology? This is a complicated historical issue which would require a comprehensive study of the relevant exegetical texts. It later becomes clear, however, that the expressed intentions of the pre-modern exegetes are quite irrelevant to the main lines of McEvenue's argument. He suggests, for example, that even if the editors of the Book of Isaiah used 'a hermeneutic with some flexibility of application . . . *we* could not allow ourselves to go along with them'.[22] He seems to be arguing that, in the judgment of modern critical interpreters, pre-critical exegetes did not *in fact* illuminate the Book of Exodus.

McEvenue's claim is probably representative of a widely held view; he, at least, seems to consider it self-evident. One should notice, however, that it assumes a distinction between two different kinds of interpretative interest. This difference could be roughly described by contrasting 'historical' and 'rationalist' interests.[23] 'Historical' interpretation (here in an emic sense), is focused on the *meaning* of texts in their own historical situation, while 'rationalist' interpretation is focused on the continuing *truth value* of the texts in question. Modern biblical critics are not primarily concerned with understanding the meaning of pre-modern exegesis in its own situation; this task is usually left to church historians. The modern critic is concerned primarily with whether past exegetes can contribute to the exegetical task as *we* now understand it. We are concerned with exegetical truth value that has stood the test of time. It is one thing to describe pre-modern commentators in the context of their own age, it is quite another to review their exegetical works in search of insights that might contribute to an emic description of the *biblical* material.

The distinction between 'meaning' and 'truth' is also stressed by McEvenue, and he uses it to make an important point, namely, that Childs's surveys of the history of interpretation 'abstract from, and implicitly trivialize the question of truth'.[24] Here McEvenue seems to be concerned not so much with the question of historicity but with the issue of exegetical accuracy. Childs's history of exegesis, it is claimed, has undermined the quest for what the text of Exodus is really saying.

We should concede at the outset that Childs's *theoretical* statements on the history of exegesis are expressed with unfortunate brevity, if not opacity. But I would suggest that there is enough evidence in the *Exodus* commentary to question McEvenue's judgement. What does Childs actually say about the purpose of his history of exegesis?

The history of exegesis is of special interest in illuminating the text by showing how the questions which are brought to bear by subsequent generations of interpreters influence the answers which they receive. No one comes to the text *de novo*, but consciously or unconsciously shares a tradition with his predecessors. This section therefore tries to bring some historical controls to the issue of how the present generation is influenced by the exegetical traditions in which we now stand. (1974a: xv)

This suggests that the primary purpose of the history of exegesis in the commentary is to encourage a sense of 'historicality'; all interpreters are themselves situated in a web of historical, cultural and scholarly traditions. We are all time-conditioned.

In other words, Childs is using the history of exegesis to draw attention, at least indirectly, to the historicality of our own exegesis. What has confused this basic point is Childs's implication that examples of historicality also illuminate the text of Exodus *for us*. But, as McEvenue rightly points out, this would seem to trivialize our concern for exegetical accuracy; biblical scholars have already decided – for good reasons, and after much painful argument – that there are elements in the pre-critical web of traditions, culture, and scholarship which we can no longer consider valid.

Accepting now that Childs has been somewhat less than perspicuous in his theoretical statement of purpose, what does he actually do with the history of exegesis in the commentary? One would have to say that section (5) of the standard format usually turns out to be simply a list of the exegetical options thrown up by the cultural tides of the last twenty centuries. This is of course no mean feat of research, but does it serve the purpose of illustrating historicality? Only occasionally does Childs make the point more explicitly. Thus, for example, in discussing the provision of manna in Exod. 16 he says that

It is an interesting commentary on the relation of biblical exegesis to the temper of the times to realize that, although no new scientific evidence appeared directly bearing on the manna, by the end of the nineteenth century the great majority of critical commentators simply took it for granted that the biblical manna was a natural substance. The miraculous element was attributed to the imagination of the Hebrew writers. (1974a: 299)

We find a similar point in his reflections on the Ten Commandments:

Although the Decalogue has been continually treated as if it, at least, were timeless and unchanging in value, the cultural conditioning of the interpretation appears right at this point. (1974a: 437; cf. 335)

McEvenue's criticism forces us, however, to look beyond these intimations of historicality: has the history of exegesis trivialized the search for an accurate interpretation of the Book of Exodus? I would say that it has not. Buried amongst the lists of exegetical options in section (5) we find some clear signs to support this conclusion. Childs says of Exod. 19 that

The history of the interpretation of Ex. 19 is of particular interest in showing the rise and development of a variety of new questions which are only indirectly connected with the biblical account itself. (1974a: 378; cf. 437)

He can even say in his excursus on the despoiling of the Egyptians that

In striking contrast to the entire history of exegesis, the Old Testament text makes no attempt whatever to justify the act. (1974a: 177; cf. 1979: 82)

In fact, the history of pre-critical exegesis rarely influences Childs's own exegetical judgment on the final form, and the same may be said of his discussions of the New Testament – he repeatedly points out where the New Testament authors have moved beyond the limits of the Exodus text (e.g. 1974a: 82, 162–3, 303). His own exegesis in section (3) is significantly placed *before* both the general treatment of the history of exegesis in section (5) and the discussion of the New Testament in section (4). When he does agree with a pre-modern judgment, as in the case of Exod. 4: 24–6, the exegetical option is already discussed critically in the preceding section on literary, form-critical and traditio-historical problems (section 2). It would be entirely wrong to infer from Childs's positive attitude to the history of exegesis that he has somehow been constrained in each of his exegetical judgments by a democratic vote taken amongst pre-Enlightenment authors.

I would suggest, however, that Childs has over-stated his originality in the use of the history of exegesis. Although the classic commentators are only rarely cited in critical commentaries, modern critics are surely not so arrogant that they will, on principle, reject a valid exegetical observation simply because it was expressed before the Enlightenment. Childs himself supplies a case in point: Wellhausen explicitly accepted Ibn Ezra's precedent in emending the text of Exod. 3: 14 (Childs 1974a: 62). Similarly, Wellhausen's reading of Gen. 1 is partly founded on observations made by Rashi.[25] If the canonical critic has more reason to look at pre-Enlightenment exegesis it is perhaps because the classic commentators were less disposed to elaborate reconstructions of textual prehistory (cf. Childs 1979: 82).

We may infer, therefore, that the history of exegesis may serve two functions for the canonical critic: (1) it may serve to illustrate the historicality of interpreters, and (2) it may bring to light exegetical options for final form exegesis. However, there is an important question which needs to be asked with respect to

point (1): is a commentary the most appropriate place for
illustrations of historicality?

I would suggest that it is not. Childs's efforts in this direction
are far too thin to make the point persuasively. It would seem
that the major purpose of a commentary should be to provide
plausible readings of the biblical text, that is, plausible *for the
commentator's audience*. Commentaries should be in this sense
'rationalistic'. The history of exegesis, on the other hand, needs
to be much more 'historical'; it needs to be written with much
more detailed attention to the surrounding cultural context,
and perhaps even to the socio-economic context of the interpreter. What the interpreter says about any particular biblical text
will only be one source of evidence in this kind of history. A
properly 'historical' study should also guard against anachronistic criticisms that draw on the achievements of more recent
exegesis. Historical critics may be happy with rationalistic
histories of exegesis which barely touch the centuries between
Jerome and Luther, or between Luther and Gabler. But
historians of exegesis should not be; their task is not to tell history
from the perspective of the hermeneutical winners but from the
perspective of the interpreter they choose to study.

As already noted in chapter 1, Childs has made an entirely
legitimate point about historicality. A consciousness of our time-
conditioned efforts should make 'rationalistic' commentaries far
more humble in their exegetical judgments than they often are.
Unfortunately, Childs's own histories of exegesis are too thin to
serve this purpose. The thicker and more 'historical' our
histories of exegesis become, the more humility we should learn.
However, commentators cannot give up the attempt to provide
the best arguments *vis-à-vis* the interpretive goals they set for
themselves. Contemporary exegetical judgment should, in the
light of our own historicality, be a humble attempt to provide
the best arguments so far, given the evidence to hand.[26] I do not
believe that Childs's *Exodus* commentary has contravened this
principle. He has, however, deflected attention from his Old
Testament exegetical work by not being clear enough about the
function of the history of exegesis in the canonical approach. It is
perhaps not surprising that this element in his programme has
played only a minor role in subsequent publications.

CHAPTER 3

'Introduction' and Old Testament theology

THE DISCIPLINE OF INTRODUCTION

Five years after the appearance of the *Exodus* commentary, Childs published his influential *Introduction to the Old Testament as Scripture* (1979). His unpublished Sprunt Lectures of 1972, which had emphasized final form studies for the first time, were also reworked into this text (1979: 17). The first issue to be considered is whether, as some have suggested, the *Introduction* reflects any changes in the canonical approach. Second, I will describe the distinctive features of a canonical 'introduction' as opposed to earlier scholarly works in this genre. Third, we shall investigate the relationship between Childs's *Old Testament Theology in a Canonical Context* (1985) and his previous publications.

Changes in the canonical approach

Up until the appearance of the *Introduction* Childs had consistently stressed that consideration of the New Testament was an essential part of his approach. Yet, as James Barr has correctly pointed out, there is comparatively little talk of the New Testament in the *Introduction*: 'the Old Testament has not been interpreted as *Christian* scripture after all'.[1] Childs's response to this observation was thin. He protested that he 'was not writing a biblical theology but an introduction to the Hebrew Scriptures . . . the larger task clearly needs to be done' (1984b: 70; cf. 1979: 72). He had, however, already written in his Exodus commentary that the sections on 'New Testament context' and

58

'theological reflection within the context of the Christian canon' belonged to 'the heart' of the commentary (1974a: xvi). Barr had good grounds to think that New Testament study was an indispensable part of the canonical approach.

Barr also detects another shift in so far as the later Childs apparently attaches a different value to the ideal of objective description. Childs had earlier sought to redefine 'description' so that it was never entirely separated from the 'constructive' task of theological exegesis (1964: 433, 438; 1970a: 92–3, 141; 1974a: xiii). But the Childs of the *Introduction* 'seeks to describe as objectively as possible the canonical literature of ancient Israel which is the heritage of both Jew and Christian' (1979: 16). Barr sees in this shift an 'obvious confusion'.[2]

The ideal of description certainly enjoys a higher profile in the *Introduction*, but it is questionable whether we should see here a change in the formulation of the canonical approach. Even on the basis of his previous publications, Childs could have argued in response to Barr that the lack of New Testament material and the more descriptive stance of the *Introduction* were interrelated. It will be instructive at this point to see just how such an answer could be formulated.

Even in 1964 Childs had envisioned three stages of theological commentary: (1) the *descriptive task* of interpreting the 'single text in light of the whole Old Testament' (1964: 438); (2) the movement between the Old and New Testaments; and (3) theological reflection on the theological reality or 'substance' to which the texts pointed. These three stages were expanded in the *Exodus* commentary into a standard format of six sections: (1) translation, textual and philological notes; (2) literary, form-critical and traditio-historical problems; (3) Old Testament context; (4) New Testament context; (5) history of exegesis; (6) theological reflection in the context of the Christian canon. Childs identified sections (1) and (2) as more technical, calling sections (3), (4) and (6) the heart of the commentary. In 1964 he had no clear emphasis on the final form – the distinctive focus of section (3) in the *Exodus* commentary. Nevertheless, this third section roughly corresponds to what in 1964 was called the descriptive task of interpreting the 'single text in light of the

whole Old Testament'. Thus, under section (3) – 'Old Testament Context' – of Childs's discussion of Exod. 24, we find the
expressed intention 'to describe as *objectively* as possible what the
final editor actually accomplished with his narrative' (1974a:
503, italics added.) Thus, even before the publication of the
Introduction, Childs's position could be summarized as follows:
final form exegesis of the Hebrew Bible can be descriptive, but
not the theological reflection on the whole Christian canon.

If we compare the format of the *Exodus* commentary with that
of the *Introduction* then it is clear that the six-part format of the
earlier work has been severely truncated. As with most introductions, there are no comprehensive translations, textual or
philological notes; these are the foundational tasks of a commentary. There are no separate sections on the New Testament, and
the history of exegesis is generally relegated to a brief bibliographical note at the end of each chapter. The standard format
for treating each of the biblical books is thus reduced to three
parts: (1) historical critical problems; (2) canonical shape; (3)
theological and hermeneutical implications. Sections (1) and
(2) of the *Introduction* therefore correspond to sections (2) and (3)
of *Exodus*. In both works, the historical issues are treated just
before a reading of the Old Testament final form. Except for
perhaps a more polemical tone in the later work, we would
argue that there is no substantial difference here in method. The
Introduction is, for obvious reasons, simply less detailed. Both
works are comparatively descriptive in these sections. In neither
work do New Testament developments play a role in interpreting the final form of the Old Testament text.

The real difference, and in this respect Barr is correct, lies in
the section on theological implications. Section (6) in the *Exodus*
commentary encompasses final form readings from both Old
and New Testaments and can thus be considered a step towards
Christian biblical theology in the canonical mode. The corre-
sponding section in the *Introduction* restricts itself primarily to the
Old Testament and may thus be considered a step towards a
canonical theology of the Hebrew scriptures. The difference is
that Childs now seems to be conceding that a theological
exegesis need not extend itself over the full extent of the *Christian*
canon. But he seems also to be implying that such a theological

exegesis is not yet a Christian biblical theology, and thus a more descriptive stance is appropriate;[3] a theology of the Christian canon is the 'larger task' yet to be done. He had decided that his earlier work had not provided the adequate groundwork for a theology of both testaments (Childs 1980a: 199), this seems to be the motivation for a more descriptive introduction to the Old Testament.

Thus, we should conclude that Childs has always had a descriptive element in his exegetical theory and practice, and he has always given up his claim to purely descriptive science as soon as he begins to speak as a Christian biblical theologian. He would depart from this basic position if in the future he produced a theology of both Testaments that claimed to be purely descriptive. However, he was not inconsistent to produce a more descriptive introduction to the Hebrew scriptures. His view seems to amount to this: a theology of the Hebrew scriptures should be descriptive, whereas Christian biblical theology is confessional. The sections in the *Introduction* headed 'theological and hermeneutical implications' are little more than summaries of the first two sections, often simply reinforcing the gains of a canonical approach and the problems with hermeneutical competitors. Only once, in his comments on Leviticus (1979: 188), does he point out the divergence of Jewish and Christian biblical theology in the context of their larger 'canons', but this kind of issue moves beyond the boundaries of his descriptive aims in the *Introduction*.[4]

In summary, the difference between the Childs of the early monographs and the Childs of *Exodus* is that a reading of the final form is added to the list of 'descriptive' tasks which were previously considered the preserve of historical criticism. The difference between the Childs of *Exodus* and the Childs of the *Introduction* is not so great: theological reflection is now founded on descriptive interpretation of the Hebrew Bible, but this kind of reflection does not yet yield a Christian biblical theology. A comprehensive biblical theology in the canonical mode could be built directly on the kind of theology found in the *Exodus* commentary, but only indirectly on the kind found in the *Introduction*. We are now in a position to examine the distinctive features of a 'canonical introduction'.

The practice of
canonical introduction

Childs's *Introduction to the Old Testament as Scripture* is a monu-
mental attempt to reformulate the questions asked by the
discipline of 'introduction', a technical term of long standing.
Instead of focusing on the traditional questions of authorship,
dating, historical background and the development of the
literature, his emphasis falls on 'the effect which the use of the
material as scripture has left on the final form of the tradition'
(1979: 661; cf. 1977a: 69). The book is effectively a hermeneutical manifesto, and Walther Zimmerli was not far wrong when he
suggested that it bordered on a kind of 'scholarly messianism'
that purported to resolve a long list of critical impasses by
attending to the 'really relevant' question of Canonical Shape.[5]

In advocating the 'really relevant' question of canonical
shape, or final form, Childs attempted to solve two different
kinds of problems at once. The first kind of problem is historical
in nature: by reciting all the critical problems and controversies
associated with the traditional questions of introduction he
repeatedly demonstrates how historical-critical conclusions
cannot escape the charge of being 'hypothetical'. The second
kind of problem is theological: *even if* historical-critical conclusions can be granted a high degree of plausibility, the effect of
these conclusions has been to tie the biblical texts more firmly in
their original contexts – thus making theological appropriation
more difficult (e.g. 1979: 79, 324, 510). Childs's formulation of
this second problem reflects a fundamental hermeneutical belief
which has shaped the exegetical goals of the canonical approach
but which has not itself been rigorously examined.[6] The next
chapter is devoted to this issue, but in this section we will focus
more on the first kind of problem – the role of reconstructed
historical background in exegesis.

Childs's solution is roughly this; *if historical reconstruction*
(*whether etic or emic*) *is too hypothetical, then a type of exegesis is needed*
that makes such reconstruction largely irrelevant. Such an exegesis will be
focused on the 'canonical shape' of the Masoretic text. This is, of course,
a crude summary of Childs's overall argument, so we will need
to examine the main premises of his programme in more detail.

First, we need to examine his claim that canonical exegesis is, in spite of the criticism of historical reconstruction, a kind of 'historical' interpretation.

The basic issue at stake is, Childs insists, the *nature* of the Bible's historicality (1979: 71), and here he seems to have two points in mind. First, although biblical revelation is inseparable from the experience of historical Israel, it is not the experience of *each generation* that is in itself significant. It is not that all the biblical communities were equally faithful before God; the biblical generations betray both faith and lack of faith. Political, sociological and economic factors were also at work in Israel's history, but these were subordinated or obscured in the long process of theological reflection and religious usage of the biblical literature (1979: 61, 78; cf. 1985: 56). In this 'canonical process', the stress falls on the collective experience of all the biblical generations who struggled for truthfulness before God. This collective experience is contained in the final form of the biblical text which 'alone bears witness to the full history of revelation' (1979: 76). Far from being an attempt to recover the unity of biblical texts by positing single authors, Childs's view leads in the opposite direction. The biblical books are 'traditional, communal and developing', rather than the product of individual, idiosyncratic authors (1979: 574; cf. 223, 236). Yet a lack of the relevant historical evidence means that the canonical process is 'largely inaccessible to critical reconstruction' (1979: 67).[7] Nevertheless, since the final form of the biblical text contains, for Childs, the purified residue of generations of theological reflection, this text is not only the sufficient but also the preferred object of exegesis.

Second, Childs's notion of 'historicality' includes the continuing history of the text itself. It is the continuity of usage which justifies his preference for the Masoretic text, not the diverse actual usage of the biblical period. The historicality *of the text* includes not only the prehistory of the canonical process but also the continuous history of the Bible's effects after the stabilization of the Masoretic text. These two aspects of Childs's theory of historicality do not co-exist easily, and it will be useful at this point to examine some signs of tension between them.

Childs claims to be describing 'the form and function of the

Hebrew Bible in its role as sacred scripture for Israel' (1979: 16), or yet more ambiguously, 'the features of this peculiar set of religious texts in relation to their usage within the historical community of ancient Israel' (1979: 73). But as pointed out in chapter 1, ancient Israel could not have used *the final form* of the Hebrew text since this was not stabilized, according to Childs himself, until the end of the first century CE (1979: 97). Indeed, the process of textual transmission and the process of canonization overlapped, and the Greek Old Testament remained in a fluid state long after the stabilization of the Hebrew text (1979: 94, 97). It follows from this that an exegesis focused on the final form of the Hebrew text cannot simply be identified with a description of the texts used by actual communities during the biblical period, and in this respect some of Childs's methodological statements are just misleading.

However, this recognition in no way damages Childs's overall argument, since his exegetical interest does not rest on a reconstruction of the canonical or textual processes. The main lines of his argument rest rather on a theory of continuous textual usage:

> Why should the one community which finally supported the Masoretic text be singled out? The reason is that only this one historic community has continued through history as the living vehicle of the whole canon of Hebrew scripture. The Greek-speaking Jewish community of Egypt died out. Similarly the community of Qumran ceased to exist in the first century. Although the Samaritan community has continued in a very restricted sense, it has retained only a portion of the Hebrew scriptures. (1979: 97–8)

Hence, it becomes clear that the complexity of the *actual* usage of the biblical period need not be reconstructed: 'The proto-Masoretic tradition was at best one among many competing traditions' (1979: 102), and its significance cannot be defended by a descriptive history of textual usage during the biblical period. Rather, its significance appeared only retrospectively as belonging to that golden thread of continuous usage which extends to the present.

In the light of this argument, it is not surprising to find that Childs stresses the value of continuity with the history of exegesis

(1979: 105). But his preference for the Masoretic text forces him to say that neither the New Testament's freedom with textual traditions nor the church's use of Greek and Latin translations calls into question 'the ultimate authority of the Hebrew text for church and synagogue' (1979: 99). It begins to look as if the golden thread of continuous usage passed into Judaism rather than into early and medieval Christianity, a strange turn of events for a library of books earlier described as Christian scripture.

However, Childs's argument concerning the use of the Hebrew Bible after its stabilization is not simply a descriptive one; the argument also has an evaluative and theological aspect. With the addition of this evaluative element it becomes clear that although the canonical approach has fostered an interest in the *actual* use of the Bible in church and synagogue, its central concern is finally not the reconstruction of this history either. In the *Exodus* commentary Childs compared exegetical 'posthistory' with the 'prehistory' of the Bible's formation, emphasizing that both these aspects of textual historicality are finally of interest only in so far as they contribute to understanding the final form of the text itself (1974a: xv). In the *Old Testament Theology* eleven years later, his prescriptive stress on the text itself has quite clearly overshadowed the descriptive historical question of how the Bible has been actually used by biblical communities:

> the theological issue of how Christians relate to the Jewish scriptures cannot be decided biblicistically by an appeal to New Testament practice . . . The debate transcends the historical moment of the first-century encounter, and turns on the church's ongoing relation to the authoritative scriptures which Israel treasured . . . It remains an essential part of the church's theological reflection on the Old Testament to continue in dialogue with the synagogue which lives from the common biblical text. (1985: 10)

Both here and in the *Introduction*, Childs's preference for the Masoretic text rests as much on prescriptive arguments as on historical ones (1979: 99, 665). The historical complexities of text criticism are thereby greatly reduced. The contemporary dialogue between Christianity and Judaism is held to determine the goal of text criticism as the recovery of the stabilized Hebrew text of the first century (cf. 1987a).

Having relativized both the prehistory and the posthistory of the Hebrew text, it is not difficult to see how Childs's account of the Bible's historicality can easily be construed as a theological version of literary formalism. His arguments seem to assume, rather than defend, a theory of 'classic' and 'eminent' texts.[8] Eminent texts are not strictly comparable, as Childs says, to 'inert sherds which have lain in the ground for centuries' (1979: 73).[9] They are not strictly comparable to texts 'which never had any effect on any historical community' (1979: 105). Yet although it is this history of effects which makes a text canonical for biblical communities, the effects are of secondary significance compared to the text itself. Post-stabilization *Wirkungs-geschichte* becomes 'targum' and 'commentary' rather than being inscribed on the text (1979: 101). Interpretation is the medium in which the text is preserved, but it does not lay claim to the eminence of the text itself.[10] Moreover, the theory of eminent texts would suggest that interpretation need not be restricted to recovering the intention of authors and tradents (1979: 79, 259, 326); it is the text which achieves eminence, not the agents of its production and reception. That these agents give life to and preserve the text is not denied; what is denied is the idea that all texts are nothing but the fleeting meanings of individual agents. To put the point positively: some texts mysteriously acquire perpetual modernity. We shall return to these issues in chapter 5, but for the present we need to focus more closely on the 'earlier' dimension of historicality in Childs's *Introduction* – the relationship between the prehistory of the biblical text and final form interpretation.

Although Childs reviews the historical-critical problems pertinent to each biblical book, he does not allow historical reconstruction to constrain his exegesis. A long list of scholars are criticized in the *Introduction* for allowing their work to be so constrained. Yet there is a sense in which some of Childs's own claims are not purely synchronic. He frequently speaks of canonical or redactional 'shaping' rather than 'shape', and the former term is often connected to hypotheses concerning editorial activity which took place *before* the text reached its final form.[11] This has puzzled reviewers like Zimmerli who cannot see why, for example, it is legitimate to speak of the Elihu speeches in Job as 'supplement and commentary' (1979: 541) yet it is illegitimate to reconstruct the 'commentary' inscribed on the book of Ezekiel (1979: 370).[12] This issue is of special interest to Zimmerli, since it was his own theory of *Nachinterpretation* in Ezekiel that Childs attacked. The difference between them is worthy of some close analysis, since Zimmerli's rehabilitation of 'secondary' material is the sort of thing one might expect canonical interpreters to applaud unreservedly.

First, it must be pointed out that Zimmerli's direct quotations from the *Introduction* are slightly misleading. Childs fully agrees with the idea that the book of Ezekiel shows clear evidence of editorial expansion (1979: 369). The basic issue at stake is the exegetical approach to this expansion. Childs praises Zimmerli for understanding this material as commentary rather than as worthless accretion, but the precise details of the *Nachinterpretation* rest 'on the same precarious subjective basis as does all such reconstruction' (1979: 370). In other words, there is sufficient evidence to speak generally of textual expansion but insufficient evidence to reconstruct it – this is Childs speaking as an historical critic, albeit a somewhat sceptical one. But then he goes on to speak *qua* canonical interpreter:

> But there is an even more serious objection: Zimmerli's method . . . has missed the significance of the canonical process in which the experience of Israel with the use of its authoritative writings has been incorporated into the text itself as part of the biblical witness. The canonical shaping not only registered that history by its shaping of the tradition, but it also brought that process to an end when it fixed its canon. Everything thereafter was commentary, not text. (1979: 370)

In other words, there is a difference between pre-stabilization and post-stabilization *Wirkungsgeschichte*, and it is only the latter kind that may properly be called 'commentary' by practitioners of the canonical approach. In so doing they affirm a golden thread of textual reception which includes the history of exegesis. Zimmerli's method breaks this thread by reconstructing a different original text (*Grundtext*) and creating a new watershed of 'text' and 'commentary'. Moreover, this new watershed 'often destroys the synchronic dimension of the text'. Continual judgments as to which verses are early and which late represent an historical exegesis that often blocks an understanding of the final form 'which has consciously intro- duced theological elements into the text in order to blue the common historical perspective' (1979: 370). Indeed, the idea that theological elements or 'constructs' have blurred historical developments is one that Childs constantly affirms.[13]

Thus, although Childs in his part-time role as historical critic knows that the biblical books have undergone development, his preferred object of exegesis *qua* canonical interpreter is the end result of this history. He does not, therefore, need to reconstruct this process in any great detail (although, in his role as historical critic, he occasionally does diachronically reconstruct a tra- dition whenever there is sufficient evidence). Although this point is theoretically quite clear, in actual exegetical practice Childs is constantly swapping hermeneutical hats – even in his sections headed 'canonical shape'.

His analysis of the book of Daniel provides a good example of this exegetical schizophrenia. He begins with the question of how the book, 'which apparently predicted the end of the world with the death of Antiochus IV Epiphanes could have been canonized in a period after the Greek danger had passed' (1979: 613). This effectively displaces one of the primary historical critical questions – the question of how the material in Daniel was understood during the reign of Antiochus IV – and reveals that much of Childs's criticism of previous interpreters is misplaced: he is usually asking a different kind of exegetical question. Nevertheless, Childs *qua* historical critic goes on to make a number of claims concerning the 'midrashic' author of chapters 7–12 who was 'confirming and elucidating the visions of Daniel in ch. 2 for the benefit of his Maccabean audience' (1979: 616–17). This judgment then receives an important qualification:

Although the modern historical critical scholar can characterize the description in ch. 7 as a prophecy-after-the-event, the biblical writer came to his material from a totally different perspective . . . He was firmly convinced that what he now saw was intended by the original vision . . . He had no new prophetic word directly from God. Rather, he understood the sacred writing of the past as the medium through which God continued to make contemporary his divine revelation. His own identity had no theological significance and therefore he concealed it. (1979:618)

But even this is not a description of the final form as such; it is an emic claim about the Maccabean author's self-perception. This is still part of what one might call diachronic emic description – a legitimate part of the historical criticism that is focused on tracing Israelite tradition. The *distinctive* aspect of the canonical approach appears in Childs's attitude toward this self-effacing Maccabean author. Rather than providing an interpretation of Daniel based on a reconstructed Maccabean situation, he focuses on the communicative intention of the *text itself*[14] without correlating this intention with a particular historical period, social group or author (a point which could be made *mutatis mutandis* for the whole of Childs's book). This allows him to reject both an etic sociological explanation that would account for Daniel as a typical response for a Hellenistic minority group under persecution (1979: 621) as well as any emic reconstruction that would sketch the conflicting theologies in the post-exilic period (1979: 613).

In a new section headed 'The canonical reinterpretation of Daniel', Childs notes that unlike the editing process of Second Isaiah the canonical process of Daniel has retained 'all the historical particularity of chs. 8, 9 and 11'. Nevertheless, even in the Roman period the book of Daniel 'was still being understood eschatologically', and he cites II Esdras 12. 10ff., Matt. 24 and Mark 13 as evidence for this. He concludes that the 'period of indignation' under Antiochus was understood typologically; Antiochus became a 'representative' of the ultimate enemy rather than the fulfilment of the vision himself (1979: 619).[15] This reinterpretation of Daniel was assisted by what I have called referential ambiguity: 'nowhere did the original author actually identify Antiochus by name with the evil one . . . the vision itself remained veiled' (1979: 620). Thus, his formalist tendency in treating referential ambiguity (i.e. a refusal to use background historical information in making inferences about authorial intention), allows Childs *qua* canonical interpreter to answer the questions of how Daniel could have been canonized long after the Greek threat and how the book was still understood eschatologically in the Roman period.

In discussing the theological and hermeneutical implications of Daniel he suggests that the book 'continues truthfully to instruct and to admonish the people of God in the crisis of faith' (1979: 622). Apparently we are in the same position as the canonical editors who, in Childs's judgment, thought that if Antiochus was not the 'contemptible one' then 'it was not the prophecy that was at fault, but the earlier identification with those specific events' (1979: 620). Thus, Childs is critical of Jewish and Christian exegesis which has transformed the prophetic vision into a mathematical game (1979: 622).

This is a noteworthy judgment since it is arguable that there were at least some canonical editors who also indulged in mathematical speculation, adding their conclusions to the text itself in Dan. 12: 11–12. In treating these verses, Childs is forced to conclude that since the numbers were 'allowed to stand uninterpreted' they should be considered subordinate redactional elements inscribed on the text after the 'major' canonical shaping. Zimmerli finds that Childs has here made an exegetical judgment 'that does not keep strictly to the final form of the book'.[16] This remark would also apply to many of the theological judgments which Childs takes to have continuing validity. But the problem is also a purely exegetical one: he tends to allow certain textual details – 'subordinate' elements – to fall into the background. Most of these details are legacies of textual prehistory which are of vital interest to historical critics. Dan. 12: 11–12 are, on the other hand, arguably the youngest verses of the book, but they reveal the same embarrassment of historical particularity that besets the vestiges of textual prehistory.

Childs seems to be reluctant to see that the canonical approach might need to view these vestiges as unexplained curiosities – elements which might have been forgotten were they transmitted in the medium of oral tradition.[17] There are surely many textual details that cannot be interpreted by attending only to the final form of the Hebrew text, and once again we should probably conclude that Childs is most coherent when he is a hermeneutical pluralist (e.g. 1979: 76, 128, 262, 334, 438) rather than a hermeneutical monist (e.g. 1979: 151, 177). His disagreement with historical-critical exegetes is hardly surprising if they have different exegetical goals. The substantive disagreement turns on why 'canonical shape' should be an exegetical goal in the first place. And this disagreement cannot be resolved by simply producing more and more canonical exegesis. We shall return to this issue in the following chapters, but first we need to discuss Childs's understanding of the discipline of Old Testament theology revealed in his *Old Testament Theology in a Canonical Context* (1985).

OLD TESTAMENT THEOLOGY

I have already suggested that a comprehensive biblical theology in the canonical mode could be built directly on the kind of theology found in the *Exodus* commentary, but only indirectly on the kind found in the *Introduction*. The bracketing of the New Testament in the *Introduction*, and accordingly the more descriptive profile, means that although the later work is more comprehensive in its scope it is more limited in its fulfilment of the goals set by the canonical approach – the *Introduction* begins the task of descriptive final form study of each biblical book, without bringing the results of this exegetical task into 'constructive' conversation with the New Testament. In the 1970s the following comment from James Barr would have been an adequate description of Childs's vision for Old Testament theology:

Biblical theology is not so much a statement of the essence or core of the Bible; rather, it is predominantly an exegetical procedure, which works on the final form of the text and observes the canon as the boundary of that final form.[18]

If the boundaries of the *Hebrew* canon were observed then it would be natural to think that 'Old Testament theology' should be discussed under the more accurate rubric of 'theology of the Hebrew scriptures' – just as the *Introduction to the Old Testament* was actually conceived by Childs as an introduction to the 'Hebrew scriptures' (1979: 72; 1984b: 70). Why then did Childs produce an *Old Testament Theology* (1985), knowing that the title of his *Introduction* had proved so confusing?

First, we should note that Childs clearly distinguishes his approach from the history of Israelite religious ideas. Once again, this is important to recognize lest he be too swiftly rejected for the wrong reasons. There is no genuine competition here with historical and analytical 'theologies' which, using the biblical literature *as the primary source*, seek to describe the history of individual ideas and theological tendencies within ancient Israel. If we had the good fortune to have other literary sources from the period, then these would need to be used as well.[19] In this respect, there is nothing peculiarly *biblical* about this kind of historical interest and nothing particularly surprising about the fact that post-Enlightenment critics with this kind of interest found it necessary to polemicize against the canon. As Barr and Robert Morgan have rightly pointed out, much of the theological research in this tradition is best understood as contributing to the history of religion.[20] (I would want to refine this point slightly and say that historical 'biblical theology' should be thought of as that part of the history of religion which is devoted to diachronic emic description; it would simply confuse matters to call etic history of religion 'biblical theology'.)

In so far as biblical theologians wish to resist this conclusion, they cannot do so on *historical* grounds. Historians of Israelite theology cannot give any privilege to the canonical literature without lapsing into methodological confusion; they cannot simply restrict themselves to the theology which happened to be preserved in the canon. Their dependence on the Bible is, from a consistently historical perspective, simply a contingent result of the lack of relevant source material.

Childs seems to be aware of these considerations when he criticizes those who present their descriptive studies under the historically illegitimate rubric of 'Old Testament' theology, 'without any true reference to the canonical fc rm and function of the literature' (1985: 6). One should concede to Childs that questions about the form and function of the *canonical* literature are not simply identifiable with questions that concern historians of ancient Israelite theology. However, his argument is still question begging. The history of exegesis of canonical texts is also a legitimate part of the history of religion,[21] and it is arguable that the 'function' of canonical literature can be understood in a number of different ways, e.g., by etic sociology as preserving social identity and so on. In other words, it is still not clear that we need to have a discipline called 'Old Testament theology' as opposed to an area of religious studies which deals with the phenomena of canons and their usage.

There is, however, one more essential element in Childs's overall argument: we can only legitimately lay claim to the rubric of 'Old Testament theology' when it is recognized that we are speaking of a Christian discipline which is ultimately interested in the *present* function of the literature 'as a witness to Jesus Christ precisely in its pre-Christian form' (1985: 9).

Although Christians confess that God who revealed himself to Israel is the God and Father of Jesus Christ, it is still necessary to hear Israel's witness in order to understand who the Father of Jesus Christ is. (1985: 9)

In other words, the Hebrew Bible is to be understood as an independent witness and not to be simply Christianized. Since 'Israel remains the prime tradent of this witness' the Christian use of the Septuagint in no way undermines the fact that the primary object of study is a *Hebrew* witness (1985: 10).[22] But although the church needs therefore to maintain a common text with the synagogue, Old Testament theology reflects on this text as Christian scripture (1985: 9). Hence, even given a common text, this necessarily selective discipline will be bound to reveal Christian interests (cf. 1985: 8).

The *selective* nature of this kind of Old Testament theology is worthy of some comment. As pointed out above, Barr was correct in his understanding of the early Childs as espousing a biblical theology which is 'predominately an exegetical procedure'. The theological sections of the *Exodus* commentary, for example, are appended to each exegetical chapter. *Old Testament Theology in a Canonical Context*, on the other hand, is not bound to biblical texts in the same manner as a commentary

(1985: 1). In this later book, Old Testament theology moves into a second, systematizing stage reminiscent of a procedure classically formulated by J. P. Gabler. In his inaugural lecture at Altdorf in 1787, Gabler suggested that after analysing texts with respect to their different authors, ideas and periods, biblical theology should, in its second stage, organize the material under thematic headings. It is not altogether clear what Gabler himself meant by this, but 'organization under thematic headings' is a procedure that has been adopted by many biblical theologians who have set out to describe the 'essentials' or 'core' of a Testament between two covers, and Childs's *Old Testament Theology* is no exception. Nor would Childs want to resist Barr's evaluation of such theologies:

In general, the wider the range of a study the farther it is likely to diverge from the purely descriptive task and the more it is likely to verge upon the more strictly 'theological' task of implying norms for present-day faith.[23]

Indeed, Childs is explicit in his claim that canonical biblical theology cannot be purely descriptive; the theological stance of the modern interpreter cannot be ignored (1985: 12). In selecting the 'essentials' of Old Testament theology the canonical interpreter not only describes the ancient texts but also confronts 'the subject-matter to which scripture continues to bear testimony'. This formulation evokes some of his earlier views on how constructive exegesis is ultimately concerned with 'theological reality'. Theological truth claims and values are at stake here, and a purely descriptive biblical theology is therefore eclipsed.

However, Childs never tells us exactly *how* theological truths and values can be recovered from ancient texts. The simplest solution would be, of course, to say that the Bible contains truths and values which are valid for all time, but this he explicitly rejects. The canonical approach does not discover a kernel of 'abiding truths' from which time-conditioned husks can be separated (1985: 14). (This was precisely the procedure advocated by Spinoza and Gabler, as we shall see.) Childs recognizes that biblical theology will always have a time-conditioned quality (1985: 14, 25), i.e., that it will always be characterized by historicality, and that each generation must therefore take up the task anew. Even before his *Old Testament Theology*, Childs had repeatedly rejected the idea that 'eternal truths' could be sifted out of the Bible (e.g. 1970a: 101, 131, 134; 1974a: xii, 336, 396, 438, 496; 1979: 73). He seems to think, however, that the fusion of a time-conditioned past and a time-conditioned present has been adequately described by Calvin's doctrine of the Holy Spirit (1985: 12), a perplexing conclusion in view of the fact that Calvin was writing before the real problems of modern historical consciousness had even arisen. We must conclude, therefore, that in spite of Childs's attempt to make the Old Testament more accessible for the Christian church, he has not adequately dealt with the issue of theological appropriation.[24]

It has been suggested that Childs is in fact still haunted by the theological scheme articulated by Gabler. Ben Ollenburger has argued that this can be illustrated by Childs's assessment of historical particularity as the central hermeneutical problem for the present use of the Bible. This is a complex claim which requires, among other things, a careful analysis of the theological and philosophical ideas of historical particularity since the Enlightenment. It is to this issue that the next chapter is devoted. I shall attempt in chapters 4 and 5 to reconstruct Childs's canonical approach as charitably as possible. The final chapter will then be a critique of what I hope, perhaps immodestly, is a theoretically stronger version of the canonical approach than has actually been presented by Childs himself.

CHAPTER 4

Has Childs fallen into Gabler's ditch?

HISTORICAL PARTICULARITY AND BIBLICAL AUTHORITY

The purpose of this chapter is to examine one type of objection which has been raised against the canonical approach: Childs, it is often said, fails to take 'historical particularity' seriously enough. As we have already pointed out, it is especially the treatment of Second Isaiah in the *Introduction to the Old Testament as Scripture* which has incensed reviewers. Bernhard Anderson is representative of this response when he claims that the

transhistorical quality of the biblical material did not eclipse the anchorage of the texts in real life with its concrete particularity and historical referents . . . the message of the prophet, and hence the meaning for future generations, is essentially related to that historical situation into which the prophet spoke Yahweh's word of consolation and hope.[1]

Anderson is, of course, referring to the historical situation of the Babylonian exile and arguing that Second Isaiah must be seen against that background of authorship.

One must ask Anderson to specify, however, exactly which 'future generations' read Isaiah 40–55 as exilic prophecy? Surely this original background was quickly forgotten. *Our* understanding of ancient Israelite prophecy is quite different to the Jewish perceptions of prophecy from the Persian period onwards.[2] In other words, the origins of Second Isaiah were indeed swiftly eclipsed and did not play a decisive role in the meaning of the text for future generations. However, other critics have put the objection concerning particularity less ambiguously than Anderson. Sean McEvenue, as we have seen, has argued that *even if* the editors of the Book of Isaiah had 'a hermeneutic with some flexibility of application . . . we could not allow ourselves to go along with them'.[3] In other words, exegesis in *our* generation must concern itself with the particulars of historical background, no matter how few clues are retained in the text. This kind of view is widely shared among historical critics, whether their interest is in source, form, redaction or sociological criticism. Childs is well aware of this view, and he has summed it up as the principle that 'the sharper the historical focus, the better the interpretation' (1980a: 205, cf. 1974a: 19). And it is precisely this principle which he rejects.

Childs regards this principle as too doctrinaire. His own exegesis of the final form is guided by another rule: go into as much historical detail as is warranted by the text. Thus, he finds that the canonical shape sometimes preserves a great deal of historical particularity (e.g., Amos and Nahum). The issue, for Childs, can only be decided by exegesis of particular texts. Shortly after the publication of his *Introduction*, he even conceded that in the case of Second Isaiah he had 'failed to do full justice to the historical features from the sixth century'. This concession did not, however, undermine his general rejection of the historical critical 'axiom of particularity'.[4]

One might question, however, whether all historical critics are really united by the hermeneutical principle that 'the sharper the historical focus the better the interpretation'. It could be argued, for example, that Childs's work has, in some respects, simply accentuated a tendency which was already latent in form criticism. In spite of the characteristic stress in form criticism on a text's locus in life (*Sitz im Leben*), it seems that this stress often simply amounted to positing a highly generalized social or cultic location, e.g., 'legal contexts', 'the New Year festival', and so on. James Muilenburg spoke for many when he found a resistance to historical commentary in form criticism which he attributed to an overemphasis on 'the typical and representative' as against the unique features of a particular historical context.[5] Thus, the canonical approach is certainly not the first of the modern schools of Old Testament studies to attract this kind of objection.

One should also recall the revealing dispute in the early 1960s between G. E. Wright and Gerhard von Rad over the significance of original historical background. Wright was convinced that theological interests should be focused on 'the actual course of events' in Israelite history, and accordingly he attached great value to the discipline of archaeology. He suggested that historians of tradition, who reconstructed only biblical perceptions of Israelite history by means of 'internal methodologies', were not dealing with 'history itself'. A more objective use of external archaeological evidence revealed, for Wright, the fact that historians of tradition were generally far too sceptical about the historicity of biblical material and that, for example, 'patriarchal tradition is at least authentic in the sense that it can be fitted into an actual historical era'.[6]

Von Rad replied to these criticisms in a way that anticipates some of the claims of the canonical approach. He argued that the older stages of the patriarchal narratives were theologically secondary, and that these traditions 'first reached their real authority of witness in the realm of the Yahwist faith, which succeeded the time of the patriarchs'. For example, where Wright concludes that Gen. 22 'must once have been concerned with the abolition of child sacrifice',[7] von Rad responds by saying that this original historical referent is of little theological value. Wright is accused of going back to a stage which is 'theologically speechless',

to a stage in the tradition of the material which lies long before the one which now speaks to us in this story, where surely the whole *kerygma* is anchored . . . [Gen. 22 is] rather about problems which lie in the promise of God.[8]

Here is at least one critic who would question the value of simply heaping up putative facts about a text's historical background. It would be more accurate (if somewhat question begging) to say that historical critics are concerned to recover *relevant* historical background. This is a point to which we shall return.

In spite of these lines of continuity with earlier scholars, it is clear that Childs considers the reconstruction of historical particularity to be one of the central obstacles to the use of scripture in the modern period (cf. e.g. 1979: 79, 324, 510), and in this respect his work is distinctive. Childs has not, however, defended this hermeneutical view in any detail, an oversight which has rightly troubled his critics.

Perhaps the most illuminating examination of this issue is to be found in a recent article by Ben Ollenburger. This article not only identifies the problem of particularity in Childs's work but goes on to diagnose the root of the problem. Ollenburger's diagnosis reaches as far back as the eighteenth century to one of the fathers of modern biblical theology, Johann Philip Gabler. The diagnosis may be roughly summarized as follows: (1) Gabler was led by certain philosophical assumptions to a low view of historical particularity; (2) Childs has unwittingly inherited Gabler's problem and has attempted to circumvent historical particularity by creating a new type of exegesis; (3) but since Gabler's philosophical assumptions no longer apply, we should be free, suggests Ollenburger, to embrace the particularity of biblical traditions, both in exegesis and in theology.[9] These arguments might seem to be an excessively circuitous way of criticizing Childs's programme, but the more detailed discussion that follows will hopefully show that Ollenburger has touched on some issues of fundamental importance. Although the validity of (1) will be defended, I will try to show that there are problems with (2) and (3).

Gabler's view of biblical authority is indeed intimately related to the cultural conditions of biblical interpretation which prevailed during the early modern period. Enlightenment critics who wished to retain some account of biblical authority had to reconcile the historically diverse biblical traditions with the standard criterion of the age – the universal claims of reason.[10] Gabler's influential solution was simple: not all biblical texts need be considered authoritative. Many of the biblical ideas should be considered transient in significance and were thus only relevant to the earliest generations which preserved them. Texts which intransigently retain the marks of historical particularity could be allowed to sink quietly into the past; they are primarily the interest of biblical historians rather than dogmatic theologians. According to Gabler, one of the primary tasks of biblical theology is to separate those biblical ideas which were transient and 'particular' from those which

were of abiding significance and 'universal'. The universal ideas
could be considered authoritative, and all the rest was of
historical – one might even say antiquarian – interest. Gabler
proposed that only these 'certain and undoubted universal
ideas' could become the 'firmly established foundations' of
biblical authority. They constitute 'the unchanging testament
of Christian doctrine, and therefore pertain directly to us'.[11]

Ollenburger claims that he has found a similar understanding
of biblical authority in the canonical approach, and there is
some evidence for his case. Childs repeatedly affirms that the
governing intention of the canonical process was the transmission of tradition 'in such a way as to prevent its being moored
in the past' (1979: 79). In the case of Second Isaiah, for example,
this implies breaking the text free from the historical anchorage
in the sixth century. The loss of this original historical particularity means for Childs that the prophetic word is 'not tied to a
specific historical referent, but directed to the future'. It is not a
'specific' commentary on the needs of exiled Israel, for 'its
message relates to the redemptive plan of God for all of history'
(1979: 326). The 'new and non-historical framework . . .
severed the message from its original historical moorings and
rendered it accessible to all future generations' (1979: 337).
Childs has not, however, *unwittingly* inherited Gabler's idea of
biblical authority. He is well aware of the 'theological trap of
polarizing the accidental and the eternal' (1974a: 336), and he
has explicitly rejected attempts to strip off time-conditioned
husks from a kernel of abiding biblical truths (1985: 14). Yet
there seems to be no practical difference between an 'eternal'
truth and one which, according to Childs, pertains to 'all of
history'. In the case of Second Isaiah, he has indeed effectively
polarized the particular and the eternal.

In the final analysis, however, Ollenburger's comparison of
Gabler and Childs is not persuasive. Ollenburger reads Childs to
be saying that for texts to be theologically useful they 'must be
removed as far as possible from the particularities of their own
history'.[12] But this is not the case. Childs does not argue that the
canonical process always and everywhere dehistoricizes the
biblical tradition. In his discussion of the canonical shape of

Nahum, for example, he claims that 'this shaping did not require the dehistoricizing of the time conditioned oracles. Indeed, they remained virtually untouched in their particularity' (1979: 445). While the oracles of Nahum 2–3 'retain all the sharp historical individuality of the seventh century', the redactional psalm of chapter 1 has 'relativized the historical particularity of Nineveh's destruction by viewing it as a type of a larger and recurring phenomenon in history' (1979: 444). Nineveh's destruction is not simply dissolved into a universal idea, but neither is it frozen into a 'static, lifeless bead strung on a chronological chain'.[13] The effects of this *particular* event, theologically interpreted, reverberate beyond their chronological origin. Ollenburger is certainly correct in emphasizing that historical particularity need not be a barrier to continuing theological significance; this seems to be Childs's own argument in the case of Nahum. It would therefore be incorrect to say that Childs consistently downgrades particularity; where he does recognize historical particularity he tries to show how the final form points to a continuing significance for unique events.

We should conclude, then, that the canonical approach is not simply a quest for universal ideas, but Childs is indeed always looking for clues in the final form of biblical texts to how historical particulars might have continuing significance. For this reason, his exegesis often does circumvent an investigation of historical background for its own sake. We shall examine the validity of this circumvention in due course, but for the present our focus will fall on Ollenburger's third argument, namely, that since Gabler's philosophical assumptions no longer apply, we should be free to embrace the particularity of biblical traditions, both in exegesis and in theology.

I have argued in chapter one that historical interests should, in the context of pluralist biblical studies, be given free rein. But there is a *theological* danger in Ollenburger's third argument: it may end up trading cultural assumptions of the eighteenth century for equally dubious ones stemming from the nineteenth. In order to illustrate this danger we will need to discuss what happened to the idea of history when European intellectual culture shifted from Enlightenment rationalism to nineteenth century historicism. This discussion will also help to illuminate the mixed fortunes of historical particularity in its path from being devalued by Gabler to being axiomatic with more recent critics.

A BRIEF HISTORY OF 'HISTORY'

Ollenburger has correctly pointed out that Gabler's attitude to historical particularity was in large measure tied to a rationalist epistemology. In the final section of his famous inaugural address on biblical theology (1787), Gabler remarked that 'the nature of our age urgently demands that we then teach accurately the harmony of divine dogmatics and the principles of human reason'.[14] Similarly, he was in accord with contemporary intellectual currents when he prescribed a search for the 'eternal truths' of history; the majority of Enlightenment thinkers before him were not primarily concerned to uncover the diversity of history, but rather, to uncover what was universal in history.[15] Indeed, we can properly begin our survey by turning to a text which is much older than Gabler's address, but which shares the same intellectual spirit. Spinoza's *Tractatus theologico-politicus* of 1670 was published eight years before Richard Simon's more famous introduction to the Old Testament and 117 years before Gabler's inaugural address. It is Spinoza's work which is often taken to contain the first outline of a modern Old Testament 'introduction', or at least the first comprehensive combination of previous biblical criticism with the Enlightenment critique of religion.[16]

In the context of bloody religious strife, Spinoza set out to provide a comprehensive argument for religious freedom, claiming to rest his argument on pure and unprejudiced reason. He writes,

As I marked the fierce controversies of philosophers raging in church and state, the source of bitter hatred and dissension . . . I determined to examine the Bible afresh in a careful, impartial and unfettered spirit, making no assumptions concerning it.[17]

As in Gabler's inaugural address, the nature of biblical authority was an issue of central importance in the *Tractatus*; the Bible's

authority had been misunderstood, and for the sake of 'the
public peace' it needed rethinking. In taking up this task,
Spinoza set the enlightening power of presuppositionless reflection over against the powers of unreason, which were personified
in his book by a flat character called 'the multitude' who cared
'more for shreds of antiquity than for eternal truths' (p. 9).

Spinoza proposed a fundamental distinction between 'meaning' and 'truth', with different methods for arriving at each. A
scriptural text only achieves a clear *meaning* 'when we examine it
in the light of its history'. Understanding the history of a text
implies for Spinoza examination of the original language, the
situation of author and audience, the transmission of the work,
its versions, and the details of who accepted it into the canon.
The contents of each biblical book were also to be organized
under appropriate headings for analysis of its ideas (p. 101). All
this was part of the analysis of meaning. But the clear historical
meanings derived from such study may be quite obscure 'in
relation to reason and truth' (p. 102). Accordingly, this first
stage of historical study leads to a second stage of inquiry:

> It is true that Scripture should be explained by Scripture, so long as we
> are in difficulties about the meaning and intention of the prophets, but
> when we have elicited the true meaning, we must of necessity make use
> of our judgment and reason in order to assent thereto.[18]

But if the truth is only illuminated by reason at the second
stage of inquiry, what kind of reason is at work, and what kind of
truth is at stake, in the first stage of study – the 'history of
Scripture'? Spinoza seems to assume actually two kinds of truth:

> The truth of an historical narrative, however assured, cannot give us
> the knowledge nor consequently the love of God, for love of God
> springs from general ideas, in themselves certain and known. (p. 61)

Spinoza is assuming here a Cartesian doctrine of clear and
distinct ideas, a doctrine that runs like a *leitmotif* through his
entire book. Clear and distinct ideas, as such eternal truths, are
the only kind of truth with abiding significance. History, on the
other hand, is only concerned with particularities.

This distinction provides the background for Spinoza's
conception of the central purpose of historical study:

That we may not confound precepts which are eternal with those which served only a temporary purpose, or were only meant for a few, we should know what was the occasion, the time, the age, in which each book was written. (p. 103)

The discovery of the widest possible historical diversity served the broader aim in the *Tractatus* of showing that the necessary and eternal requirements of faith were actually quite minimal. This provided the foundation of the political argument that people should be allowed the liberty of the widest variations of faith. The eternal requirements of faith could be induced from the 'history of scripture' in the same way that Francis Bacon thought that the general laws of natural science could be induced from 'natural history'.[19] Thus, although Spinoza clearly distinguished between eternal truths and historical truths he allows for the possibility of an overlap. His epistemological distinction is not so sharp as we find in the later writings of Lessing and Kierkegaard who found an 'ugly ditch' between the contingent truths of history and the necessary truths of reason.[20]

Although Gabler's critical assumptions may be different in many respects from those of Spinoza, a number of points of comparison may be made. Both have a two stage process of interpretation that first recovers historical particularity but then strips it off in order to discover a kernel of eternal truths. For both, the properly 'critical' task of historical criticism belongs to the second stage,[21] which uncovers the universal truths that are the sure foundation of biblical authority. For Spinoza, the 'clear and distinct' knowledge of eternal truths permitted the widest variations for faith. For Gabler, the careful excavation of 'certain and undoubted universal ideas' provided the stable foundation for successive dogmatic theologies which may be tailored to suit the needs of the 'times, age, place, sect, school, and other similar factors' subject to change.[22] In effect, the investigation of historical particulars was only important because it provided the means for overcoming their transience.

Whether Spinoza actually influenced Gabler directly is a question we may leave to biographers of Gabler, but it is clear that both saw an epistemological distinction between *particular* truths and *universal* truths. This distinction was an important feature in the two works we have examined, works which are often considered to be among the founding documents of modern Old Testament 'introduction' and biblical theology. As already pointed out, however, in spite of the similarities between the epistemological 'ditch' formulated by Spinoza and Gabler and the more famous 'ugly ditch' constructed by Lessing and Kierkegaard, there is at least one important difference: both Lessing and Kierkegaard thought (for different reasons) that the *garstige Grabe* between the 'accidental' truths of history and the necessary truths of reason could not be crossed; the epistemological gap was not so much a ditch as an unbridgeable chasm. Lessing drew the conclusion that historical particularity had nothing to do with authentic religion which, as such, enjoyed the certainty of necessary and eternal truths. Kierkegaard, on the other hand, held on to both the certainty of necessary truths as well as the particularity of the historical Jesus, concluding that Christian faith was essentially a paradox which could not be defended by reason. Spinoza and Gabler had not yet gone to such extremes. They were both inclined to think that the 'eternal truths' sifted out of the Bible by careful historical study would not conflict with the claims of reason.[23]

Spinoza and Gabler both represent a world view which was characteristic of the Enlightenment, a 'world view which emphasized the unchanging nature of ultimate reality'.[24] With the rise of historicism this concept of reality was to be decisively challenged, but the groundwork for this challenge was ironically laid by a philosopher who in some ways shared this Enlightenment assumption about the unchanging nature of reality. In his widely influential work on epistemology, Immanuel Kant laid the foundations of so-called 'transcendental idealism'. The complex details of his philosophy are not our present concern, but I should perhaps note in passing that his influence on the Old Testament studies of W. M. L. de Wette was considerable. De Wette's attitude to history was shaped in particular by J. F. Fries, who revised Kant's idealism in the context of the philosophy of religion.[25]

However, there were other, more 'historical' or 'evolutionary' versions of post-Kantian idealism which were developed by de Wette's contemporaries, Schelling and Hegel. It was especially Hegel's evolutionary account of history, introduced into Old Testament studies by J. K. W. Vatke,[26] that has become notorious. In the wake of the many caricatures of 'speculative' idealism it is hard for us to appreciate what a powerful attraction Hegel was. He replaced the static Enlightenment view of reality with one that was dynamic and thoroughly historical. Accounts of Hegel's grand scheme of development, with historical reality moving towards its goal of becoming Absolute Spirit or Idea, have overshadowed the role which historical particularity played in this philosophy.

In Hegel's scheme, the development of the Absolute Idea was entirely dependent upon the driving force of historical 'particulars', especially the peculiar spiritual principles which were held to underlie nation states. Hegel's doctrine of Absolute Spirit bridged the ditch between particular history and absolute truth precisely by means of historical 'particulars' organized into a pattern of development. This is clearly evident, for example, in his view that there is an underlying Spirit which carries forward the eternal aspects of each successive nation in history while allowing the *merely* particularist tendencies of degenerating nations to subside into the past:

If thought develops to the point where the particular principle of the nation in question is no longer essential, that nation cannot continue to exist; for another principle has meanwhile emerged . . . World history then passes over to another nation.[27]

The idea that nations are enlivened by peculiar spiritual principles is one that Hegel shared with the majority of nineteenth-century German historians.[28] Where historians such as Ranke differed from Hegel was not so much in this notion of national particularity but in the idea that history could be pressed into a single narrative of development (a point to which we will shortly return). Even one of Hegel's most notable critics, Ernst Troeltsch, praised Hegel for his formulation of the 'closest thinkable interconnection' between the rational Idea and the historically concrete.[29]

In the long run, the philosophical baggage imported into Old Testament studies by de Wette and Vatke became an unnecessary burden for later critics. Wellhausen purged his predecessors' exegetical and historical insights of philosophical abstraction and restated their advances in the more concrete language of his own literary criticism. But with the rise of the 'History of Religion' school we encounter a new set of assumptions about the nature of history.

The 'History of Religion School' is now a technical term in biblical studies that refers to a loose association of German scholars which included in its number two Old Testament critics, Hugo Gressmann and Hermann Gunkel, as well as the eminent theologian Ernst Troeltsch. One encounters in the writings of this group a new attitude to historical particularity, but this attitude is not so much radically new as an extension into religious studies of earlier ideas. We shall examine in particular the influence of Leopold von Ranke and J. G. Droysen.

Perhaps the clearest statement of the assumptions of the *Religionsgeschichtliche Schule* is Troeltsch's article, 'On historical and dogmatic method in theology' (1898). Here Troeltsch pronounces dead any dogmatic theology that promulgates universal, ahistorical ideas. In a flat denial of the approach taken by Spinoza and Gabler, Troeltsch claims that since history is an ever growing process there is no possibility of discovering an ahistorical core at the centre of historical studies.[30] Cultural and historical traditions are far too varied for that to be possible.

Troeltsch is not so much concerned in this essay with isolated results of historical inquiry as with the general effect of modern historical method on conceptions of Christian faith.[31] The nature of biblical authority is once again a crucial issue. His first principle of historical criticism is that historical inquiry can only produce results of greater or lesser probability. This had been stressed many times before, but no great force had been attached to the point since several strains of Enlightenment tradition had argued that faith was in any case not simply founded upon historical inquiry. But for Troeltsch and his school, religious ideas have no source other than history; the necessary and certain ideas proposed by Spinoza and Gabler were excluded by a thoroughly historical point of view. The properly 'critical' part of historical criticism comes in judging the relative reliability of particular historical traditions, not in sifting out universal and ahistorical ideas.

It is interesting to notice the shift from Enlightenment vocabulary in Troeltsch's article: there is no more talk of 'clear and distinct' or 'certain and undoubted' ideas. The *religionsge-schichtliche* scholars are interested in religious 'intuitions' and in the intuitions necessary for historical reconstruction.[32] In this respect, however, the History of Religions school followed a broad trend of historical thinking in nineteenth-century Germany which is best characterized as 'romantic historicism'. As both Friedrich Meinecke and George Iggers have shown, historians in this tradition spoke less of clear explanatory concepts and more of intuitive understanding.[33]

Common terms for describing the historians intuitive art of 're-experiencing the past' were 'Nachempfindung', 'Nachfüh-lung' and 'Ahnung'. This language pointed to a species of intuitive yet empirical knowledge which was the characteristic conception of historical understanding formulated by influent-ial historians like Ranke and Droysen. In his comprehensive study of this historicist tradition, Iggers argues that one of its central tenets was 'Anti-Begrifflichkeit', an antipathy towards conceptual thinking in historical explanation.[34] The historicists denied the relevance not only of the universal truths or concepts of philosophy but also of the general laws of natural science; such laws, they argued, may be relevant to nature but not to history. In his *Grundriss der Historik* (1858), the historian of Hellenism J. G. Droysen contrasted the more intuitive, historical 'Verstehen' with a stricter notion of 'Erklären' proper to the natural sciences.[35] The Verstehen–Erklären distinction was associated with a contrast between the 'Geisteswissenschaften' (human-ities) and the 'Naturwissenschaften' (natural sciences), and nineteenth-century German historians relied on such distinc-tions in resisting the encroachment of positivist social science into their discipline. Thus, for example, Droysen wrote a stinging review of H. T. Buckle's *History of Civilization in England*

(1859/61) which was inspired by the positivist philosophy of August Comte.[36] Droysen stressed that historians should attend to the individual and the particular and not to the general laws beloved by positivists.[37]

In this German tradition of historiography, the category most appropriate to history was one borrowed from Herder and the Romantics, the idea of 'individuality'. The aphorism *individuum est ineffabile* summarizes the Romantic rebellion against the reduction of the human spirit to general truths, whether in the medieval doctrine of Natural Law, the Enlightenment doctrine of Reason, or the positivist vision of scientific laws at work even in the realm of human history. Meinecke has argued that it was precisely the idea of 'individuality' that was the foundation of historicism.[38] In this tradition of historiography, historical 'individuals' were held to have their own peculiar laws of organic development which cannot be reduced to the general laws of mechanical causality. The historicist individual is never simply an instance of a general law. It cannot be 'explained'; it can only be understood by sympathetic intuition (*Ahnung* or *Nachempfindung*).

In this connection it is interesting to compare Spinoza's rejection of miracles with the rejection formulated by Troeltsch in the essay mentioned above. For Spinoza, the laws of nature were the clearest reflection of the essence of God. Their eternal and immutable nature reflected the eternity and immutability of the divine. Hence, he rejected miracles because they undermined a clear perception of the immutability of God.[39] Troeltsch, on the other hand, did not reject miracles by reference to natural laws but by reference to a common human spirit which is the necessary presupposition of the historian's art of *Nachempfindung*. Absolute uniqueness cannot be re-experienced since it would fall outside this commonality; understanding of the past presupposes, therefore, at least some analogy with the present.[40] For historicists like Troeltsch, divinity is not to be found in general laws, but in the full diversity of historical individuals. The historicist doctrine of individuality could never allow historical particularity to be swallowed up into general laws.[41]

In their search for the antecedents of this attitude to history, historians of ideas have, as already noted, pointed to Herder and the Romantics who followed him. But it was Leopold von Ranke who brought the historicist vision to maturity. Herder's exhortation to study every detail of the past with equal attention[42] was taken up by Ranke in his prodigious historical writings and underpinned by a virtual theology of history.[43] His famous maxim, 'Every epoch is immediate to God', represents an enormous methodological gain for historiography. In effect, Ranke broke the Enlightenment connection between the divine and the general. If every particular epoch is in itself directly related to God then its particularity or contingency is no longer a problem. God was on the historical side of the 'ugly ditch' – if indeed there had ever been a ditch in the first place; there was no need to strain after eternal truths. For the *religionsgeschichtliche* school, this meant that all religious phenomena of the past had their own particular value and integrity. One could not isolate particular events or entire periods (e. g., miracles or Salvation History) as being alone 'of God'.[44]

One should note, however, the polemical context of Ranke's maxim. Its polemical intention is actually a good deal clearer than the meaning of the maxim itself. The maxim is found in his essay 'On Progress in History' (1854), a direct attack on the Hegelian view of historical development.[45] Ranke's central argument was at least in part concerned with Hegel's theology of history. The Hegelian view presupposed an 'utterly unworthy idea of God': the Absolute Spirit used the earlier epochs of history as mere 'stepping stones' to the later epochs of self-development. But these earlier epochs, so Ranke argued, had their own particular integrity. This judgment was later echoed by Troeltsch, who argued that Hegel's synthesis of the rational Idea with the concrete historical individual finally remains a contradiction; the 'individual' becomes a mere plaything of 'the cunning of Reason'.[46] The way to counter Hegel's view of evolutionary development was, according to Ranke, to appreciate the equal integrity of all historical individuals before God.

Ranke also responded to Hegel's evolutionary views, however, by citing examples of historical degeneration. But this tactic just raises a new question: would not degeneration represent a regression from the immediate connection with God? This is where a systematic ambiguity in the notion of 'individuality' becomes clear. An historicist 'individual' is a *collective* expression of the human spirit.[47] It can be a state, a nation, a people, a religion, a family, and for Troeltsch, even a profession or class.[48] This kind of particularity is not simply identifiable with an individual historical fact; the historicist individual is a collective structure with its own peculiar laws of organic development from birth to maturity and decline. For Ranke, the highest expressions of individuality were nations, which each have their own peculiar 'spiritual force' or 'principle'.[49] Thus it seems that only these vital spiritual forces need be considered immediately related to God, and these are best expressed by the *genius* in art, poetry, science, statecraft and religious thought.[50] The genius, the 'great personality', inspired the growth of communities and nations. But the loss of the underlying spiritual principles brought degeneration. Ranke, for example, thought that the Hellenistic kingdoms after Alexander had 'no individual principles of existence' but were based upon 'money and soldiers alone'.[51]

Considering the views of this patriarch of German historical studies, it is perhaps not surprising that in stating his aims as a religious historian Hermann Gunkel said that he sought the 'inmost nature' of the Israelite nation and set a high priority on understanding its great religious 'personalities'.[52] Comparative religious studies were not pursued for their own sake; they would finally reveal, according to Gunkel, 'the peculiarity of the Israelite spirit'. Gunkel seems to be most famous for his rejection of the idea of Israelite religion as something *absolutely* distinctive, but this did not prevent him from emphasizing the peculiarity (*Eigentümlichkeit*) of Israelite tradition.[53] This applies also to Gressmann, who could claim that every people (*Volk*) has an individual soul with specific qualities that distinguish it from every other.[54]

Although a number of Gunkel's contemporaries, such as Bernhard Duhm, criticized him for neglecting the great personalities, this criticism is more relevant to the form-critical work on

the sagas and the psalms. As Werner Klatt has pointed out,
Gunkel's aim to understand the 'hidden inner life' of the
prophets is in many respects indistinguishable from Duhm's own
attempts to understand these 'great personalities'.[55] Similarly,
Troeltsch's critical principles were not designed to eliminate the
creative originality of the great religious personalities. He
argued, for example, that

All human religion is rooted in religious intuition or divine revelation
which acquires community-building power in specific religious personalities and which is re-experienced by the community of believers
with less originality.[56]

It seems that this kind of view was widely assumed in the
'romantic idealist' tradition of historiography. The communities which followed the great historical personalities were
credited with somewhat less originality, and perhaps a less direct
connection with the divine.

It is therefore not surprising that we have much modern study
of Israelite prophecy which has been concerned to separate the
authentic words of a prophet from 'secondary', less vital
accretions. This kind of interest has, of course, antecedents in the
early modern period, but it was greatly encouraged by scholars
(as different as Wellhausen and Gunkel) who were influenced
by romantic idealism. This would account, at least in part, for
the sometimes exclusive exegetical interest in the *ipsissima verba*
of the prophets, and the consequent disregard for 'secondary'
material.[57] The historicist 'individuals' were organic; they could
be captured by narratives of birth, maturity and decline. Given
such a view, the particularities of the degenerative phase would
not attract the same kind of interest, a point which is clearly
evident in Gunkel's account of Israelite literary history.[58]

Gunkel, however, went a step further than Wellhausen by
contrasting the later, written and 'artificial' stages of tradition
with the vital, original *Sitz im Leben* or in *Volksleben*.[59] In focusing
on oral folk tradition, Gunkel was following in the footsteps of
Herder and the Grimm brothers who thought that the peculiar
spirit of the people (*Volksgeist*) could be discerned through
examination of folk legends. (Werner Klatt has rightly pointed
out that Gunkel did not import a ready-made system of genres

from contemporary studies of German folklore, but he concedes that the influence of Herder and the Grimm brothers cannot be denied.[60]) The written stage of oral tradition often represented a decline, since it was far removed from the vital, creative wellsprings of the peculiar Hebrew spirit. Not only did Gunkel wish to uncover the particularity of the Hebrew Geist, he was anxious to preserve the particularities of the Bible's oral literature. The saga, for example, had its own peculiar laws, (or 'Eigengesetzlichkeit') which were not to be confused with the written genre of historiography.[61] Here again, in this stress on literary particularity, one can trace lines of continuity with Herder. In *The Spirit of Hebrew Poetry* (1782–83) Herder had defended the distinctive features of Hebrew poetry, encouraging his readers to divest themselves of their habits of comparison and attempt to understand the biblical materials entirely on their own individual terms.[62]

I have argued so far that Gunkel continued in the historicist tradition of constructing large scale historical 'individuals'. In spite of his detailed form criticism, it seems that he was still able to see the whole sweep of Israelite history as the story of a single Hebrew spirit which fell into decline in the post-exilic period. We could compare this with Ranke's view that the Greek spirit went into rapid decline after Alexander. But not all the historicists were uncritical of the idea that collective historical individuals could be captured by narratives with such convenient beginnings and endings. Indeed, Droysen could be said to have reformulated the notion that 'every epoch is immediate to God' precisely in his pioneering work on the Hellenistic period, where he argued against the assumption of an 'historical vacuum' between the height of Greek civilization and the formation of the Roman empire. In assessing Droysen's works, Meinecke argued that there is in fact a natural connection between the research on Hellenism and Droysen's more theoretical criticisms of the tempting illusions of 'beginnings' and 'endings' created by narrative representation of the past.[63] Droysen's critique of narrative unities in historiography was an omen of things to come.

The History of Religion school made great methodological

advances by adopting the historicist view that history is a
plethora of collective and organic individuals, each with their
own integrity and value. But after the two world wars German
historicism went into rapid decline. Historians still do, of course,
describe any period or dimension of history *for its own sake*. But
some of the elements of romantic idealism which supported
Ranke's initiation of this attitude have lost their validity.[64]
Thus, for example, Frank Frick is drawing attention to a widely
held view amongst sociologists when he suggests that historicists
over-emphasize uniqueness at the expense of objective gen-
eralization.[65] Both Frick and Gottwald hold that genuine
historical explanation requires the synthesis of particulars into
general laws. One would be justified in seeing here a revival of
the positivist view of historical particularity.

Further, the historicist marriage of the empirical and the ideal
has proved to be an unhappy one. Nations, states, peoples, and
religions are now less likely to be seen as ideal, organic
individuals than as uneasy conglomerates of groups and fac-
tions. One historian of ideas has claimed that in our current
situation, 'Power has been hypostatized and given the status
that spirit once enjoyed in an earlier, humanistic dispen-
sation'.[66] It is certainly the case that the nineteenth-century
model of history writing based on philology and 'intuition' has
been supplanted by a much closer relationship between historiography and the social sciences.[67]

Similarly, in Old Testament studies we have seen the demise
of the idea of a peculiar Hebrew spirit and an encroachment of
social scientific explanation. Some scholars still claim that at
least some biblical material is resistant to such explanation, but
this seems to be special pleading. Just as Ranke could envision
the loss of spiritual principles and a regression to 'money and
soldiers alone', so many historians cannot now rise above the
level of 'money and soldiers alone' because their belief in vital
spiritual principles has died.

If, however, Ranke's romantic idealism has died, his affirmation of the integrity of each epoch has not. Historians of biblical
tradition have recently emphasized the *theological* value of each
'generation' or 'stage of tradition'.[68] Douglas Knight is even

critical of von Rad who emphasized the 'middle' stages of tradition over against Gunkel's emphasis on the earliest stages. According to Knight, *all* stages of tradition have their own integrity and have a potential value for contemporary biblical theology. This kind of argument represents, it seems to me, a new theological refinement of nineteenth-century historicism. The historical individual is here reformulated in terms of a particular Israelite 'community' or 'stage' in biblical tradition, and it seems that each one is 'immediate to God'. These notions are certainly at a lower level of abstraction than 'nation' or 'Volk'; a generation or stage of tradition is not so large an individual. This newer language also avoids the tired opposition between the genius and the social. Tradition history has provided an important corrective to the History of Religion school's predilection for origins by bringing serious attention to the 'secondary' material previously considered too far removed from its vital origin. The vocabulary of 'actualization' (*Vergegenwärtigung*) played a decisive role in this change of attitude; later reappropriations of traditional material need no longer be seen as necessarily lacking in creative originality. But we need to ask ourselves whether these newer traditio-historical categories still retain certain idealizing elements.

For example, in his recent article on biblical theology and sociological interpretation, Bernhard Anderson has pointed out that although many biblical scholars have been critical of the ideological tendencies in royal covenant, Zion and priestly theology, a consistent implementation of sociological method can find ideology in all the major biblical traditions.[69] Only a residual idealism would suggest that certain individuals, most often the prophets, stood outside any particular ideological tradition. Indeed, the influential French historian Michel Foucault is insisting that 'every discourse bears within itself the anonymous and repressed actuality of highly particular arrangements of power and knowledge'.[70]

Anderson's attempt to escape the problem seems to reverse the priorities of romantic historicism:

But, the power of the symbolization of each of these covenantal ideologies was not limited to the initial social setting out of which it arose and to which it gave meaning and legitimacy. Each of these linguistic patterns became a major 'trajectory' whose path can be traced into situations far removed from the original sociological setting.[71]

Anderson seems to be arguing that the biblical traditions have a 'metaphorical power' which lifts them up out of the sociological constraints of their origin. Sociology has apparently polluted the language of 'original historical settings' and a theological recovery is now rested on the history of a tradition's reception. This is precisely the kind of strategy used by Hans-Robert Jauss in his attempt to save literary tradition from the hands of Marxist critics, but to no avail: the history of reception can, as we shall see, also become subject matter for Marxist and other types of sociological analysis. Literary reception has its own historical particularities which are only in recent years beginning to be analysed.[72]

It seems to me that even this highly selective survey of ideas of history can throw some light on the debate about the canonical approach. The question that needs to be asked is this: has the debate been clouded by unexamined assumptions? When Childs is accused of neglecting historical particularity, there is, to be sure, more than one kind of issue at stake, but one kind of issue is theological. Knight, for example, has insisted against Childs that earlier stages of tradition have 'as much right to their own integrity as does the canonical form'; the canonical approach deprives the earlier stages of their own independent theological value.[73] Even the canonical critic J. A. Sanders separates himself from Childs by recommending attention to 'each sequential generation'. Childs's stress on believing communities is paradoxical, according to Sanders, because he effectively denies the humanity and integrity of those very communities.[74] These arguments put forward by Knight and Sanders against Childs bear a striking resemblance to Ranke's moral and theological argument against Hegel. As we have seen, Ranke affirmed the integrity of each epoch against the immoral, Hegelian Spirit which used earlier epochs as mere stepping-stones in the process of self-development. Similarly, Knight and Sanders affirm the integrity of each generation against a canonical approach which threatens to turn earlier generations into mere stepping-stones in the development of the final form of scripture.

On closer analysis, of course, tradition historians have two different goals, one descriptive and the other evaluative. First, there is a descriptive goal behind the attempt to re-expand and separate out all the particular stages of tradition that have been telescoped into the canon's final form. As I have argued in the previous chapter, this goal of traditio-historical work can be most accurately described as an attempt to write the emic history of Israelite religion. But beyond this emic description, tradition historians often insist on the potential theological value of all the traditions they reconstruct. They are more sketchy about this evaluative goal, apparently feeling more at home with the descriptive task. But it is clear that they see theological value in their work.

It is not quite so clear, however, exactly what this theological value is. Expressing warm feelings about history is not enough. When we examined Ranke more closely we found that it was really the *genius*, rather than a whole epoch, who is immediate to God, and a similar point applies here. Tradition historians occasionally give us hints that the real value of uncovering the various layers of biblical tradition is that they are opened up for fresh critique and evaluation. Sometimes earlier traditions will be preferred and sometimes later ones.[75] A point that is often stressed is that modern biblical theologians should have the right to remake decisions about the relative value of different theological traditions. We need to retain this right because the biblical generations may have been misguided in their decisions. As Rudolf Smend has put it, '*We* . . . may see something they never saw'.[76] Thus, apparently, all generations and stages of biblical tradition need equal attention precisely because their theological judgment cannot be trusted.

For the canonical approach, on the other hand, the Bible is not a source book for the history of Israelite religion but the product of a long evaluative process of selecting and ordering the most valuable traditions. Childs has not arbitrarily privileged the canonizing generations over all the others; he has repeatedly affirmed that much old material has found its way into the final form. However, he is disposed to accept the decisions of the successive biblical communities as both theologically and exegetically important. He has shown no desire to remake decisions about the relative value of the variety of theological traditions found in the Bible. Accordingly, if this evaluative process has left original and particular historical contexts blurred, a canonical approach does not demand their recovery. The approach can properly be called a hermeneutic of consent – consent to the decisions made in the process of canon formation. There is still a role for theological critique, Childs has recently argued, but this should take place using categories supplied by the canonical tradition, not categories supplied by modern sciences (1985: 11–12). In other words, contemporary theological judgment should preserve an 'emic continuity' with our classic texts.

One should recognize that Childs has not disallowed the separate task of writing a history of Israelite religion or literature (1979: 60–2). The most he has said is that this work will be speculative and of little *theological* value. This judgment, I would suggest, should not trouble a 'pure' historian. However speculative their work turns out to be, historians of Israel are responsible to the evidence, methods and questions appropriate to their own scholarly community. Given the categories and questions of their discipline, they will try to tell the best story possible with as much particularity as the biblical and extra-biblical evidence allows. As pointed out in chapter 1 even the results of the hard sciences can be understood as conjectural. The sticking point for some biblical historians is that they *also* want their results to have theological significance, something Childs denies. And indeed some historians have suggested that history writing designed to have practical significance *is not history writing at all*.[77] Nevertheless, the question remains: has Childs oversimplified the evaluative task of biblical theology by accepting the decisions of earlier traditions which are embedded in the final form? What are the other options for approaching this evaluative task? I shall discuss these issues further in the final chapter, but at this point a few brief remarks are in order.

One would have to say that the most popular option in

evaluating the past is to accept the criteria of one's own culture, age, or interpretative community. This was indeed the kind of solution that was explicitly offered by Ranke, and his evaluative attitude is, therefore, best described not as relativism but as conservatism.[78] Ranke not only claimed that each nation has its own peculiar spiritual principles, he also discouraged the importation of foreign ideas and institutions, especially those stemming from the French Revolution. What was needed, in Ranke's view, was a 'balance' of the great national powers; 'a mixture of them would destroy the essence of each one'.[79] In this respect, an exclusive fidelity to the spirit of one's own nation, age, culture, or interpretative community implies a conservative position that resists the criteria offered by other communities. In Ranke's view, other historical individuals may be studied and contemplated for their own sake; they may interact with but need not transform one's own outlook. The irony in this kind of descriptive approach is that history becomes an antiquarian exercise with no decisive bearing on the present.[80] History is finally unimportant in any normative sense; only the present 'spirit of the age' counts, or to put it less abstractly, only the criteria of one's own community count.

Ernst Troeltsch, on the other hand, became critical of the contemplative attitude to history advocated by both Ranke and Meinecke. Although the belief in the essential equality of all religious insights had great methodological value for historiography, most of the History of Religions school seemed to assume some kind of normative value in the Jewish-Christian tradition. Just how this normative value should be articulated was a problem they left up to Troeltsch.[81] Whatever we may think of Troeltsch's solutions, he must be credited with a clear view of the *implications* of relativism in the historicist tradition, and this is the problem that dominated all his later writings.[82]

The problem of theological evaluation is still usually addressed by biblical critics only in an *ad hoc* way, and this would not be a problem if biblical studies was purely concerned with the history of Israelite religion. But if the biblical traditions are to be considered in some sense normative, then explicit discussion is needed as to how their diversity is to be evaluated. Even if Childs's solution is simplistic, it is not sufficient to reply to him by warmly affirming the diversity and particularity of biblical traditions. Such a reply is entirely appropriate for an historian of Israelite religion, but it cannot serve as criticism for the interesting and difficult task which Childs has set himself, namely, how the Old Testament can still function as normative literature for the Christian church. There may well be good *theological* reasons for reconstructing the history and religion of Israel, but I would suggest that any such reasons should not be allowed to retain an implicit dependence on romantic histori- cism. The affirmation of historical 'individuals' certainly played an important role for historians responding to Enlightenment rationalism, but with the decline of both Enlightenment rationalism and romantic historicism, our theological attitudes to historical particularity cannot rest on these nineteenth- century foundations.

To summarize: vague invocations of historical particularity cannot be used in theological arguments against the canonical approach. We need to separate two different issues here, one that concerns theological evaluation of biblical traditions and one that concerns the methodology of historical reconstruction. Theological evaluation of the canonical process is indeed a genuine problem, and we shall return to it in the final chapter, but Childs cannot be refuted by simply invoking the integrity and particularity of the individual biblical traditions. The question of whether the Bible can still supply theological norms needs a lot more detailed discussion than that. Leaving aside the theological issue for the time being, we are now in a position to consider the second problem – the role of 'background' in historical studies.

THE PROBLEM OF 'BACKGROUND' IN HISTORICAL STUDIES

In some ways, Childs was quite justified in rejecting the exegetical assumption that 'the sharper the historical focus, the better the interpretation' (e.g. 1980a: 205). In order to defend him, one would not even need to draw on the kinds of arguments about literature advanced by the New Critics. One could begin, for example, by emphasizing the plurality of methods in biblical studies. It is not clear that *all* textual interpretation has to be historical in the sense that it is bound to the non-linguistic context of a text's production. The choice of a method will depend on one's interpretative goals, interests, purposes and affiliation to scholarly communities. If one wishes to argue for the superiority of one method over another, this will need some detailed comparison, not a question-begging assertion that one needs to recover a text's historical particularity in order to discover its 'true intelligibility'.[83]

Let us assume, however, for the moment that we wish to be 'historical' critics and not, say, New Critical or structuralist ones. Just how much detail do we need before we can claim to have accurately described an historical context? Take for example a text which has its origin in a cultic festival. Was that festival celebrated for generations or for a few years, all over Israel or only in specific parts? And were the social relations or economic structures different in each case, or the same? Sociological and economic historians might want to know this kind of detail. Do we need to know the author's family, or just the clan? Would the author's socio-economic status be relevant? A psychoanalytic historian might want to know the details of the author's relationship to his mother, or to her father, in order to tell us what was *really* being intended. And what about temporal particularity: is the generation enough, or might we need to know the year of authorship, the month, or even the time of day?

The point is, of course, that more and more historical detail will not necessarily give a better interpretation. This is often overlooked because of the scarcity of our sources. But if one looks at works on contemporary history where there is an overload of information, the issue is clear. More information only solves one type of interpretative problem. There seem to be more arguments over how the information is to be construed and which historical details are relevant or significant.[84]

Here we are touching on one of the most fundamental issues in historiography: criteria of relevance. Just which historical particulars are to be considered relevant will depend on the kind of explanation an historian wishes to offer. It is important to see that the search for criteria of relevance is a matter for constant debate; it is not something to be simply assumed. It is not enough to say that the more details the better. Feminist, economic, psychoanalytic, sociological or political historians will, in all likelihood, offer competing interpretations of the same events. The *Annales* school of French historiography has even produced criteria of relevance which give priority in historical explanations to environmental conditions that persist for hundreds of years. My basic point here is that the bi-polar opposition between historical particularity and 'abstract time-lessness'[85] is itself far too abstract to be of any real use.

If we consider the canonical approach in the context of this wider debate about historiography we see that Childs is willing to accept the criteria of relevance used by the communities that preserved the biblical literature. These communities have deemed some traditions and some historical details more relevant to their ongoing concerns than others. Less relevant details were subordinated or forgotten. Childs wants to accept these decisions whereas historical critics want to recover more and more of the forgotten detail which they deem relevant to an adequate understanding of the texts. The recovery of this detail is especially acute problem for certain types of literature, like wisdom and the psalms. Form criticism has been forced into saying only the most general and speculative things about the 'Sitz im Leben' of such texts. Even with respect to prophetic texts and narrative material the background posited in exegesis often consists of highly generalized references to 'the' post-exilic, or pre-exilic periods (sometimes rounded off to the nearest century), or to a northern instead of a southern provenance.

Yet it is still arguable, against Childs, that the biblical authors intended their meaning to be inferred not simply from their text but from a knowledge of the specific historical context which they shared with their audience. Speakers often intend their audience to draw out implications which they have not *explicitly* articulated. In analysing such cases, linguists have referred to the 'mutual knowledge', shared by speakers and hearers but not explicit in speech, which is necessary if the correct implication is to be drawn out.[86]

Two things may be said here in defence of Childs. First, even if the task of discerning an author's intention is a legitimate goal of historical exegesis, it need not (unless one is a hermeneutical monist) be the only aim of interpretation. Second, even if we could be certain about all the details of an author's historical context it is extremely difficult to know how this evidence should be used in emic description. The matter is considerably simplified in etic research since the 'native' description of a context does not need to coincide with that of the researcher. Emic description, on the other hand, is constrained to ask whether the native sees the context in the same way.

The central problems for emic description in this area are bound up with notoriously complex debates about reference and allusion. A comprehensive discussion of these issues would require a separate study, but here I will simply try to clarify the relevance of these debates. One should begin with the basic insight in linguistics that there is no intrinsic connection between linguistic 'meanings' and actual referents in the world;[87] i.e., different languages divide up the non-linguistic world in radically different ways. Consequently, a non-native observer's account of supposed referents – whether these referents are events, practices or objects – does not constitute direct evidence for 'the native point of view'. This would be even more true of scholarly *reconstructions* of events, practices, objects and situations which belong to the distant past. I am not suggesting here that 'there is nothing outside of the text'.[88] The linguistic practices of referring are not so easily disposed of; reference is a genuine problem, not a pseudo-problem.

John Lyons provides one of the clearest articulations of this point, and it will be instructive to quote him at length:

Not all the observable, or observationally salient, components of the actual situation of utterances are linguistically relevant, and in some cases very few of them are. Moreover, the linguistic relevance of much of what is observable is apparent only to those who are familiar with a given language system and culture . . . It is not being denied that some correlations between certain features of utterances and components of actual situations are discoverable by external observers . . . Linguists and anthropologists in the field may start by doing this. Subsequently, however, they work from within the culture, and more or less successfully in proportion to their success in identifying the culturally and linguistically relevant distinctions.[89]

In other words, the emic correlation of text and context is an extremely difficult task which requires a great deal of sensitivity and patience on the part of the field-worker. Some authors have even doubted whether successful cross-cultural understanding can be demonstrated in any strict sense at all.[90] Add to this the problem of dealing with languages and cultures which have been dead for thousands of years, and the scepticism of the canonical approach towards historical background and 'referential readings' becomes a good deal more plausible.

However, it is one thing to concede that emic description of Israelite tradition is a very difficult task, and it is quite another to conclude from this that one should always give priority to the explicit content of biblical texts in their final form. I would prefer to say that emic historians have different interpretative interests. Although it is true that more and more historical background will not always give a better interpretation, emic historians need to reconstruct the *relevant* features of historical background (including social practices) before they can formulate their hypotheses about how native Israelites saw things. I will also argue in the next section that the reconstruction of relevant historical background is as important for synchronic interpretation as it is for diachronic studies. The sense in which the canonical approach is synchronic, as Childs has sometimes claimed, will therefore require some careful qualification. This, then, is the next stage in our clarification of the relationship between the canonical approach and historical research.

WHAT IS SYNCHRONIC INTERPRETATION?

'Synchronic interpretation' is an umbrella term for a large number of disparate intellectual movements which are counterposed to 'diachronic' approaches, and although some types of synchronic interpretation, including the canonical approach, have often been regarded as anti-historical, this is not necessarily the case. Synchronic interpreters are united by their opposition to a view, widespread in the nineteenth century, that

an adequate understanding of the nature of any phenomenon and an adequate understanding of its value are to be gained through considering it in terms of the place which it occupied and the role which it played within a process of development.

This quotation is actually the definition of 'historicism' provided by Maurice Mandelbaum in a major study of nineteenth-century intellectual history.[91] Such a broad definition of historicism (perhaps overly broad) reflects Mandelbaum's focus on the idea of *development*, an idea shared by diverse movements in the nineteenth century which one also meets under the labels of 'positivism', 'romanticism', 'speculative idealism', 'materialism', or 'evolutionism'.

Two of the most important twentieth-century movements opposed to historicism in this broad sense have been 'functionalist' social science and 'synchronic' linguistics. Again, the broadest characterization of these complex movements will be sufficient for our purposes. Functionalism reacted in particular against the evolutionary doctrine of 'survivals'. This doctrine was reflected in a tendency to account for puzzling cultural phenomena as legacies of earlier stages of evolutionary development which had somehow survived and been preserved by later generations.[92] Functionalists would insist, for example, that one does not account for the use of horse-drawn hansom cabs in present day New York City by explaining the invention of such vehicles and the original contexts of their usage. Rather, the contemporary usage of hansom cabs should be understood as serving the *present* function of nostalgia or 'retrospective sentiment'.[93] Such a social scientific explanation is synchronic rather than diachronic. Note that there is no denial here of the fact that social phenomena have a history, or that social agents are interested in their history; rather, it is argued that the best kind of social scientific explanation seeks to understand the function of phenomena within a contemporary social system. This was, at least, the characteristic style of explanation developed by the influential British school of 'structural-functionalism'.[94]

One of the characteristic features of synchronic linguistics may be described in the same way. Especially since the publication of Saussure's *Cours de linguistique générale*, linguists have emphasized that the meaning of a word may bear little relation to its prehistory. To put the point positively, a lexical item (which may be larger than a single word) is most adequately understood as a function within the synchronic system of which it is a part. Over the past three decades, this point has been repeatedly stressed by biblical scholars like James Barr and John Sawyer who have been anxious to correct the misuse of diachronic hypotheses formulated by comparative Semitists. Once again, the point has not been to deny that words have a history; rather, it is emphasized that synchronic semantic description, which seeks to understand language within its contemporary linguistic system, has methodological priority. Diachronic semantics is strictly speaking dependent on the results of synchronic description, and not the other way around.[95]

Although I have been speaking at a rather high level of generality, it would be fair to say that structural-functionalism and synchronic linguistics share a common stress on 'synchronic interpretation'. Now we need to look more closely at how such ideas have been applied analogically to exegesis. In recent years, several advocates of the so-called literary approach to biblical study have been directing their attention to the final form of biblical texts. Although the expression 'final form' carries the implication that the text has indeed passed through *prior* forms, the newer literary interests have sometimes been associated with anti-historical rhetoric.[96] The impression created by this rhetoric was that if diachronic critics had dissected biblical texts into earlier and later stages, then conversely, synchronic critics represent a different kind of literary interest in the unified final form. But such a notion leaves a great deal to be clarified.

The label itself, 'the literary approach', is unfortunately misleading. First, it is easily confused with the literary criticism which has as its goal the analysis of written sources, as opposed to oral tradition. This kind of approach has also seen a revival in recent years, and, in spite of the vigorous debate which it has generated, the goals of the new literary or documentary criticism stand firmly in the tradition of historical criticism. Second, 'the' literary approach wrongly implies a homogeneity of interpretative interests, perhaps most notably a common focus on the final form. But even if the various versions of the literary approach have often concentrated on the final form, there is no necessary reason why this should have been so.[97] There is nothing contradictory about literary interests being brought to reconstructed texts, however hypothetical these texts may be. Instead of speaking about 'the' literary approach we should speak of a diversity of literary approaches which are identified by their characteristic set of analytical concepts like theme, plot, character, scene, repetition, structural opposition, point of view, style, metaphor, indeterminacy and so on.

Given the fact, however, that these concepts have often been applied to the final form of biblical texts, in what sense is such interpretation synchronic? The central problem is that the text being interpreted usually does not stem from a single specific period; there are frequently textual elements (whether ideas or linguistic archaisms) which, like hansom cabs in present-day New York, derive from earlier cultural-linguistic systems. This, at least, is the general consensus of historical criticism, even if it is difficult to find agreement about details.

The simplest response to this problem would be to draw an analogy between exegesis and structural-functionalism or synchronic linguistics: legacies of earlier systems have to be explained in terms of their contemporary function in the final form. But this response is not really a precise analogy at all, since a text – in this case the final form – is not itself a system. (In Saussure's terms, texts are *parole* rather than *langue*; they are examples of communication made possible by a language system). Rather, one would need to say that the elements of the final form should be understood within the context of their contemporary social and linguistic *systems*, and this could mean one of two things: (a) one should understand the final form within the social and linguistic systems which were the original context of its *production*, or (b) one should understand the final form within the social and linguistic systems which were the successive contexts of its *preservation*. This, however, just raises a new problem for anti-historical literary approaches, since (a) can be understood as a task for redaction criticism broadly conceived, and (b) can be understood as a task for historians of Judaism and Christianity. In other words, a strict application of the analogies with structural-functionalism and synchronic linguistics leads us back to historical (though not, in Mandelbaum's sense, historicist) disciplines.

This argument can be made more concrete if we examine the work of John Sawyer, who has explicitly dealt with final form semantics in the light of synchronic linguistics. Sawyer introduces one of the main principles of his semantic theory by arguing that words have meaning only within the specific 'historical contexts within which they have been understood'.[98] He goes on to insist that there is no reason to privilege one synchronic context over another, and he makes the 'quite arbitrary decision' that

the final form of the text as preserved in masoretic tradition and transmitted to us in the Codex Leningradensis, should be the literary corpus in which the terms to be discussed occur, and how the masoretes themselves understood the text should be the subject for semantic analysis. (p.11)

It seems, then, that Sawyer's monograph is not a final form study in sense (a) above – the final form studied within the social and linguistic systems which were the original context of its production. His work is, at least ostensibly, more in line with sense (b): it sets out to be a study of the text's preservation within one of the subsequent contexts of its reception, i.e., within 'the' masoretic period. It is therefore conceived as an historical study, albeit one that gives methodological priority to synchronic description. Sawyer finds a direct analogy between the successive audiences of the biblical period, and the successive audiences who preserved the biblical text after that period. 'We are not concerned', he writes,

in defining meaning, only with what the original author meant, but also with how his original audience or readers understood him; and if we allow this, then we must also grant that the interpretations of later readers (who may or may not have discovered the author's meaning) have as much claim on our attention as his original audience. (p.5)

The medieval masoretes, in Sawyer's view, are to be considered one of those later audiences. Since this particular audience provided a number of religious communities with the standard text of the Hebrew Bible, and moreover, 'the text is as a rule quite intelligible as it stands' (p.12), Sawyer chooses the MT as the object of his semantic description.

This argument is, however, built on some tenuous analogies. The medieval masoretes, for example, were attempting to preserve a fixed text in a language which was, from a synchronic perspective, already 'dead'. There is a broad consensus among linguists that language systems can, and normally do, change from generation to generation.[99] Although it might be arguable that Hebrew changed only very slowly, it would be misleading to think of the masoretes as 'native speakers' of biblical Hebrew, or more precisely, of any of the linguistic systems within which the biblical text came to be. Nor were the masoretes participants in the social systems of the biblical period. There is in fact some equivocation in Sawyer's semantic principles and here it will be useful to focus on two problematic issues in his work which are relevant to an understanding of the canonical approach: (a) how the MT relates to the actual language systems of the biblical period; (b) how 'historical setting' determines a 'semantic context'.

As already indicated, the first principle of Sawyer's monograph is that words have meaning only within the specific 'historical contexts within which they have been understood'. However, Sawyer points out that the language of the Old Testament originated in various distinct historical contexts, and therefore semantic studies which take in the whole of the biblical corpus cannot be used 'as a guide to any one historical situation' (p.41). 'The corpus is not a representative cross-section of the Hebrew language at any one time' (p.114). For example, by working on the semantic field of words for salvation in the final form of the MT Sawyer has avoided the historical changes to the field of salvation during the biblical period. Thus, although the size of the field has through time been enlarged – e.g., *psh* and *prq* are probably loan words from Aramaic (p.42) – Sawyer's method does not require him to specify the size of the field at any one time during the biblical period. The synchronic slice of his choice falls long after these changes have occurred, in a time where 'the' language system exists only in a fixed written corpus.

In what sense, then, has Sawyer interpreted the MT in the 'historical context' of the masoretes? The issue is very unclear. It is difficult to see how the historical context of the masoretes can be *semantically* relevant; the linguistic features of the Hebrew Bible cannot be understood as functions within medieval language and socio-cultural systems. Surely, the most that can be said is that the *exegesis* of the MT should be understood within the context of medieval language and socio-cultural systems.[100] To say that the study focuses on the meaning of the final form as the masoretes understood it, or 'as contextualized in masoretic tradition' is just ambiguous (pp. 19, 26). Masoretic tradition is not a linguistic system, nor is it an historical context.

In practice, the 'context' of Sawyer's synchronic description in this monograph is the corpus of the Hebrew Bible, not the historical context of the masoretes, and in later essays he has been more consistent in explicitly opposing 'settings in literature' to 'settings in life'.[101] The problem here might be illuminated by an analogy: modern English speakers stand in a similar relation to the language of Shakespeare as the masoretes stood to biblical Hebrew. We can understand Shakespearean English, with perhaps a little study, and even occasionally use it, but it is not in itself our *langue*. A synchronic study of, say, British English in the 1980s would need to recognize uses of Shakespearean language as *antiquated*, designed to have certain 'literary' effects, and so on. The evidence for such a study could never be restricted to the literary corpus of Shakespearean English. Yet that is precisely the kind of restriction that Sawyer has adopted in order to understand the contextualization of the Hebrew Bible in 'the' masoretic period. In short, Sawyer's *Semantics in Biblical Research* contravenes its own first principle: lexical items are not here understood within historical contexts at all; they are understood within the literary context of the whole Hebrew Bible. It would be more accurate to say that Sawyer has developed a semantics for *formalist literary theory*, a point to which we shall shortly return.

I have argued, then, that it is misleading to compare contextualization of the Hebrew Bible during 'the' masoretic period with the synchronic contextualization of Hebrew spoken during the biblical period. In so far as the masoretes were understanding the text, and not simply transcribing it, they were *reconstructing* the language of the biblical text into a meaningful system. Not possessing the spectacles of Enlightenment criticism, they did not see that the text might be the product of a complex history of tradition, and not possessing the spectacles of synchronic linguistics, they did not see that the language might be a hybrid of many successive linguistic systems. To speak anachronistically, they reconstructed the *langue* of the Bible on the basis of its *parole*. This is, indeed, precisely what modern linguists do, but there is a difference: the *langue* of the Old Testament corpus, as Sawyer himself points out, does not correspond to the *langue* of any one community of speakers in ancient Israel. These ancient systems of Hebrew might be reconstructed not only with the aid of the MT but also with the help of contemporary Israelite inscriptions.[102] Sawyer, then, has followed the masoretes in reading the MT *as if* it were the product of a single, historical language system.

What, then, does all this mean for the canonical approach? I have already pointed out that the goal of textual criticism is, for Childs, to recover the Hebrew text which was probably stabilized around the end of the first century C.E., and he takes the medieval Masoretic Text to be the primary witness to this goal. But what are the implications of this goal with respect to linguistics? One possibility is to say that the aim is to understand the biblical text *in the context of the linguistic system of Hebrew in use around the end of the first century*. Taking this line of approach, archaisms and the like must be understood precisely as *archaisms*, i.e., within the contemporary linguistic system rather than within the context of their origin. (Note, however, that earlier *ideas* or *concepts* could well be retained in the text and simply recast into contemporary language. The arresting of this process of linguistic contemporizing could then be understood as a part of textual stabilization.)

The difficulty with this approach, however, is that the process of stabilization extended over a period of indeterminate length. The Torah probably achieved an indisputably authoritative status before the other books, and its textual transmission seems therefore to be more stable. On the other hand, there are both 'conservative' and 'updated' recensions of prophetic texts at Qumran, reflecting a situation of textual fluidity just before 68 C.E. This has been contrasted with the more unified profile of the biblical texts found at Murabba' at and dated around 132–35 C.E.[103]

What would it mean, then, to say that one is working with 'the' linguistic system of the entire stabilized Hebrew Bible? It would seem difficult to say that this system is simply identical with the Hebrew used at the extreme end of the biblical period. Given the length of time that the canonization process took, it seems clear that the corpus includes more than one system of Hebrew. The distinctive features of later Hebrew are often pointed out, for example, in studies of Chronicles, Ezra and Nehemiah, Esther and Ecclesiastes. 'The' Hebrew of the canon is simply not identical with the Hebrew spoken in the late first century C.E.; it is a literary hybrid. All language systems are, of course, in some sense hybrids of previous ones – this fact is not in itself an obstacle to strictly synchronic semantics. The distinctive feature of 'canonical Hebrew' as a linguistic system, however, is that it is a *literary* hybrid; it was never spoken by a single community of speakers, including the speakers of Hebrew at the end of the first century, and this makes it difficult to study in a strictly synchronic way.[104] It was certainly understood by Hebrew speakers at the end of the first century, but these speakers of Hebrew were already making a transition to Mishnaic Hebrew (and, indeed, many Jews needed Aramaic translations as well). Strictly synchronic semantic studies of the first-century Hebrew canon could not, therefore, focus simply on the corpus itself; such studies would need to place the canon in the historical context of a reconstructed language that shares some of the features of Mishnaic Hebrew.

Childs has not, however, drawn out the linguistic implications of his work in these strictly synchronic terms. He seems to assume a much more flexible approach to linguistic description which might actually require (whether he approves of this suggestion or not) some formalist literary theory. It will be useful, therefore, to examine how such a theory can throw a different light on these linguistic issues.

Scholars such as Childs and Sawyer have explicitly refused to restrict their exegetical goals to the intention of actual historical authors, and this would be supported by a number of schools of literary theory. Sawyer has, in effect, gone a step further and attempted to create a semantics which is not restricted to individual, historical language systems. Neither scholar has engaged with post-structuralist theories of language, which might have been useful to them, but both have revealed a decided inclination towards the formalist linguistics that was implied by New Criticism.[105]

Although New Critics stressed the integrity of literary artefacts, they did not see these artefacts as entirely 'autonomous' of the linguistic conventions within which they were produced. Texts could become autonomous with respect to authors but not with respect to linguistic systems. It is simply not true to say that a New Critical approach to the Bible is essentially ahistorical. The main New Critical point is that meanings are precisely *conventional*, the sort of thing one can look up in 'grammars, dictionaries, and all the literature which is the source of dictionaries'.[106] The fact that 'the interpreter of the Bible must double as linguist far more often than an interpreter of modern literature need do'[107] does not undermine this point at all. Modern literature is historical in precisely the same sense as ancient literature is. The only difference is that when interpreters turn their attention to ancient texts, as well as to contemporary but *foreign* texts, they necessarily consult grammars and dictionaries much more often.

However, in an important footnote to Wimsatt and Beardsley's classic essay on the 'intentional fallacy' we find the following remark:

the history of words *after* a poem is written may contribute meaning which if relevant to the original pattern should not be ruled out by a scruple about intention.[108]

This suggests that New Critical interpretation need not be restricted to the single linguistic system within which a poem is produced. New Criticism need not, therefore, be a strictly synchronic style of interpretation after all; it allows for a certain degree of interpretative play between cognate language systems.

This kind of theory has obvious advantages for biblical interpretation. Given a hybrid text in which different historical stages have been fused together, it is extremely difficult to reconstruct the different linguistic systems of ancient Hebrew which are embodied in the canon. But the approach of Wimsatt and Beardsley would allow us to circumvent the problem. Nevertheless, what is a virtue for some will be a vice for others, depending on the prior interpretative interests brought to the text. It is obvious that a New Critical approach to language will never enjoy universal appeal. New Criticism is manifestly of no use, for example, to historians of the biblical period; given their interpretative goals, they will naturally and properly reject it. However, given a pluralist philosophy in biblical studies, it is not necessary to rule out the utility of New Criticism altogether. Indeed, such a flexibility in linguistic description would seem to be more practical in studies of the Hebrew Bible than strictly synchronic semantics.

In the case of the canonical approach, it would be fair to conclude that Childs has developed a style of exegetical practice which bears a clear resemblance to New Criticism: his final form interpretation is not tied to specific historical intentions or even, apparently, to specific historical language systems. His exegetical practice seems to allow a certain degree of interpretative play between the cognate languages which have left their stamp on the Bible. Childs has quite explicitly been working with a hybrid text in which various historical elements have been fused together. Perhaps we should understand his endorsement of a 'synchronistic' interpretation as *metaphorical*; his is not a synchronic method in the stricter senses discussed above. He is not, for example, attempting to relate all the elements of the final form to the social and linguistic systems inhabited by the final redactors of the Bible. The most one could say is that his approach is akin to synchronic methods in so far as canonical exegesis is not made to rest (at least when Childs is being consistent) on reconstructions of historical development. In other words, the canonical approach may not be strictly synchronic, but neither is it 'historicist' in Mandelbaum's sense of the term.

Childs has not, however, advocated his philosophy of interpretation as a part of a general theory about literature. His formalist approach to biblical texts is founded on theological reasoning, as well as on a distinctive account of the process of canonization. John Sawyer is right to insist that 'The "canonical approach" cannot claim exclusive rights to work on the final form of the text',[109] but we must remember that 'literary' critics and linguists have usually chosen this exegetical object for different reasons.

To summarize: Childs's approach to exegesis is formalist rather than strictly synchronic. He cannot be faulted for not having the right kind of historical interest, whether emic, etic, synchronic or diachronic; these are simply different interpretative interests. The theological value of these various interests is a separate issue, which needs a lot more discussion than historical critics have so far offered.[110] The goal of the canonical approach is to provide fresh readings of the final form of the biblical texts as such. Childs has adopted this formalist goal partly on the grounds of his understanding of the canonical process and partly on theological grounds. In the next chapter, we shall examine the validity of these grounds, and investigate further the relationship between the canonical process and 'canonical intentionality'.

CHAPTER 5

Textual intentions and histories of reception

One of the distinctive features of Childs's work is his stress on the reception and ordering of traditions within the biblical period – the canonical process (e.g. 1985: 23). He resists, however, the practice of reconstructing earlier layers of the text 'apart from their reception and transmission within the community of faith' (1985: 11–12). The *end products* of the canonical process are the object of exegetical attention, and the earlier layers of a text are not to be understood independently of later editing and redaction. The final composition of a biblical text is greater than the sum of its parts. This also applies to the parts played by individual biblical editors; their merely individual contributions have been effaced so that attention can be focused on the text itself. Yet more than this, canonical exegesis can also examine textual effects which may or may not have been intended by particular redactors (1984a: 49; c.f. 1979: 79, 661). As if to soften this exegetical licence to seek out unintended effects, Childs also speaks of 'the intention of the text' or of 'canonical intentionality' (cf. 1979: 79, 300, 393, 486, 645). In this chapter we shall address the issue of whether all these separate arguments about reception and textuality can be held together in a coherent whole.

Can we, for example, make any sense of the idea that communicative intentions can be attributed to texts, rather than to human agents, or is this, as Barr and Oeming suggest,[1] just a 'mystic' anthropomorphism? And how does the idea of textual intention relate to Childs's claims about the intentions of the actual biblical editors? First, we should stress that the idea of canonical intentionality is one implication of Childs's view that the Old Testament is the product of a long communal process of reception. He explicitly opposes the 'modern' idea of books produced by individual authors with the Old Testament books which are 'traditional, communal, and developing' (1979: 574; cf. 223, 236). In this sense, the idea of canonical intentionality is simply a new way of expressing the long familiar idea that Old Testament texts are more often a deposit of tradition than the product of individual authorship. But Childs's exegetical pract-ice is explicitly focused on the final biblical text, and this focus cannot simply be identified with an emic description of Israelite tradition during the biblical period. An emic history of tradition would need to *reconstruct* the beliefs and practices of historical Israel, and this is precisely what Childs refuses to do. His exegetical practice is, as argued in the previous chapter, formalist if not synchronic.

In this chapter I shall attempt to unpack this set of problems and provide a defence of the canonical approach. It will become evident that my defence has distinct limits, but nevertheless, Childs has received some unjustified criticisms. We will begin by analysing James Barr's argument that the canonical approach, in working with the final text, falls into anachronism. After showing that the kind of anachronism at issue here is not so damaging as it seems, we will move on to the puzzle of textual intentions. Beginning from an analogy between the canonical process and progress in science, I will suggest that even the recent work of E. D. Hirsch gives some credence to the idea of 'meaning without an intending subject';[2] texts *can* become relatively independent of their authors and a legitimate goal of interpretation in themselves. I will suggest that both authorial intention and 'textual intention' are valid – but different – interpretative goals, without yet implying a preference for either. I will, however, attempt to give a defence of Childs's preference for textual intention by interpreting the canonical approach in the light of Gadamer's hermeneutics. The final section on Gadamer will draw together a number of the themes in previous sections.

CONCEPTS OF CANON AND THE IDEAL EYE WITNESS

The concept of canon is notoriously difficult to define, and it must be confessed that Childs has himself helped to confuse the issues. Hans Barstad has complained that the word 'canon' often functions in Childs's writing as 'une espèce de formule magique'.[3] Indeed, James Barr has argued that Childs's attempt to hold together both a *final* canon and a *canonical process* (a canon in the making) has led to frequent confusions and ambiguities unified only by 'the principle of attraction, value, and satisfaction that makes everything about canons and canonicity beautiful'.[4] Barr's analysis is often illuminating, but I shall argue in this section that his discussion does not actually undermine the canonical approach.

Consider the first thesis advanced in Barr's book, *Holy Scripture*:

In what we call 'biblical times', or in much of them, there was as yet no Bible . . . A scripture, in the sense of an already existing, defined and delimited, written guide for the religion, did not yet exist.[5]

This is a puzzling claim. If Barr is simply saying that there was no immutable corpus of authoritative writings during the biblical period then the point seems quite uncontroversial: the expression 'biblical times' denotes the period within which the Bible came to be, not the period *after* its formation. One could hardly expect a 'defined and delimited' set of books to exist before the events which gave rise to these books had actually transpired.

Barr goes on to argue that by taking its stand on the canon as a complete entity the church fell into 'a deep anachronism'.[6] This assertion also requires a lot more analysis than it receives. There are a number of difficult theological problems connected with the use of a canon, but I would suggest that Barr's argument about anachronism is not one of them. The kind of anachronism found in the religious use of scripture (whether Catholic, Protestant or Jewish) can also be found in modern history writing. This point can perhaps be best illustrated by beginning with a familiar example, a single event, and then multiplying descriptions of it until we reach a description that Barr's argument would require us to regard as an anachronism.

There was, in 1914, a murder in the town of Sarajevo. Gavrilo Princip pulled the trigger of a gun, shot the Archduke Franz Ferdinand, and killed him. In so doing, Princip avenged Serbia against Austria. Problems for retrospective observation have begun to appear even at this point. We could not say that Princip 'avenged' Serbia until the archduke had actually been shot. There was a time, of course, when it would have been anachronistic to say that Princip had achieved this end, even though it may have been true to describe his *intention* to avenge Serbia. As John Searle puts it, 'Princip moved only his finger but his Intentionality covered the Austro-Hungarian Empire'.[7] But now the real problems begin. This event is most often described not by reference to finger movements but by reference to a colligatory conception[8] that unites a period of four years: it is often said that Princip 'started' the First World War, but this is where even Searle draws the line. Was this really an action of Princip's or was it not (if the notion has any sense at all) an unintended consequence of his action? Certainly the contemporaries of the murder in Sarajevo could not have known the event *under the description* 'the beginning of the Great War', and still less under the description 'the beginning of the First World War'. Descriptions which incorporate later consequences are, in Barr's sense, anachronistic, but few would suggest that they should therefore be expunged from the vocabulary of historians. Such descriptions need to be expunged only if one were attempting to provide an emic account of how the contemporaries of the murder saw the original event. But this kind of interest would be far too restrictive for most historians.

This example illustrates a central thesis of Arthur Danto's *Analytical Philosophy of History*:

For there is a class of descriptions of any event under which the event cannot be witnessed . . . The whole truth concerning an event can only be known after, and sometimes only *long* after the event itself has taken place, and this part of the story historians alone can tell. It is something even the best sort of witness cannot know.[9]

Danto drives this point home by imagining an Ideal Chronicler who could, with absolute precision, tell us every detail of historical events *as they were happening*. But, Danto argues, this ideal record of what really happened would not be enough.

Historians would need to go on to select significant details and colligatory conceptions that are relevant to their interests. These interests and colligatory conceptions are most often arrived at retrospectively, and hence no historian – not even the Ideal Chronicler – could write in 1618 'The Thirty Years War begins now.'

Danto's work, although focused on history writing, has a direct bearing on the matter at hand. If the biblical generations could not have known scripture under the description 'a pre-existing, complete, and delimited guide' to faith and practice, they could well have known some biblical texts under a description like 'authoritative traditions' (one can hardly imagine a society *without* authoritative traditions). Moreover, some Israelite communities would have known, say, prophetic oracles, before they had actually acquired an authoritative status, i.e., when a prophet could at most make a *claim* to authority. But again, is this really a controversial point? The biblical texts concerned with true and false prophecy provide evidence enough for this kind of situation.

Biblical scholars have rightly pointed out that the retrospective criterion for true prophecy offered in Deut. 18: 21–22 and Jer. 28: 9 would not be much use to the original audiences of the prophets, but an exiled community would have had considerably less difficulty in deciding whether a prophet of doom had been correct or not. John Barton is surely close to the mark when he writes:

the tendency to reapply prophetic utterances to new situations . . . can also suggest that the prophet had proved so successful that people expected his book to be endlessly pregnant with new meanings.[10]

This is precisely the kind of argument Childs uses when he suggests that if there had been confusions regarding Jeremiah's authority during the prophet's lifetime, the authority of his book after the fall of Jerusalem would no longer have been so problematic (1985: 133–42). To say that Jeremiah's authority in later Jewish history led to an anachronistic perspective on his book would be to block out the later consequences of the prophet's speech and action. Whether the historical Jeremiah intended these consequences is a different kind of historical question. Prophetic speech and action can have unforeseen consequences in exactly the same way as Princip's action in avenging Serbia had such consequences.

It is clear, then, that the religious use of a canon is only anachronistic in so far as it takes into account the later effects of events during the biblical period. But even Barr seems willing to see a 'principle of canon' at work in early Old Testament times if this is to be understood as a 'core of central and agreed tradition' which functioned in the early communities in a way that may be compared to the later function of scripture.[11] What then, is the point of his argument about anachronism? It seems that Barr's strongest argument against Childs in this context is that one cannot describe a 'principle of canon' at work in Israelite history *and at the same time* concentrate exegesis on the final form of the text. Reconstructing the prehistory of the canon requires historical criticism, not the canonical approach.[12]

If this is indeed Barr's point, then I can only agree with him. I would, however, go on to point out that Childs, at his best, is not actually doing both tasks at the same time. He consistently separates 'historical critical problems' and 'canonical shape' into *two different sections*, and only the second of these has any legitimate claim to exegetical distinctiveness. Indeed, one should probably distinguish canonical criticism and the canonical approach in just this way: the work of Sanders, for example, does indeed attempt to reconstruct the prehistory of the canon with historical-critical interests and tools. In so far as his approach is distinctive, Childs takes a more formalist approach to the final shape of scripture, but not because he is simply recapitulating Protestant orthodoxy as Barr seems to suggest, Childs writes in a review of *Holy Scripture*:

my understanding of canon was offered as a major criticism of late seventeenth and eighteenth century Reformed orthodoxy which tended to place the authority in a divinely inspired book apart from its reception by the community through the work of the Spirit. (1984b: 67)

Childs goes on to say that this inspired process of reception is to be seen in both the oral and literary stages of Israelite tradition, but that it finally resulted in 'a fixed form of relative stability'. Historians of religion are also interested in describing the use and development of canons in various religious traditions,[13] so the distinctiveness of Childs's claims here would seem to turn on his doctrine of the Holy Spirit. If the canonical process was guided by the Spirit, then, according to Childs, the *product* of this process, rather than the history of reception itself, will be more significant for later biblical communities. The final text encompasses the full history of 'the peculiar relationship between text and the people of God'; it alone bears witness to the full history of revelation' (1979: 75–6).[14] Even if the process of reception could be reconstructed, and we have seen that Childs is generally sceptical on this point, the canonical approach does not do so.

Unlike James Barr and Hans Barstad, I find nothing *conceptually* wrong with this argument. There seems to be no reason why a more formalist exegesis should not attempt to interpret the final products of the canonical process as they have been handed down to us. The conceptual problems only arise when diachronic reconstructions of the canonical process are used to explain the text in its present form. However, as suggested in chapter 1 above, the issue of revelation is a logically separable issue. There are a number of reasons, without having to invoke a providential Holy Spirit, why the products of the canonical process might be independently interesting.

In the next section we shall consider whether the canonical process could embody a refinement of biblical tradition analogous to progress in science. In order to explore this analogy we shall examine the work of Karl Popper who, in a similar way to Childs, has stressed the importance of the autonomy of scientific texts over against the individual intentions of those who produce them. I shall argue that Popper's work offers some intriguing parallels with the canonical approach. However, many theologians, including Childs, would find any comparison between theology and science misleading. The following section will therefore attempt to show that Popperian insights have also been taken up in Hans-Robert Jauss's literary aesthetics. Popper's philosophy is not restricted simply to the natural sciences, as he himself has stressed. In the next two sections, therefore, I will be attempting to demonstrate the relevance of

Popper and Jauss to Childs's view of the canonical process as a progressive refinement.

FROM AUTHORS TO TEXTS: THE MODEL OF PROGRESS IN SCIENCE

The growth of scientific knowledge presents a number of difficult philosophical problems, among the most difficult of which is the theory of reference. How can an outdated theory which refers, for example, to phlogiston be referring to the same reality denoted by 'oxygen'? How can two groups of scientists, who have advocated competing and incommensurable theories, have been talking about the same thing? Theorists who are unhappy with the image of science as a series of incommensurable research paradigms have attempted to give some account of the continuity of language usage across scientific revolutions. In order to do this, it has been suggested that newer theories have to reinterpret the elements of older theories 'whether or not this interpretation would have been endorsed by preceding generations'.[15] For example, on this view, much of the earlier talk about phlogiston was *really* about oxygen, although earlier generations could not have known this. Indeed, it is commonplace in the history of science to find that the later reception of theories often 'has very little to do with the intentions which guided their original formulation'.[16]

Given the considerations above, some philosophers have argued that scientific reference is always subject to revision; the possibility remains, for example, that talk about oxygen will become as antiquarian as talk about phlogiston. As a consequence, they have argued that reference must be *independent of conscious intentions*, and in this sense meaning is tied to the true state of affairs even where the speaker or writer turns out to be mistaken. Reference is primarily a matter of causal links that run from the world to language. Any departure from the original intentions behind a theory's development is, on this view, only to be expected; any particular *mental* act of referring is always subordinate to the future growth of knowledge, and indeed, ultimately eliminable.[17]

In chapter 1 above, I noted that E. D. Hirsch has recently

drawn on an influential reference theory of this kind, developed
by Saul Kripke, in order to revise his analysis of literary
meaning. Hirsch now argues that authors, like scientists, intend
their texts to have future, if not entirely foreseeable, applications. Some of these future applications can legitimately be
called a 'meaning' of the text, even if these were not part of the
author's consciousness. Hirsch's new theory of meaning suggests
that even if authors cannot foresee the future reception of their
text they can at least fix 'the *principles* of further extrapolation',[18]
principles which can save a text from becoming irretrievably
dated. Hirsch, I should stress, explicitly recognizes that his use of
Kripke's work is only analogical. He could not accept Kripke's
sharp distinction between meaning and conscious intention
without destroying the fundamental thesis of *Validity in Interpretation*. Hirsch does not wish to give up his emphasis on conscious
intention entirely, rather, he wishes to leaven his intentionalism
with just enough Kripkean reference theory to support the
expansion of his notion of meaning to include unforeseen
applications. Whether or not Hirsch has been successful in
drawing the anti-intentionalist sting from Kripke's theory is a
question we may leave to one side; I have mentioned the new
Hirsch in order to show that even he, an eminent intentionalist,
has now come to question an exclusive stress on the conscious
intentions of authors.

The philosophical analysis of progress in science has also been
a central concern in the writings of Karl Popper, and in this
connection one finds a striking similarity between Kripke's idea
of 'reference without mental content' and Popper's notion of
'knowledge without a knowing subject'. Popper not only
provides good reasons for speaking of 'the intention of the *text*'
(rather than of an author), his work is also relevant to the issues
of motives and ideology which will be addressed in the next
chapter.

A great deal of Popper's writing is devoted to exploring the
consequences of his refutation, in the 1930s, of Baconian
induction (crudely, the idea that scientific laws can be inferred
from a stock of pure facts). Popper replaced this understanding
of science with the model of conjecture and refutation: if a theory

cannot be inductively derived, it can at least be subjected to rigorous attempts at refutation and falsification. Although there is still considerable disagreement as to the nature of falsification, this basic idea has been enormously influential. My interest in the present context is with one of the implications of this idea which Popper has himself suggested, namely, that objective knowledge exists independently of any particular knower, indeed, that it exists in texts and computers rather than in human minds.

Popper's argument rests on a distinction between three 'worlds':

first, the world of physical objects or physical states; secondly, the world of states of consciousness, or mental states, or perhaps behavioural dispositions to act; and thirdly, the world of *objective contents of thought*, especially of scientific and poetic thoughts and works of art.[19]

'Thought' is here understood as a public and objective content, rather than as a subjective act of thinking, and this distinction is specifically tied to the practice of science. The objective contents and structures of thought are, of course, *produced* by human beings, but Popper argues that these 'produced structures' have a kind of epistemological priority over the processes of production.[20] The *linguistically formulated* contents of 'world three' give rise to new and unexpected problems which were not part of the producer's consciousness.[21]

Moreover, the idea of world three is a key instrument in Popper's defence of science against charges of ideology. Beginning with the idea that science is advanced by conjectures and refutation, he argues forcefully against Karl Mannheim's notorious suggestion that objectivity in social science can only be achieved by select intellectuals operating in relative independence of general social prejudices. Popper insists against this that objectivity does not rest upon the objectivity of individual scientists; it rests instead upon the results of mutual criticism. Accordingly, a brilliant Robinson Crusoe cannot produce objective knowledge because there is no one to refute his results, 'nobody but himself to correct those prejudices which are the unavoidable consequence of his peculiar mental history'.[22] According to Popper, the details of 'the social or ideological habitat of the researcher' tend to be consumed in the fires of refutation, although these details 'always play a part in the short run'.[23] The relative autonomy of world three is, therefore, for Popper an essential ingredient in his defence of the objectivity of science.

Popper has not only argued for the relative autonomy of scientific texts, he has also applied his theory to the humanities and to hermeneutics. He suggests that 'the activity of understanding consists, essentially, in operating with third-world objects'.[24] He explicitly recognizes that this thesis flies in the face of the widely held view that texts simply express subjective mental states. Nevertheless, he insists that

It is the understanding of objects belonging to the third world which constitutes the central problem of the humanities. This, it appears, is a radical departure from the fundamental dogma accepted by almost all students of the humanities . . . I mean of course the dogma that the objects of our understanding belong mainly to the second world, or that they are at any rate to be explained in psychological terms.[25]

My own argument in this section does not attempt to prove so much. I am simply concerned to show that interpreting 'the intention of a text' is just as intelligible a goal as that of understanding an author. It may well be the case that in practice we often cannot distinguish between the ideas of a text and the ideas of an author, but the two interpretative goals are nevertheless methodologically distinct. This point can be illustrated by reference again to Saussure's *Cours de linguistique générale*, which first appeared in 1916.

This enormously influential book was not actually prepared for publication by Saussure himself, and indeed, a critical edition has been recently produced which, on the basis of scattered notes and other sources, attempts to be more faithful to Saussure's intentions. After pointing all this out, one of the leading authorities in current linguistics goes on to say that although the original edition may not be a faithful representation of all Saussure's ideas, 'It is, however, the *Cours* as published, that has been of historic importance'.[26] In other words, the scholarly discipline of linguistics in this century has

been deeply influenced by a book that was relatively autonomous of the author who 'produced' it. An historian of ideas, who
may be centrally interested in the actual intentions of the
'historical Saussure', will need to treat the original *Cours* with a
good deal of circumspection. Linguists, however, are not simply
historians of ideas; they have been more interested in the *truth
content* of the original *Cours*, and they have therefore taken the
communicative intention of Saussure's text as a contribution to
their 'rationalist' rather than 'historical' interests.[27]

I would suggest that this discussion of a textual world three
can shed some much needed light on Childs's programme. The
Popperian focus on texts, rather than on individual minds,
makes the idea of 'the communicative intention of a text' a good
deal more plausible. Not only does Childs think of biblical
tradition as a story of progressive refinement, he also thinks of
the biblical texts as a kind of 'world three' which can yield
implications unforeseen by individual authors. Whether Childs
makes exegetical claims in terms of 'redactional intention', or in
terms of 'the effect which a particular rendering has on the
literature', in either case the focus is on *the explicit* and '*objective*'
content of the biblical texts – rather than on the mental contents of
authors or redactors.[28] Moreover, Childs also has enough
Popperian optimism to suggest that the development of biblical
tradition has filtered out the influence of the original 'ideological
habitats' of biblical authors and redactors.

I shall return to the issue of ideology in due course, but first we
need to explore some of the implications of Popper's philosophy
in the domain of literary aesthetics. We have seen that Popper
considers his idea of world three to be relevant not only to
science but also to the humanities. This relevance is especially
demonstrated by Hans-Robert Jauss, who draws an analogy
between the conjectures and refutations of scientific texts, and
the reception of 'fictional' literature.

RECEPTION AESTHETICS AND THE CANONICAL PROCESS

In recent decades we have seen a marked increase in the number
of studies dedicated to what might loosely be called the
reception of literature. Although many of the questions being

pursued in these studies are not entirely new, it is clear that there is a much wider consensus as to their importance. Thus, for example, a polemical essay published by Hans-Robert Jauss in 1967 has become enshrined in some quarters as 'the origin of modern reception theory',[29] and only ten years later one German scholar was able to produce sixty-five pages of bibliography relevant to questions of literary reception.[30] The spectacular growth of interest in these questions is worthy of a few words of explanation, but my main concern here will be to show how Jauss's reception aesthetics can contribute to an understanding of the canonical process.

During the middle decades of this century, formalist or 'text-immanent' approaches were widely influential in literary criticism. The focus was on the *text itself*, and information extraneous to the text (except perhaps for the wider literary canon) was considered irrelevant to its interpretation. Information derived from an author's biography, including the author's intentions and social location, were expressly excluded from consideration. This kind of *purely* literary approach to literature was, in many respects, a new variation of an aesthetic theory that took shape during the eighteenth century in reaction to the impressive gains made by natural scientists. According to the historian P. O. Kristeller, before the modern rise of the natural sciences there was, for example, no systematic attempt to separate practical and 'fine' arts, and in this sense there was no important distinction between carpentry and poetry. The activities named on modern lists of the fine arts were simply not considered an autonomous realm of human experience.[31]

This thesis has been confirmed in a different way by M. H. Abrams who claims that the pragmatic tradition of literary theory – which views the work of art as primarily a means to a practical end – was the principle aesthetic attitude of the West up until the late seventeenth century, when a more exclusive interest began to be directed toward the psychology and creative genius of authors.[32] Although the twentieth-century New Critics turned away from the psychology of authors, they maintained the early modern view that literary works belong, in some sense, to an autonomous realm of human experience and communication. But New Critics distinguished themselves by not only condemning the search for authorial intentions as irrelevant to the literary work itself, they also rejected, with the aid of the so-called affective fallacy, the experience of *reading*.[33]

Hans-Robert Jauss's *Literaturgeschichte als Provokation der Literaturwissenschaft* (1967) was one among several reader-oriented works which contributed to the decline of formalism.[34] Jauss argued forcefully that the study of literature needed to focus once again on historical contexts, both the context of the work's production and, more importantly, the successive contexts of its reception; this procedure would recover the 'historicality' of literature. In developing this case, Jauss invoked biblical form criticism as an exemplary method that emphasizes the correlation of literary forms with their social and historical setting, and he has applied form-critical questions to the study of medieval genres. He has stressed, however, that this kind of correlation between text and context should stop short of the orthodox Marxist doctrines which saw a literary work as simply a self-portrait of the groups which produced it, and some recent studies in the sociology of reading support Jauss's critique.[35]

Jauss's work is thus directed both against formalism and against reductive sociologies of literary production that cannot account for the fact that some works exercise powerful influences upon generations and cultures far removed from the work's origin.[36] Jauss does not entirely reject the role of the original audience; he simply denies it privilege. He first plays the role of a historical critic, bringing out the differences between former and current understandings of a work and foregrounding the text 'against those works the author explicitly or implicitly presupposed his contemporary audience to know'.[37] But reconstructing the original 'horizon of expectation' (roughly, the set of expectations the first audience would have brought to the work) is seen as simply the first task in a history of reception.

In speaking of a horizon of expectations Jauss does not mean only an original and fixed frame of reference. Rather, he sees it as more like a scale against which deviation can be measured, a scale which can develop and change shape as a result of assimilating literary innovation. This idea of a mutable horizon owes much to his former teacher Gadamer, but what is more important in this context is that Jauss has explicated the idea specifically with reference to Popper's philosophy of science.[38] As already pointed out, Popper does not attribute progress in science to induction from pure facts, but rather, to modifications of previous knowledge, or more precisely, previous conjectures. He argues that all learning is guided by expectations which may be conscious or subconscious. Expectations are not only a matter of conscious psychology or explicit scientific hypotheses since 'we become conscious of many of our expectations only when they are disappointed'. Thus, Popper suggests that

At every instant of our pre-scientific or scientific development we are living in the centre of what I usually call a 'horizon of expectations'. By this I mean the sum total of our expectations, whether these are subconscious or conscious.[39]

Similarly, according to Jauss, works of art are understood within a conscious or subconscious set of expectations which may be disappointed or modified by the work of art itself. Literary history shares some features with all human learning, scientific or 'pre-scientific'.

Jauss stresses, again following Popper, that a horizon of expectations is the sum total of expectations, and not just the sum of *literary* expectations as the Russian formalists tended to imply. Literary history, for this Russian school, was primarily a history of innovations of literary technique which are only perceivable against the background of previous texts, a view which was expressed in an exemplary fashion by Viktor Shklovsky. But in addressing Shklovsky's position, Jauss emphasizes that

the new literary work is received and judged against the background of other works of art *as well as* against the background of everyday experience of life.[40]

Literary innovation is then not considered for its own sake, but rather, in relation to everyday life and social change.

In Jauss's view, there is an important relationship between the narrower horizon of literary experience (which is formed by pre-understandings of genre, form and themes of already familiar works) and the wider horizon of life experience. He argues that the relationship between aesthetic and practical experience is not simply an opposition of 'fictional' and 'real' horizons; rather, aesthetic experience projects 'no longer' or 'not yet' actualized forms of life, and thereby offers the reader the possibility of appropriating these projected horizons.[41] This rather abstract argument may be illustrated by a famous example. Flaubert's novel *Madame Bovary* was widely condemned by its original audience, yet it is now considered a modern classic. Jauss correlates this shift in appreciation with significant changes in both social and literary expectations. Examples like this suggest that some works 'break through the familiar horizon of literary expectations so completely that an audience can only gradually develop for them'.[42] In this respect (and perhaps only in this respect) one can draw an analogy between *Madame Bovary* and the Israelite prophetic oracles which only became canonical retrospectively.

How, then, are these phases of reception to be studied? Jauss is sympathetic towards the kind of research that illuminates the historical and socio-economic contexts which may influence a horizon of expectation. He also agrees that we need to examine the social groups which are the bearers of dominant literary norms and canons, but his primary interest is in a specific and partial question, namely, how aesthetic experience can change the communicative patterns of everyday life.[43] It is precisely this question, however, which turns out to be controversial. It is difficult to judge whether a literary work has exercised influence beyond its original setting or, on the contrary, whether earlier literary works have been simply caught up in historical developments which are essentially determined by socio-economic processes. Those who advocate the latter view would suggest that social processes determine literary taste and not the other way around.[44]

There is, however, one other element of Jauss's reception theory which is particularly relevant to a discussion of the canonical process. Jauss maintains that

The reconstruction of the original horizon of expectations would nonetheless fall back into historicism if the historical interpretation could not in turn serve to transform the question, 'What did the text say?' into the question 'What does the text say to me, and what do I say to it?'[45]

This implies that the subject matter and truth content of literature cannot finally be suppressed in the name of a purely descriptive literary history. Interpretation must finally become a genuine conversation, and in this respect Jauss preserves a central hermeneutical emphasis of his teacher Gadamer. If texts from the past are to reform the horizon of the present then they need to maintain their veracity in the face of questions which may have arisen since the time of their production. Accordingly, Jauss speaks of a 'progressive understanding, which necessarily also includes criticizing the tradition and forgetting it'.[46] This is also what Childs says about the canonical process before the stabilization of the Hebrew canon.

In summarizing Jauss's position we would need to say, then, that he conceives of literary history as a progressive mediation of literature and life within which the truth content, or perhaps authenticity, of the aesthetic tradition is continually evaluated and reformed. Let us suppose, as many historians of the biblical traditions do, that the communities who transmitted the biblical documents were similarly concerned with continually mediating their sacred traditions with new experiences of life. The texts would then be reworked in the face of new questions, and traditions found wanting would be either subordinated or forgotten.

One might plausibly infer that inauthentic traditions transmitted orally would be easily forgotten and eliminated from the Israelite cultural repertoire,[47] whereas problematic written traditions might linger on as subordinate vestiges. Given this scenario, long-lived written traditions might finally become canonical because they had continually demonstrated their truthfulness. These canonical traditions could be distinguished from other writings which had not so proved themselves. In order to maintain social coherence the biblical communities would need to exclude some traditions, while other traditions no doubt fused together during the process of transmission.[48] From the historian's point of view, the final form of the biblical text would then represent a nightmare of confusion, but on the other hand, the final form could also be understood as the outcome of a necessary social process. As Alasdair MacIntyre puts it,

A living tradition . . . is an historically extended, socially embodied argument, and an argument precisely in part about the goods which constitute that tradition.[49]

It would not be surprising if in an ancient literate society this historically extended argument should give rise to a written canon which although excluding some traditions altogether allowed other traditions to be either inseparably fused together or unsystematically 'listed' one after the other.

What I have just described may be considered a charitable reconstruction of the canonical process. If this reconstruction has any plausibility at all (it was, of course, hypothetical) then we are now in a position to pose another kind of question. *Would it not make some sense for later religious communities to regard the Bible as the product of the best theological 'science', or critical reflection, to come out of the biblical period?* This seems to be what Childs wants us to believe. He is insisting that if historical critics wish to continue their antiquarian search for abandoned and defective Israelite theologies, they should recognize that such an interpretative interest is not the one which animates the present communities of faith. Rather, religious communities are seeking in the Bible a Word of God which is still valid.

Two questions cry out for articulation at this point. First, leaving aside (at least for the time being) the interests of academic historians, how can Childs be so sure that all the discarded or displaced traditions were of no value to communities who continue to hold the Bible as in some sense authoritative? It may be that the final form is simply a monument to the victors of vicious conflict and to the social groups who exercised most power not only in the canonization process but during the entire history of reception.[50] Secondly, how can Childs attribute to the Bible the power to answer any question put to it by subsequent generations? In other words, why should the process of theological 'science', or critical reflection, stop with canonization?

Childs's responses to these questions have been perhaps the

least satisfactory aspects of his writing. First, he recognizes that sociological factors were at work in the canonical process, but argues that these were subordinated to purely theological ones in the course of time. Secondly, he regards the Bible as the locus of divine revelation while stressing that this revelation needs to be appropriated afresh by each new generation under the guidance of the Holy Spirit. The biblical canon therefore marks a watershed in critical theological reflection; theological critique becomes a commentary on the classical biblical literature.

The question that arises at this point, however, is whether Childs is invoking a doctrine of the Holy Spirit in order to circumvent important theological problems. I would suggest that in order to answer the two questions articulated above the canonical approach need not make recourse to such question-begging theological arguments. Gadamer's philosophy of interpretation, and especially his understanding of 'the classic', provides a better response in both cases. Gadamer's work is not, of course, free of controversy. Jauss, among others, is very critical of the doctrine of the classic in *Truth and Method*; he suggests that hiding under all Gadamer's talk of 'historicality' lies a dogmatic classicism which simply assumes the superiority of an ancient canon.[51] Childs may well turn out to be guilty of the same charge, but before we can deal adequately with this issue we will need to examine Gadamer's doctrine of the classic in some detail.

To summarize this stage of our argument: even if we can grant to Childs that there is something like a progressive refinement in biblical tradition, he needs to explain how narrow social interests and prejudices can be filtered out of a living tradition. In answering this question he might follow Popper in stressing that the filtering medium is to be found precisely in 'world three'; the biblical *texts* provide the medium of a continuing critical process of reception. But why, then, does this process stop with the stabilization of the canonical texts? Here Childs needs to develop the notion of a classical text which has the power to demonstrate continually its truthfulness in new circumstances. And at this point, the canonical approach might gain some assistance from Gadamer's hermeneutics.

GADAMER AND THE CANONICAL APPROACH

The central thesis of the second part of Gadamer's *Truth and Method*,[52] in which the example of the classic is discussed, is this: human life is deeply marked by historical influences which can never be totally illuminated by critical reflection. The classic text is taken up as an *example* to illustrate the fact that our lives have an 'effective substratum' of historical influences (p. 258, S. 274). Indeed, according to Gadamer, 'there culminates in the classical a general character of historical being, preservation within the ruins of time' (p. 257, S. 273). Although the concept of 'the classical' has often been reduced to a merely descriptive designation for an historical period or an aesthetic style, Gadamer argues that classical works are those that have continued to demonstrate their normative authority – especially in the idea of a humanistic or liberal education. (Indeed, he suggests that Droysen's rehabilitation of the hellenistic period was made necessary by a long-standing humanistic prejudice in favour of classical culture.[53]) In other words, the literary works of classical antiquity have, according to Gadamer, deeply influenced the developments of Western culture even where this normative influence has not been explicitly recognized.

The second part of *Truth and Method* is also directed against an older school of romantic hermeneutics which presupposed an 'unhistorical substratum' of common human nature (as opposed to an effective substratum of tradition) on the basis of which an interpreter could re-experience the thoughts of an author from the past. Gadamer argues that this presupposition of a common human nature overlooks the limitations placed on interpreters by their own historical conditions. He suggests that an act of interpretation is as much an historical event as, for example, the murder of Archduke Ferdinand: both have immensely complex pre-conditions, some of which remain unknown to the historical actors, as well as unforeseen consequences. Interpretation or understanding is just another species of historical action. And, according to Gadamer, we belong to history in a much stronger sense than history belongs to us. Our attempts to master history through critical reflection are finally less significant than the effects which our own family, society, culture, or research tradition have upon us (pp. 244–6, S. 260–1). This, then, is the context within which the following pithy claim at the end of the section on the classic is set:

Understanding is not to be thought of so much as an action of one's subjectivity, but as the placing of oneself within a process of tradition. (p. 258, S. 274–5)

In his foreword to the second edition of *Truth and Method* Gadamer stresses that this notion of situated understanding cannot be simply reduced to a conscious and conservative 'assimilation of traditional opinion', yet this is precisely the way his argument concerning the classic has often been taken.[54] It will be instructive, then, to examine in more detail exactly what he *does* say about the role of tradition in human understanding.

Enlightenment thinkers were deeply mistaken, Gadamer argues, when they drew a sharp distinction between reason and tradition. While it may be taken for granted that traditions may contain illegitimate prejudices (p. 246, S. 261), some element of tradition is at work in all understanding. The Enlightenment's polarization of authoritative tradition and the 'freedom of reason' has proved inadequate even with respect to the most rigorous processes of reasoned reflection.[55] The rational ideal of being free from all prejudices was itself founded on an illegitimate prejudice; human understanding requires at least some 'prejudice', and not all traditions can be subjected to critique at the same time. Gadamer attempts, therefore, to articulate a conception of understanding which embraces our dependence on tradition and which 'opens the way to an appropriate understanding of our finitude' (p. 244, S. 260).

This awareness of human finitude leads Gadamer to argue that it is entirely *reasonable* for an individual to accept the limits of reason, and indeed, to accept that others may be 'superior to oneself in judgment and insight'. This is especially true of a tradition which has acquired its authority by continuing to demonstrate its truthfulness:

authority . . . is based ultimately, not on the subjection and abdication of reason, but on recognition and knowledge – knowledge, namely,

that the other is superior . . . authority cannot actually be bestowed,
but is acquired . . . Thus the essence of authority belongs in the context
of a theory of prejudices free from the extremism of the
enlightenment.[56]

The classic is therefore to be understood as a special instance of
authoritative tradition: it is the most obvious (one might also say
the most *extreme*) example of the preservation of tradition.

Gadamer does not, however, simply return to a dogmatic
position which would uphold the legitimacy of tradition over
against every reasonable argument which is brought against it.
On the contrary, such a dogmatism would maintain the very
polarity of tradition and reason which he is anxious to
overcome; it would amount to an *irrational* preservation of
tradition. 'But preservation', Gadamer insists, 'is an act of
reason, though an inconspicuous one' (pp. 249–50, S. 264–5).
This point also applies to the classic:

the classical . . . does not seek to be a suprahistorical concept of value.
It does not refer to a quality that we assign to particular historical
phenomena, but to a notable mode of 'being historical', the historical
process of preservation [Bewahrung] that, through the constant
proving of itself [Bewährung], sets before us something that is true . . .
The classical is what resists historical criticism because its historical
power . . . precedes all historical reflection and continues through it.
(p. 255, S. 271)

The classic therefore continually demonstrates its value through
the vicissitudes of time, taste and criticism, and if any particular
work does not so continue to prove itself, it can no longer be
called classical.

I have so far been able to reformulate these arguments from
Truth and Method into a relatively coherent whole. But certain
obscurities begin to appear as soon as one attempts to analyse
Gadamer's account of historical criticism. He clearly endorses
the necessity of criticism in preventing naive and premature
appropriations of tradition (p. 273, S. 290). Yet his main
argument is that *criticism itself is a process or 'event' of tradition*, and
this seems to mean at least two different things. First, it means
that modern critics stand within scholarly traditions which
determine the kinds of method and modes of questioning

deemed appropriate by the scholarly communities to which they belong. These traditions constitute a web of historical effects which is often concealed by appeals to critical method (p. 268, S. 284). 'Effective history . . . determines in advance both what seems to us worth enquiring about and what will appear as an object of investigation' (pp. 267–68, S. 284). Second, Gadamer suggests that the prejudices of historical criticism also need to be called into question by a genuine conversation with tradition. Given this kind of argument the classic may not in fact be able to maintain its veracity in the face of *every* criticism; rather, the truth value of the classic may only become evident when the critic has entered into a genuine dialogue with the past and has indeed been transformed by this conversation (p. 341, S. 360). This transformation may then be understood as a new event in the life of a tradition (*Überlieferungsgeschehen*).

The notion of understanding as a process or event of tradition seems therefore to be used in two different ways – first, in reference to research within a particular paradigm, and second, in reference to a more transformative encounter with tradition. Both these senses of 'tradition' refer to living tradition and not simply to the content of past opinion, yet the connections between the two senses of living tradition are by no means self-evident. Although one might agree that the routine questions of a particular research programme (like, for example, form-critical study of biblical texts) embody a certain kind of tradition, it is questionable whether being transformed in conversation with a classic is an 'event of tradition' in the same sense. Gadamer does, however, provide a connection between the two.

Scholarly research, according to *Truth and Method*, has to be disciplined by 'effective-historical consciousness', that is, by the recognition that the interpreter's own situation is marked by complex historical influences, some of which may be hidden from immediate view. The question of how these influences can be brought into consciousness is probably the most important, and most controversial, issue in Gadamer's hermeneutical theory. His central contention is that the prejudices of the present, including those of the scholar, have to be tested in encounters with classical tradition (pp. 266 & 273, S. 283 & 290). Just why an encounter with tradition should have a purifying effect is something I will take up below, but for the present we should note that bad prejudices are rarely, according to Gadamer, filtered out by technical research procedures, i.e., by 'method' in the narrow sense. He seems to be claiming, rather, that the bad prejudices of a particular research programme are more effectively tested by actual dialogue with classic texts than by purely technical refinements in modern methodology. It would, however, be a caricature of his position to suggest that Gadamer is simply anti-method. His main point seems to be that a method, no matter how rigorous or scientific, is only as good as the question which guides it. His favourite example here is statistics, which allows the facts to speak with an apparent objectivity which 'in reality depends on the legitimacy of the questions asked' (p. 268, S. 285). The well-formed question is a thing of greater value.

These considerations lead to one of the most distinctive elements of Gadamer's hermeneutics. Historical reconstruction is, in *Truth and Method*, considered only one phase in the process of understanding, a phase which should not become solidified into a *purely* historical understanding (p. 273, S. 290). If the task of interpretation is restricted to reconstructing the original horizon of the text then historical thinking

makes an end of what is only a means. The text that is understood historically is forced to abandon its claim that it is uttering something true. (p. 270, S. 287)

For Gadamer, the purely historical question is not well-formed. This claim marks a decisive departure from the broad consensus of hermeneutical theory since the Enlightenment.[57] Gadamer is rejecting both Spinoza's distinction between meaning and truth and Schleiermacher's emphasis on understanding authors for their own sake. Reproducing the intention of an ancient author would be for Gadamer – if he thought the task possible – only the *means* of entering into a genuine conversation about the truth claims of the author's text. In this sense Gadamer stands much closer to Kripke's theory of meaning than he does to Hirsch's.[58]

Gadamer's account of interpretation is based on his belief that authorial meanings cannot be captured within a fixed context, and even if they could, this would not be a desirable way to pursue the truth content of texts from the past. Human life – both past and present – 'is never utterly bound to any one standpoint, and hence can never have a truly closed horizon'. The idea of a closed horizon is as fictional and unattainable as Robinson Crusoe's island (p. 271, S. 288). We are caught up in a 'play' of tradition which places individual psychology in a subordinate role to the mutable webs of social interaction.[59] Gadamer has also made this point in his critique of Schleiermacher's romantic hermeneutics:

> Schleiermacher has withdrawn into the psychological out of fear of a theory of inspiration, and has thus surrendered hermeneutical possibilities. The superior . . . justification for the individualization of the New Testament authors, which he offers in opposition to pneumatic exegesis, cannot conceal that the determinateness of historical effects in our understanding of these texts also includes higher units of meaning, such as the unity of faith represented by the early community . . . which led to the formation of the canon.[60]

As he later makes clear, Gadamer is not here denying the existence of intentionality; he is simply emphasizing (in a similar way to Danto[61]) that the goal of historical understanding cannot be reduced to individual intentions.[62] Similarly, in *Truth and Method* he writes: 'we miss the whole truth of the phenomenon when we take its immediate appearance as the whole truth' (p. 268, S. 284).

In spite of explicit disclaimers to the contrary, Gadamer's account of historical study seems to have not only a descriptive but a normative aspect. He suggests that unless individuals can be drawn into genuine conversations they remain at the mercy of their individual prejudices; they overvalue their immediate horizon (p. 269, S. 286). A genuine conversation is characterized by transformation into communion with others, or to put the point in a more pedestrian fashion, Gadamerian hermeneutics denotes the process of two different parties 'coming to an understanding'. For this process to be successful critical historians need to place themselves in the situation of the past. But,

Gadamer emphasizes, it is precisely *themselves*, their own prejudices, which need to be brought into play and put at risk. This
placing of oneself in the situation of the past

is not the empathy of one individual for another, nor is it the subjection
of the other to our own criteria, but it always involves the attainment of
a higher generality that overcomes, not only our own particularity,
but also that of the other.[63]

Gadamer is, in effect, trying to tread a fine line between emics
and etics. Historical study is an educative process that implies
giving up prejudices which belong to an individual's narrow
situation and acquiring a wider 'horizon' through a common
quest for the truth.

Precisely this quest for a wider horizon means that Gadamer
finds more potential truth value in traditions than in individuals: over time a tradition can become distanced from the
particular prejudices that may govern its transmission at any
particular point. In his section on 'the hermeneutic significance
of temporal distance' Gadamer argues that the passage of time
allows

those prejudices that are of a particular and limited nature to die away,
but causes those that bring about genuine understanding to emerge
clearly as such. (p. 266, S. 282)

By way of analogy, he suggests that the true content and
meaning of an art work cannot be perceived in the moment of its
appearance; we approach such a contemporary work with
uncontrolled prejudices which lend it a fleeting 'extra re-
sonance'. The true value of art works only emerges when their
merely contemporary connections have faded, 'so that the
understanding of what is said in them can claim a normative
generality' (p. 265, S. 281).

This kind of claim reappears later in *Truth and Method* when
Gadamer argues that 'linguistic tradition retains special priority
over all other tradition'. The detachment of linguistic tradition
from its origin, especially in writing, is portrayed as a positive
gain of autonomous meaning:

The understanding of something written is not a reproduction of
something that is past, but the sharing of a present meaning. Writing

has the methodological advantage that it presents the hermeneutical problem in all its purity, detached from everything psychological. (p. 354, S. 370)

What is stated in the text must be detached from all contingent factors and grasped in its full ideality, in which alone it has validity. (p. 356, S. 372)

It should be clear that Gadamer's view, albeit densely expressed, shares a good deal in common with Popper's account of a linguistic 'world three' which embodies the growth of knowledge and which eliminates, with the aid of mutual criticism, the prejudices which are attached to individual mental histories.[64]

Gadamer's view of the classic follows naturally from this account of writing and temporal distance. The classic text is an exemplary written tradition which has demonstrated its validity throughout the vicissitudes of time. It may be 'approached directly' not because it has the immediate electric touch of the contemporary work of art, but rather, because it has *retrospectively* demonstrated its truth value.

But that means ultimately that the classical is what is preserved precisely *because* it signifies and interprets itself; i.e. that which is spoken in such a way that it is not a statement about a missing past, a mere testimony to something that still needs to be interpreted, but says something to the present as if it were said purposely to it. (p. 257, S. 272)

This self-interpreting characteristic of the classic overlaps considerably with what Gadamer elsewhere says about 'eminent' texts – amongst which he includes the Bible and poetry generally. He stresses that texts become 'literary' not simply by being written down but by 'speaking in their own right'. The eminent text does not, like lecture notes, refer back to the original act of speech or to a 'more authentic experience of reality'. An eminent text 'stands written' in its own right.[65]

We may infer, then, that the classic shares the qualities of an eminent written tradition: it may be read as a compelling contribution to its subject matter, rather than as an indirect witness to the psychology of its author or to the purely contingent circumstances of its production. We might also infer that the classic (especially one that is itself the product of an authoritative tradition) has so thoroughly filtered out the bad prejudices which may have informed it, that each new generation can *reasonably* submit their finite judgement to its superior insight.

This Gadamerian account of classic and eminent texts comes very close to Childs's view of the biblical tradition. The canonical approach does not search behind the text for a more authentic saying or religious experience. There is no (relevant) missing past which still needs to be interpreted; rather, the text is treated as if it can 'speak for itself' to each new present with a truth value that continues to be demonstrated in the communities for whom the Bible is canonical. But this is not merely an ahistorical formalism; Childs is well aware that the Bible has a long and complicated history. Indeed, that history is essential to the function of the biblical classic: it allows the full effects of Israelite history to emerge. The canonical approach does not reconstruct an ideal eye witness who might bring a premature perspective on the later refinement of the biblical tradition.

With Gadamerian (and Popperian) optimism Childs regards this long history as a filtering process which has removed those *merely* particular prejudices which might have resulted from peculiar mental histories. The canonical editors have largely obscured such narrow interests:

the original sociological and historical differences within the nation of Israel – Northern and Southern Kingdom, pro- and anti-monarchial parties, apocalyptic versus theocratic circles – were lost, and a religious community emerged which found its identity in terms of sacred scripture . . . When critical exegesis is made to rest on the recovery of these very sociological distinctions which have been obscured, it runs directly in the face of the canon's intention. (Childs, 1979: 78)

Against both of these authorities – Gadamer and Childs – I would argue that historians can and do give plausible accounts of the intentions of historical individuals and of the *relatively* discreet periods of history, and in this sense they provide us with 'merely' historical interpretations. On the other hand, it also makes perfectly good sense to speak along with Gadamer, Childs

and Popper of a relatively autonomous world of texts which
have a communicative intention of their own.

One should also note the agreement between Gadamer and
Childs on how to construe the relationship between the eminent
text and its commentary. Gadamer argues that a 'literary' text is
relatively autonomous both with respect to its production and
its *preservation*:

any reproduction – even on the part of the author or reader – contains
an inappropriate contingent moment. A genuine text in this eminent
sense is never measured against the original way in which it was
originally said. There is always something disturbing about hearing a
poet reading his own works . . . The text has acquired an ideality that
cannot be obviated by any possible realization.[66]

Hence, although the Bible (which Gadamer considers an
eminent text) has become classical by being preserved in a long
history of effects, there is a sense in which the history of exegesis is
always marked by contingencies, and in this sense secondary to
the classic itself. This is almost exactly Childs's position: neither
the 'effective history' of the biblical period, nor the history of
exegesis after the stabilization of the text can supplant the
eminence of the Bible itself.

There is one important consequence which follows from this
view, and it pertains to the history of exegetical methods. Childs
writes,

the appeal to the canon does not restrict the interpreter to any one
particular exegetical method. Obviously, the tools of interpretation
will change and vary according to each age. (1970: 106)[67]

Here Childs demonstrates both a Gadamerian sense of historicality, as well as a relative indifference to method in the narrow
sense. He therefore stresses that although the canonical approach elevates an eminent classical text, it does not elevate a
particular 'hermeneutic', and this is another point which
distinguishes his work from that of J. A. Sanders (cf. 1973: 90).

Several critics have been troubled by this aspect of Childs's
position in so far as it reflects an ambivalent attitude towards the
early Church. As John Barton notes, Childs implies that 'the
very same generation of Christians who fixed the main outlines

of the canon is also a hopelessly unreliable guide to the correct
way of reading that canon'.[68] Interestingly, Barton goes on to
point out that the canonical approach is therefore not 'true to
the mind' of these early generations, a point which is wholly true
but not at all damaging to an approach dedicated to a textual
'world three'; the canonical approach is just not focused on the
minds behind the text, and Childs has nowhere advocated the
simple imitation of early Christianity.

One should also notice that in embracing the historicality of
all biblical interpretation Childs approaches Gadamer's view of
truth. Childs argues that there is a 'scandal of particularity' in
the continual reinterpretation of the biblical canon, but that
this scandal should not worry us unduly.

> The mistake lies in assuming that there is such a thing as a timeless
> interpretation. The challenge to hear the Old Testament as God's
> word in a concrete definite form for one's own age carries with it the
> corollary that it will soon be antiquated. (1974a: 438)

Hence Childs repeatedly claims that each new generation has to
study the Bible and 'anticipate a fresh appropriation of its
message through the work of God's Spirit' (1974a: xiii; cf. 1985:
12). This implies that the history of exegesis should not be
conceived of as a progressive movement toward an ideal end of
inquiry when the true meaning of the text will finally emerge.
The most we can hope for is that our interpretations will be
appropriate for our situation. By rejecting the 'progressivist'
interpretation of exegetical history Childs is able to hold on to
two ideas that would otherwise be difficult to reconcile: (1) the
best exegesis of the past was valid with respect to the interpretative aims, evidence and conceptions available at the time; and
(2) each new generation needs to interpret the Bible afresh.
Whiggish historians of exegesis are more inclined to say that pre-
modern exegetes were for the most part simply wrong – except
for a few favourite anticipations of *real* exegesis. Thus, to take an
extreme example, F. W. Farrar suggested that the School of
Antioch

> possessed a deeper insight into the true method of exegesis than any
> which preceded or succeeded it during a thousand years.[69]

Gadamer, on the other hand, would find such a judgment unhistorical. He holds that the idea of a 'progressive approximation to the truth' reflects the worst kind of Hegelianism; the idea of an ideal end of inquiry *within history* makes no sense. And if it has no cash value, within history then it can be disposed of without loss. Truth, rather, should be understood as the continuing conversational process of discovering the best questions and arguments with respect to one's own situation in history.[70] It is enough to say that later generations understand in a different rather than in a superior way (p. 263, S. 280).

To summarize: I would suggest that a comparison with Gadamer's philosophy provides the most charitable way of understanding the hermeneutics of the canonical approach. If the canonical process can be understood as a filtering of tradition, then interpretation can be justifiably focused on the classical form of the Hebrew Bible rather than the earlier layers of tradition which inevitably reveal the prejudices of particular historical periods. It is the final form which has continued to demonstrate its truthfulness in new situations to those who have been transformed and tested by their conversation with this classic text. Fresh interpretations of the canon reflect the interpreter's own situation in history rather than an ideal end of inquiry. The classical text has an inexhaustibility that resists any one interpretative method or any one understanding of it.

There are, however, some residual problems in this comparison. Let us consider, once again, Gadamer's emphasis on the truth value of classical traditions; merely reproducing past opinions for their own sake is not enough. Childs seems to echo this emphasis when he says that Old Testament theology 'involves wrestling with the subject-matter to which scripture continues to bear testimony' (1985: 12), and Old Testament theology is not therefore simply an emic description of past opinion (although a history of Israelite religion might be). He has a Gadamerian emphasis on the continuing truth claims of the text, over against 'merely' historical exegesis. But where in Childs's work is there a recognition that these truth claims have to be tested against all modern criticism? Gadamer points to the modern end of the problem when he discusses, for example, the appropriation of Aristotle's classical works: he argues that Aristotle's ethical writings are superior to any modern moral theory, but he stresses that this judgment cannot be reached on the basis of a 'historical' reading of Aristotle but only on the basis of a comparison with modern ethics. Moreover,

if this is the case, then I go on to ask: Is it not then meaningful to say of Aristotle that he could not have understood himself in the way that we understand him if we find what he says more correct than those modern theories (which he could not know)? (pp. 267–8, S. 284)

In speaking of textual intention, rather than an author's intention, Childs sometimes implies the same point: the canonical interpreter does not understand ancient Israelites in the way that they understood themselves. But if the canonical approach is concerned with the question of theological truth, then even this is not enough. The canonical theologian would need to consider all the modern theories of biblical interpretation that might undermine the explicit claims of the final form. Just as philosophically productive interpretations of Aristotle's ethics must take account of modern theories which the historical Aristotle could not have known,[71] so theologically 'constructive' exegesis, as Childs calls it, must account for the wide range of arguments thrown up by etic explanations of the biblical literature. These cannot be circumvented by claiming that the canonical approach has different interpretative interests. The classical text needs to demonstrate continually its truthfulness; its authority cannot be asserted dogmatically in the face of all reasoned critique.

If the canonical approach were simply a formalist mode of biblical interpretation then there would be no problem; formalist readings of texts do not need to make truth claims. But the canonical approach was conceived at the outset as being relevant to the truth claims of modern theology. Theologians making use of canonical exegesis need, however, to consider the results of these formalist readings in the wider context of modern theologies. Moreover, biblical studies guided by other interpretative interests may provide results of theological relevance. The diversity of approaches in biblical studies is therefore a contemporary theological problem, and it is to this set of issues that the next chapter is devoted. The arguments of this chapter, drawn primarily from Gadamer (and to a lesser extent from Popper and Jauss), have hopefully lent some plausibility to the canonical approach as one valid kind of biblical study. The theological value of this approach, however, does not immediately follow. The continuing truth value of canonical biblical theology cannot be assumed without further argument.

[illegible]

I think Barth is prejudging the difference between Popper & Gadamer (who represent two quite different systems) in order to get over the problem posed by the canon – closed, i.e. Barr's problem

CHAPTER 6

The future of the canonical approach

THE CRITIQUE OF IDEOLOGY

Having argued in the previous chapter that Gadamer's hermeneutics provides the most charitable way to understand the canonical approach, I want to stress that there are still some differences between Childs and Gadamer which prevent us from simply paraphrasing Childs's writing in Gadamerian terms. There are some residual problems which suggest that the canonical approach needs a more thorough reconstruction. Gadamer, for example, has consistently stressed that hermeneutics has a 'productive' aspect, that is, the interpreter needs to consider issues beyond the perspective of the author if the truth value of an author's text is to be taken seriously. Childs, on the other hand, wants both to emphasize the truth value of canonical Old Testament theology[1] *and at the same time* to reject etic biblical studies which reformulate biblical theologies and reconstruct Israelite history using modern analytical concepts. But how can the biblical classic continue to demonstrate its truthfulness if the critical questions raised by later generations are excluded from the outset? How can the canonical approach avoid charges of fideism or dogmatic classicism? Childs's arguments so far provide no adequate way of responding to these charges. In the first part of this chapter I will argue that one possible way forward for the canonical approach would be to follow Gadamer's philosophical response to the critics of his classicism. In the second part of the chapter I will examine other alternatives.

Both Gadamer and Childs stress that a classic text can

exercise considerable influence long after the time of its production. Moreover, they are agreed that the passage of time can eliminate the *purely* contingent factors that belong to a tradition's origin, and that the bad prejudices of a tradition can be gradually filtered out. Hence, the canonical approach focuses on the 'intentionality' of the classical Hebrew text since this is taken to be a repository of the most valuable traditions which have demonstrated their truthfulness over time. But even if we concede to Childs that the canon contains the most valuable theological reflections of the biblical period, it does not follow that the biblical texts will continue to demonstrate their truthfulness in all subsequent contexts. What if modern biblical studies discover that the communicative intention of the canonical texts is systematically distorted by precisely those 'hidden indices' – historical forces behind the text – that the canonical approach excludes on methodological grounds?[2] What if, for example, the canonical process was shaped by long-standing patterns of communicative interaction within which the powerful simply dominated the weak?[3]

Norman Gottwald has provided us with perhaps the most notable articulations of these questions. He is quite willing to concede that there was indeed something like a canonical process in ancient Israel, even from the earliest times,[4] but he is anxious to stress that this process should not be understood apart from the social matrixes within which it took place. He also seems willing to concede to Childs that the canonical process has blurred and obscured the original sociological factors behind the development of biblical traditions.[5] The difference between the two scholars turns on *the methodological significance attached to this blurring and obscuring of origins.*

In arguing that the canonical editors 'did their best to obscure their own identity' (1979: 78; cf. 393) Childs unwittingly played right into Gottwald's hands. Although there are widely differing uses of the term, one common definition of ideology is precisely a set of beliefs which *obscures* social reality.[6] Hence, it is not at all surprising to find Gottwald objecting:

one of the prime reasons for obscuring the identity of those who advocate authoritative decisions and interpretations is to make their judgments look unquestioned and ancient, even timeless, and certainly descended from divine authority. To overlook this psychosocial reality of ideology and mystification in religious assertions, canonical assertions included, is to deliver theology into an uncritical subjection to the unexamined self-interests of canonizers.[7]

There is, at least in principle, no serious disagreement between Childs and Gottwald as to the *communicative intention* of the final form of biblical texts; the difference between them cannot be resolved by simply asking 'what does the text say?' Rather, it is their different hypotheses as to the *motives* of canonical editors which leads one to a more formalist exegesis and the other to socio-historical methods.

Let us look once again at the premises of Childs's argument that exegetes should leave obscured socio-historical differences obscure. In the *Introduction* he writes:

When critical exegesis is made to rest on the recovery of these very sociological distinctions which have been obscured, it runs directly in the face of the canon's intention. (1979: 78)

Similarly, in discussing the sociological work of Otto Plöger and Morton Smith, he argues that

this historico-sociological approach to the Old Testament is deficient when it fails to reckon with the inner canonical process which, in the case of Joel, has largely obscured these historical differences among groups and replaced them with a normative literature . . . these sacred writings became the norm by which religious identity was measured . . . This observation does not imply that the historical enterprise is illegitimate, but it does call into question an exegetical method which feels itself so dependent on historical research as to overlook the explicit testimony of the literature itself in its canonical form. (1979: 393)

In these arguments, Childs is using the elasticity of the words 'canon' and 'canonical' to equivocate. In both cases, it is possible to see two quite different claims being made, and for the sake of clarity one should reformulate these two claims without using the problematic words in question: (1) the final form of the text provides no clear evidence for a background of social distinctions; (2) during the process of the literature's formation, the authors and editors have deliberately passed over social differences in order to make theological points.

To say that (1) the *final form* provides no clear evidence of social distinctions seems relatively uncontroversial. Interpreters like Gottwald take it for granted that a text may well be obscuring the socio-historical contexts of its production and preservation. At most, the text would provide only fragmentary and indirect clues as to this background. The really controversial claim turns out to be the second one. How does Childs know that the canonical editors have not allowed political strife to influence the formation of their authoritative religious texts? How does he know that less innocent motives have not been subtly concealed? At one point he even concedes that the lack of historical evidence makes it 'difficult to determine the motivations involved in the canonical process' (1979: 62). Nevertheless, he cites Deut. 31; 9ff., Exod. 12:14, and Exod. 12:26ff. in order to argue that the main motive was to lay *religious* claims upon successive generations (1979: 78).

Yet this strategy of citing the final form simply begs the question; the texts may be obscuring deeper motives below their surface meaning. The motives for a lie, for example, are not to be found in the lie itself. In judging the *motives* behind a communicative act, the explicit content of that act is not the only source of relevant evidence. One would need to collect evidence from a wide range of different sources, and in particular, one would need to see whether actual behaviour fits with the explicit content of communicative acts. Thus, to take a biblical example, in I Sam 29: 1–7 the Philistine king of Gath disagreed with his military commanders as to David's motives for living in Philistine territory, but there was no disagreement as to what David was actually telling them about his supposed raids against Judah (e.g., I Sam 27: 10). The disagreement turned on how the wider evidence of David's history and behaviour was to be construed. As it turned out, the Philistine king drew the wrong conclusion about David (I Sam 27: 12) because he took David's *communicative* acts at face value. Similarly, all kinds of darker motives could be hidden under the guise of purely religious claims.

I am forced to conclude, then, that the canonical approach *cannot itself provide the kind of evidence necessary to support one of Childs's key arguments for reading the final form.* Canonical exegesis can tell us very little about the motives of the canonical editors, yet it is precisely Childs's theological understanding of the canonical editors which legitimates his focus on the received text. He recommends that we need not recover original socio-historical differences since these have been subordinated to theological concerns (1979: 393). But he cannot draw this conclusion by simply reading the final form.

In order to defend his approach, Childs might want to be more conciliatory towards the kind of canonical criticism developed by J. A. Sanders which seeks to reconstruct the canonical process. Recall, however, his judgment on Sanders' project:

I am critical of Sanders' attempt to reconstruct the hermeneutical process within ancient Israel, which appears to be a highly speculative enterprise, especially in the light of the almost total lack of information regarding the history of canonization. (1979: 57, cf. 67–8)

Indeed, one could argue that the canonical process raises unique problems for historical study: even if we possessed a wide variety of texts from the biblical period which discussed decisions about the canon in the making (which we do not), it would always be possible to probe behind the explicit content of such texts for masked social interests. There is a sense in which *there can be no 'primary' sources for human motives*; an assessment of the motives behind the canonical process would require a great deal of inferential reasoning based on a wide range of sources of evidence. One can hardly expect scholarly conjectures to secure a wide consensus when the relevant evidence is almost entirely lacking. Childs's own emphasis on the final form is taken to be an antidote to the speculative nature of 'reconstructive' criticism, canonical or otherwise. In other words, he cannot move in the direction of Sanders without undermining the distinctiveness of his own approach.

Alternatively, the canonical approach could invoke a general principle of Gadamer's hermeneutics: bad prejudices are filtered out over time since the *merely* contingent interests of particular agents are left behind in the transmission process of a tradition. One would need to recognize, however, that this is more like a 'rule of thumb' for Gadamer and not a general law.

As a rule of thumb, it cannot be invoked against strong arguments which may be available in the case of a specific (in this case biblical) tradition. Gadamer's hermeneutics provides only a *prima facie* case for trusting classic texts.

For example, in reply to Habermas's criticisms of *Truth and Method*,[8] Gadamer emphasized that hermeneutics can indeed include the critique of ideology and reflection upon social manipulation. Habermas had construed Gadamer's account of linguistic tradition as implying that sociologists could not inquire into the material conditions within which a cultural tradition is transmitted. (One might compare here Childs's strictures against Gottwald's etic sociology.) But Gadamer's account of tradition does not envision a purely 'cultural' world of meaning which is separate from 'the economic and political realities which pre-eminently determine the life of society'. He writes:

it seems altogether absurd that the concrete factors of work and dominance should be seen as lying outside the scope of hermeneutics. What else are the prejudices with which hermeneutical reflection concerns itself? Where else shall they originate if not in work and dominance? In the cultural tradition? To be sure, there, too. But of what is that tradition compounded?[9]

One should be reminded at this point that Gadamer's account of the authority of a classic is philosophical in nature and not a defence of a particular canon. As we have pointed out above, if an ancient work does not continue to demonstrate its truthfulness, then Gadamer is not compelled to identify it as classical in his normative sense. He insists against Habermas that authority rests on the *free* acknowledgement of superior knowledge and judgment. If empirical research reveals that the past acknowledgement of an authority involved the yielding of the powerless to force then the 'authority' in question has lost its legitimacy. The critique of ideology is precisely one of the ways in which this legitimacy may be lost:

When Habermas says that 'what was mere domination can be stripped from authority [by which I understand: what was not authority in the first place] and dissolved into powerless coercion by insight and rational decision' . . . ,then I no longer know what we are arguing about.[10]

Whatever one might think about the Gadamer–Habermas debate (the interpretations of it are legion) it is important, in our present context, to see how Gadamer's position differs from Childs's. Because Gadamer emphasizes the *productive* nature of hermeneutics he is able to provide a reasonable reply to the critics of ideology. He insists that his version of hermeneutics should not simply be identified with an emic or 'verstehende' sociology,[11] or indeed with any particular method of social-scientific research. Whatever the content of a cultural tradition it is always possible to revise it; it is always possible for critical reason to 'demand proof' of the tradition's validity. Gadamer's argument is that critical reason *cannot demand proof of all tradition all at once.*[12] Thus, Gadamer's rejection of the antithesis between authority and reason does not lead to an unqualified dogmatism.

Gadamer therefore escapes the charge of dogmatism or fideism by saying that tradition is always revisable. Yet he is deliberately vague on the question of what would count as *sufficient reasons* for criticizing tradition. If, as Gadamer suggests, genuine conversation with classics transforms our view of things, it would be difficult to formulate principles of criticism in advance of actual conversation. Productive understanding is neither pure empathy with the other, nor 'the subjection of the other to our own criteria' (p. 272, S. 288). Here Gadamer seems to be undermining a purely critical or etic approach to classics and thereby placing limits on the revisability of tradition. On the other hand, the possibility of critique provides his escape from charges of dogmatism.

The theological value of the canonical approach might be enhanced by Gadamer's more subtle view of conversation with classics. Certainly, final form study cannot in itself provide the kind of evidence that would protect the canonical process against the critique of ideology. If truth claims are at stake, then it would be most reasonable to think that canonical exegesis needs to be placed in the theological arena along with alternative styles of interpretation and critique. Gadamer, among others, would lead us to think that the results of conversation in this broader arena cannot be stated in advance.

This picture of theological diversity would, however, be

unacceptable to many theologians, and no doubt to Childs himself. In the next section we shall therefore consider a school of theology which asserts the clear priority of the biblical categories for contemporary theology, and therefore stands closer to Childs's own view. The possible ways forward for the canonical approach will be discussed in theological more than in philosophical terms, and in particular we will investigate the possibility of 'intratextual' theology becoming an ally of the canonical approach.

A THEOLOGICAL CRITIQUE OF THE CANONICAL APPROACH

Another way forward for the canonical approach would be to link it with the intratextual theology developed by Childs's colleagues, Hans Frei and George Lindbeck. Ronald Thiemann's recent work *Revelation and Theology* (1985) is also relevant here, since this study attempts to construct an intratextual account of revelation. Before we examine the possible links between this kind of theology and the canonical approach, it will be necessary to provide a brief sketch of the views upon which Frei, Lindbeck and Thiemann are agreed.

The intratextual school does not regard biblical texts as simply stepping stones which lead to a more fundamental reality within history or within the human subject; referents only appear *under the descriptions* offered by the biblical traditions. Although it may be possible to redescribe historical individuals and events by means of extra-biblical categories, such etic redescriptions cannot be said to belong to the same tradition of religious belief and practice. This kind of theology is founded especially on the 'realistic' or history-like narratives of scripture which are held to shape Christian faith even if the historicity of these narratives cannot be justified by a scientific historiography. The biblical text is seen as a kind of framework, a symbolic universe given by the tradition, through which the Christian interprets the world. In Lindbeck's words:

Intratextual theology redescribes reality within the scriptural framework rather than translating Scripture into extra-scriptural categories.[13]

It is essential to recognize at the outset that the intratextual school rejects the basic conception of epistemology which took shape during the Enlightenment. Frei, Lindbeck and Thiemann all agree that the truth claims of Christianity cannot be defended in the public realm by arguments which would secure universal agreement; a recognition of the irreducible *pluralism* of our contemporary situation is finally not compatible with an apologetic strategy which purports to begin from universally accepted foundations.[14] This is not to say that individual traditions are therefore fixed in static opposition to one another; rather, the view is that if traditions change (here one would have to focus on Lindbeck's interest in ecumenical conversations) this will be through concrete, transformative conversation and not through assuming at the outset that somewhere deep down in the human spirit there is a domain, purged of the 'accidents' of tradition, where we all agree.

Critics of the intratextualists – especially the exponents of liberal theology – are tempted to see the internal focus of the cultural-linguistic model as just a new version of fideism.[15] One should recognize, however, that this theological attack on the *universal* aspirations of Enlightenment epistemology is also a characteristic feature of recent 'postmodern' philosophy.[16] We have now a wide variety of theologians, philosophers and literary critics who have subjected the vision of a pure and unified rationality to a severe re-examination. Our universities, for example, are not so much unified totalities as splintered specialities which are governed by the narrow competence of experts at the cutting edge of their own particular research tradition. Contemporary 'modernists' like Habermas suggest that we can alleviate this lamentable situation only by forging a theory of human communication with universally applicable rules of rational discourse and critique. Postmodernists, on the other hand, are suspicious of the idea that there can be a single and independent set of rational ground rules which could decisively settle any particular debate between different traditions.[17] They seem to be satisfied with 'local knowledge' and have given up what Bernard Williams calls 'the superpower view of defence' – the view that you have justified a position 'only if you can annihilate the other side'.[18] As Frei puts it:

the faith articulated in dogma is . . . indeed not irrational, 'paradoxical' or 'fideistic', but rather rational yet fragmentary.[19]

Frei, Lindbeck and Thiemann are therefore more disposed
towards what some postmodernists call narrative knowledge,[20]
which is opposed to legitimation through universally valid
argument or proof. Making their debts to Clifford Geertz
explicit, the intratextualists conceive of theology as more
descriptive than explanatory.[21] The term 'descriptive' does not
here indicate an opposition to normative claims, rather, it
indicates a task which is roughly equivalent to emic description
(which I have opposed to etic explanation), except that the
theologians stand explicitly within the tradition they are
describing. They are not so much interpretative anthropologists
– who attempt to suspend their prejudices in order to do field
work – as reflective informants who explicate their *normative*
proposals without justifying these proposals on the basis of
universally accepted explanatory theories.

The justification of Christian truth claims is, in intratextual
theology, conceived as specific to the Christian community and
tradition. Truth claims are justified primarily in terms of
'intelligibility, aptness and warranted assertability'.[22] Any
reference to an historical or ontological reality is taken to be
inseparable from the wider cultural-linguistic system within
which it is perceived. A religious claim is 'intrasystematically'
true when it coheres with the total relevant context of Christian
speech and action. Lindbeck concedes, however, that 'intrasystematic truth is a necessary but not sufficient condition for
ontological truth'.[23] It seems that although theological talk of
actual referents cannot bypass the cultural-linguistic frameworks of the biblical communities, 'it does not follow that we can
no longer make historical or ontological claims to truth'.[24]
Accordingly, Thiemann is careful to distinguish between the
logic of truth claims, and the logic of *justifying* those claims. The
postmodernist seems committed to the view that what we claim
to be true can finally be justified only by the sufficient reasons
peculiar to a particular tradition.

I should perhaps note here parenthetically that this view is
not peculiar to intratextualists. A similar point has recently been

made by Nicholas Lash in a brief discussion of the verification of
Christian truth claims. Lash suggests that we should face up to
the fact that biblical scholars cannot secure the historical
grounds of belief by the strategies of secular or 'scientific'
historiography. But he does not regard this as a great loss. If the
correspondence of Christian faith to reality eludes scholarly
demonstration, this is not the end of the story. This correspondence can

be practically, imperfectly, partially and provisionally *shown* by the
character and quality of Christian engagement in patterns of action
and suffering, praise and endurance.[25]

In arguing this position, Lash appropriates that strand of
Marxist epistemology which stresses the primacy of action over
reflection, of social existence over consciousness.[26]

One might even see an analogy here between this Marxist
epistemology and Calvin's idea – occasionally alluded to by
Childs – that the witness of scripture is confirmed by the
contemporary action of the Holy Spirit (*Institutes I, 7*). In both
cases there is an important sense in which the justification of
scriptural claims is internal to the transmission of biblical
tradition. This seems to be one of the central theses of
intratextual theology, and it leads both Frei and Lindbeck to be
critical of David Tracy's broader view of the religious classic. In
The Analogical Imagination Tracy writes:

certain expressions of the human spirit so disclose a compelling truth
about our lives that we cannot deny them some kind of normative
status.[27]

These expressions become classics, Tracy suggests, when they
reveal 'what is essential, that which endures'. Intratextualists
find these claims immodest. Lindbeck prefers to say that classics
are 'culturally established for whatever reason', and he eschews
all references to 'the' human spirit or vague references to the 'we'
who recognize a normative authority. The authority of the Bible
is actually recognized only by a particular 'sociolinguistic
community'.[28]

It would seem to follow from this that Lindbeck sees the Bible
also as culturally established for whatever reason. But surely he

would not want a biblical tradition established for *ideological* reasons to provide the framework for modern Christian descriptions of reality. The intratextualists, however, have so far shown little interest in probing for ideology behind the finished and 'objective' text of scripture. The Bible seems to occupy such a central position in the web of Christian beliefs and practices that it is 'like the axis around which a body rotates', 'the scaffolding of our thoughts', and as such it 'lies apart from the route travelled by inquiry'.[29]

It is difficult to see how this attitude toward scripture can be maintained without a doctrine of revelation to support it. Philosophers influenced by Gadamer could freely concede that our lives are structured by traditions which cannot *all* be subjected to critique at the same time. It would not follow, however, that individual biblical traditions cannot be criticized by later biblical communities – in effect, allowing the canonical process to continue. Moreover, one could agree with a great deal of what Lindbeck says about his cultural-linguistic model of religion and still disagree with his treatment of scripture. Wayne Meeks, for example, has argued that Lindbeck does not actually apply his own cultural-linguistic model *to the biblical period*.[30] Meeks reflects the interpretative interests of most biblical scholars when he asks why we need to read the final form of the Bible as part of *later* cultural-linguistic religious systems? Biblical scholars are more interested in using the biblical texts as sources for the religious systems of the ancient world.

Childs's work could be seen as a contribution to precisely this set of issues. He suggests that religious communities do not read the Bible as a source of ancient religious systems since our overriding interest is in a Word of God which is still valid. *The final form of the text is the 'objective' repository of the best theological reflection of the biblical period*; it contains 'the full history of revelation' (1979: 76), and it is relatively autonomous of the narrow social interests and peculiar mental histories which may lie behind the text in the period of its reception before stabilization. But now we have come a full circle since it is still not clear how Childs can justify this belief in the canonical process. In particular one is left with the classic problem for doctrines of revelation: what is the relationship between divine initiative and human reception? The determined sceptic can always assert that the Bible is simply a collection of literary vestiges from ancient religious systems. All talk of revelation would on this view be redundant.

Amongst the intratextualists, Ronald Thiemann has provided the most comprehensive reflection on the problem of revelation. He has suggested that although a sense of revelation-weariness has settled over the discipline of academic theology,[31] this doctrine is indispensable – especially if one wants to speak of the prevenience of God's grace (the belief that God acts before all human will). Thiemann begins by arguing that revelation cannot be defended in the public realm by universally acceptable foundations, but he sets out nevertheless to provide a reasonable account which should at least be acceptable to Christian communities. Taking up the problem of the relationship between divine initiative and human reception, he begins by citing James Barr's formulation of the issue:

The real problem, as it seems to me, is that we have no access to, and no means of comprehending, a communication or revelation from God which is antecedent to the human tradition about him . . . In attempting to found the status of scripture upon such an antecedent revelation we are explaining what is obscure by what is quite unknown.[32]

In short, the human response is the only source of our knowledge of God's initiative. The problem is by no means alleviated if we discover, for example, that ancient prophets and communities themselves stressed God's intervention over against their own will; this could simply mask a hidden motive of self-legitimation.

Thiemann goes on to suggest, however, that Barr's point really only counts against the temporal model of *antecedent* revelatory event and *subsequent* response, a model of revelation which was characteristic of the American 'Biblical Theology Movement' during the 1950s.[33] Against this, Thiemann argues that

Revelation is the *continuing* reality of God's active presence among his people. Since it is a reality 'not seen' and not fully experienced, it must be expressed by a confession of faith, i.e., an 'assurance of things hoped for, the conviction of things not seen'. That conviction is displayed theologically by showing how God's prevenience is retrospectively implied by a cluster of Christian convictions concerning God's promises, identity, and reality.[34]

On this view, God's revelation is not located in an unambiguous historical event. Rather, revelation is a continuing reality within the beliefs and practices of a religious community, on the basis of which God's prevenience is retrospectively inferred. Revelatory events do not present 'in themselves' but only under religious descriptions. The direction of interpretative flow is from language to world, not world to language.

This line of argument might seem, however, to beg the question. How do we know that the community was justified in retrospectively inferring God's prevenience? And does not the very word 'retrospective' smuggle in the temporal model of antecedent revelation under a new guise? Here I would say two things in Thiemann's defence. First, what is being smuggled in is not Danto's ideal eye-witness but the retrospective historical reflection which encompasses the later consequences of historical events. Moreover, the events that are being reflected upon in the biblical tradition have an inexpungable religious dimension which could not be empirically verified, even by ideal eye-witnesses. For example, would a newsreel report of the exodus event record the intervention of Yahweh, or at most, a sequence of coincidences which turned out to favour the Israelites? Would an independent chronicler in Jerusalem in 597 BCE agree with Jeremiah's judgment that 'this city is delivered by Yahweh into the power of the Babylonians' (Jer. 32)?[35] I would suggest that no eye-witness or historian could verify statements like this without first believing that Yahweh existed and could be active in history. In short, many of the central concerns of the Hebrew Bible *could not be verified by a purely empirical historiography*.

Thiemann's view is therefore compelling: revelation is better conceived of as a continuing phenomenon which includes communal interpretation of history, tradition and new experience – interpretation which is in some sense guided by God. The identifiability of God's presence and action in the world is, as

Thiemann says, '*intrinsically* related to Christian belief and practice'.[36] A decisive and universal validation of Christian truth claims is simply not available within history.

One could, however, concede all this to Thiemann and still wonder why intratextualists are so attracted to the final form of scripture. Why should God's providential guidance of the community's interpretation cease at the end of the biblical period? Such a view would seem to require a special hermeneutical providence for the biblical period. Some might respond by arguing that the revelation of God in Jesus Christ was so decisive that it is sufficient for all of history. But such a response would overlook the necessity for a *continuing interpretation* of the significance of Jesus Christ; it would not constitute a defence of the final form of scripture or of its history-like narrative. One might want to argue, as has Elizabeth Schüssler Fiorenza, that the canonical picture of Jesus Christ has seriously distorted the original, more fruitful, interpretations of the historical Jesus.[37] Even if one rejected Fiorenza's own reconstruction of the early church, one might want to endorse the task of critical historical research if it can provide a quite different, and less distorted, narrative interpretation of the identity of Jesus Christ. One might even argue that such critical reinterpretations of Jesus (or of Israelite history) could be thought of as retrospective reflections guided by God's continuing revelation in our own age. Thiemann's intratextual account of revelation would seem to be compatible, in this sense, with the continuation of the canonical process.

It is not clear how Thiemann would respond to this possibility. To put the point more generally, it is not clear (even if we accept the cultural-linguistic model of religion and the narrative construction of human and divine identities) how intratextualists can justify their stress on the final form of scripture. In a recent essay on ecclesiology Lindbeck has stated his position with more circumspection: 'Biblical conceptualities', he writes, 'may be supplanted or displaced, as at Nicaea and Chalcedon, but only if this is necessary for the sake of greater faithfulness, intelligibility or efficaciousness. The burden of proof is on those whose fundamental categories for thinking about the church are nonbiblical'.[38] This statement comes closer to a Gadamerian position that allows the possibility of criticizing the classic without undermining its fundamental role for those who stand in its history of effects. Lindbeck seems to have retreated, prudently, from a purely biblical understanding of intratextuality, and he is now in a better position to respond to charges of fideism. Further, in adopting his narrative ecclesiology, which is based primarily on the Old Testament rather than the New, he has shown that intratextual theology does not always need to encompass the whole Christian Bible. How the canon is used apparently depends on the particular theological task at hand, not a general rule that the entire canon is always relevant.

It seems to me that the Lindbeck represents the closest theological ally of the canonical approach, even though Childs himself seems reluctant to grant this fact (1984a: 541–6). Childs seems more concerned to rehabilitate a doctrine of biblical inspiration (e.g. 1970a: 131; 1985: 12). Although this might appeal to the more conservative elements of the church it is precisely these elements who will resist the relative indifference to questions of historicity in the canonical approach.[39] Conservative evangelicals, for example, would tend to see this as too much of a concession to the modern criticism of the Bible.[40] The canonical approach finds closer allies amongst intratextual theologians.

Nevertheless, it would be a mistake to *identify* the canonical approach with intratextual theology. It would be preferable, I would argue, for the canonical exegetes to give up all talk of revelation and turn attention to the 'objective' content (in Popper's sense) of biblical tradition, without making any claims about the canonical process. This way forward would take the canonical approach much closer to the 'literary' approaches which eschew historical reconstruction and simply read the text as it has been handed down. I should stress that this way forward would not need to rest on a particular literary theory, such as New Criticism, which sets out to find organic unities in the text come what may. There is now a diversity of literary theories which would endorse a search for tensions[41] or even contradictions[42] in biblical texts without attempting to resolve such problems into literary sources or editorial additions. Post-structuralist critics insist, for example, that all texts are 'a tissue of quotations drawn from the innumerable centers of culture'.[43] The tendency to attribute logical coherence to individual authors and literary sources (ancient or modern) is arguably an unjustified interpretative prejudice. Attention to the 'objective' content of biblical texts need not, one should also notice, preclude the critique of ideology, and here one need only cite the formalist work of Phyllis Trible.[44]

There are at least two *theological* arguments for blurring the distinction between the canonical approach and other formalist literary approaches. First, theologians of various persuasions have worried about the relationship between academic biblical study and the non-expert lay person. The issue has recently surfaced especially in Roman Catholic liberation theology, but one finds it expressed by fundamentalists, kerygmatic theologians and neo-Kantians.[45] Given a 'top-down' model of the church, a gap between expert biblical interpreters and lay people is of no special concern; the church at large is, on this view, guided by benevolent authorities. It is arguable, however, that this model is inherently authoritarian and that church leadership is no more free of vested interests than any other human institution. A more egalitarian ecclesiology would want to prevent the interpretation of scripture from becoming the preserve of learned and powerful elites. The egalitarian model might suggest that the final form of scripture should be the beginning point for all Christians (even if one goes on, like Trible, to criticize the text). If subtle reconstructions behind the text are a necessary strategy for dealing with some interpretative problems, *vis-à-vis* the *laity* such reconstructions will always have the logical status of arguments from authority.

J. A. Sanders raises just this kind of issue when he suggests that critical Protestant scholarship created a new type of 'priestly' control of religious communities, even though the Reformation had attempted to give the Bible back to the people. He also seems to imply that his own version of canonical criticism is motivated by this Protestant principle.[46] One can only wonder how he reconciles this point with his own stress on the necessity for historical and sociological reconstruction;[47] such reconstruction is clearly dominated by professional biblical scholars. The most one could claim is that professional scholarship has no *centralized* authority.

There are, of course, considerable difficulties with this theological justification for final form study. The church is always dependent on experts both for translation and for the many exegetical difficulties which even the untrained eye can discover. One should also distinguish between authorities whose social location is the church and authorities who are located in the university. It is arguable that the social matrix of the university, with its own internal system of rewards, provides a relative degree of autonomy which is necessary for criticizing church authorities. One would also need to remember, however, that university experts have vested interests in making biblical study difficult, and thus worthy of a place in the university in the first place. If final form study becomes fashionable at universities, one suspects that biblical studies will not *ipso facto* become more accessible to wider audiences. Final form studies will need to be presented as subtle and learned, borrowing insights from neighbouring disciplines and solving interesting new problems.[48] Allowing for all this, a focus on the final form of scripture could still, depending on the theological task at hand, contribute in a small way to closing the gap between experts and laity. We should, in any case, be thinking more deeply about the social location of biblical criticism.

The second argument for bringing the canonical approach closer to formalist literary approaches is related to my advocacy of pluralism in biblical studies. It seems to me that there are good *theological* reasons for relieving the canonical approach of excessive theological claims. Being primarily an approach to biblical study, it should not be used to short circuit the widest possible discussion in theology. The distinction between these two disciplines is not a simple issue, but there are nevertheless differences in interpretative interest. Even if, for example, final form exegesis can make substantial contributions to intratextual theology, theologians will need to go beyond the narrowly exegetical interests of biblical scholars and investigate the *aptness* and *applicability* of canonical theologies in the contemporary world. In undertaking this broader task intratextualists will need to consider the contributions of competing theological schools as well as the results of biblical studies guided by other interpretative interests. If theology is to remain theology, and not some other thing, this open discussion will fall short of *universal* publicness, but contemporary theology needs this wide horizon if it is to avoid the charge of fideism. Indeed, if scripture is to be proclaimed 'outside the community' as well as inside, it must be understood by the variety of audiences which are shaped by other traditions and other classics.[49]

The promotion of pluralism in biblical studies is one way of keeping our horizons wide. Childs wants to put all our theological eggs in one basket – the canonical approach. It would be more responsible, on the pluralist argument, to distribute them widely.[50] But pluralism is not an end in itself. A variety of interpretative interests may be intelligible and permissable, but not all will be edifying to the Christian community. We are in need of some attention to the ethics of interpretation.[51] Theologians should recognize the canonical approach as one fruitful way of doing biblical interpretation, but the utility of a particular approach needs to be argued in relation to concrete exegetical studies and specific theological projects. Even if we do not all become formalist interpreters of the Hebrew Bible in its 'objective' canonical shape, Childs's work will not have been in vain. Although he has not always been persuasive, we should be grateful to him for urging us to think more clearly about methodology in biblical studies and its relationship to wider concerns. Indeed, even Childs should be able to agree with what Frank Kermode has said about classic texts in another context:

however a particular epoch or a particular community may define a proper mode of attention or a licit area of interest, there will always be something else and something different to say.[52]

Notes

INTRODUCTION

1 L. Gilkey, 'Cosmology, Ontology, and the Travail of Biblical Language' *JR* 41 (1961), 194–205.
2 J. Barr, 'Revelation through History in the Old Testament and in Modern Theology' *Interp* 17 (1963), 193–205.
3 J. Barton, *Reading the Old Testament: Method in Biblical Study* (London: Darton, Longman & Todd, 1984), p. 208.
4 Comparisons between Gadamer and Childs have been briefly suggested by: S. Fowl, 'The Canonical Approach of Brevard Childs' *Expos. T.* 96 (1985), 173–76; F. Kermode, 'The Argument about Canons' in: *The Bible and the Narrative Tradition* (Oxford: Oxford University Press, 1986), pp. 78–96; M. Oeming, *Gesamt-biblische Theologien der Gegenwart* (Stuttgart: Kohlhammer, 1985), pp. 202–3 n. 49. Oeming devotes three chapters to Gadamer, but his main purpose is to make comparisons with the biblical theology of Gerhard von Rad. He also summarizes a number of common objections to Gadamer's work which, especially through comparisons with Popper, I am seeking to undermine. The most detailed theological critique of Gadamer, and the reception of his work, can be found in H. G. Stobbe, *Hermeneutik: Ein Oekumenisches Problem* (Zürich: Benziger, 1981). Gadamer's rhetorical ambiguities take on a fresh significance, however, when they are read in the context of the recent 'anti-foundationalist' movement of Anglo-American philosophy. See G. Warnke, *Gadamer: Hermeneutics, Tradition and Reason* (Oxford: Polity, 1987), esp. chs. 5–6.
5 See further my article 'Four or Five things to do with Texts: A Taxonomy of Interpretative Interests' in: *The Bible in Three Dimensions*, ed. D. Clines, S. Fowl and S. Porter (Sheffield: Sheffield Academic Press, 1990), pp. 357–77.
6 J. Barr, *Holy Scripture: Canon, Authority, Criticism* (Oxford: Oxford University Press, 1983). This book is discussed below, chapter 5, in the section on 'Concepts of Canon and the Ideal Eye Witness'.

7 See G. Lindbeck, *The Nature of Doctrine: Religion and Theology in a Postliberal Age* (London: SPCK, 1984).

8 This point has rightly been made by James Barr with particular reference to the Biblical Theology Movement. See his contribution to the Festschrift for Childs, 'The Theological Case against Biblical Theology' in: *Canon, Theology, and Old Testament Interpretation*, ed. G. M. Tucker, D. L. Petersen and R. R. Wilson (Philadelphia: Fortress, 1988), pp. 3–19.

9 The theory is familiar, at least, among phenomenological sociologists, interpretative anthropologists and Wittgensteinian philosophers. Among the most influential books in each of these traditions are P. Berger and T. Luckmann, *The Social Construction of Reality* (Harmondsworth: Penguin, 1967); C. Geertz, *The Interpretation of Cultures* (New York: Basic Books, 1973); P. Winch, *The Idea of a Social Science* (London: Routledge & Kegan Paul, 1958).

10 For an influential philosophical statement of this view, see J. F. Lyotard, *The Postmodern Condition* (Minneapolis: Minnesota University Press, 1984). The theological views of Lindbeck, Frei, and Thiemann will be discussed below, but cf. also N. Wolterstorff, *Reason within the Bounds of Religion*, 2nd edn (Grand Rapids: Eerdmans, 1984); A. Plantinga and N. Wolterstorff (eds.), *Faith and Rationality* (Notre Dame: Notre Dame University Press, 1983); N. Murphy and J. McClendon, 'Distinguishing Modern and Postmodern Theologies' *Mod. Theol.* 5/3 (1989), 191–214; F. B. Burnham (ed.), *Postmodern Theology* (London: Harper & Row, 1989).

1 DISTINGUISHING INTERPRETATIVE INTERESTS

1 See, e.g., R. Rendtorff, 'Jesaja 6 im Rahmen der Composition des Jesajabuches' *BETL* 81 (1989), 82; R. Polzin, *Moses and the Deuteronomist* (New York: Seabury, 1980), ch. 1.

2 N. Gottwald, 'Social Matrix and Canonical Shape' *TT* 42/43 (1986), 307–21.

3 Cf. J. Stout 'What is the Meaning of a Text?' *New Lit. Hist.* 19 (1982), 1–12; L. Dannenberg and H. H. Müller, 'Wissenschaftstheorie, Hermeneutik, Literaturwissenschaft' *DVLG* 2 (1984), 177–237.

4 See especially Childs's discussion paper 'Karl Barth as Interpreter of Scripture' (1969b). Childs shares Barth's criticism of modern 'theological historicism' which seeks 'to penetrate past the biblical texts to the facts which lie behind the texts. Revelation is then found in these facts as such (which in their factuality are

independent of the texts)'. The emphasis on archaeology in the Biblical Theology Movement exhibited just this kind of theological historicism. The canonical approach seems to follow Barth's recommendation that the goal of exegesis be reformulated in the light of the fact that the revelation attested by biblical texts 'is not to be sought, behind or above them but in them'; for Barth, scripture is the 'indispensable form' of the 'content' of revelation. Cf. Barth, *Church Dogmatics* 1/2 (Edinburgh: T&T Clark, 1956), pp. 492 and 494.

5 See Barr's preface to the second edition of *Old and New in Interpretation* (1966; London: SCM, 1982), pp. 13–14.

6 K. Popper, *Objective Knowledge* (Oxford: Oxford University Press, 1972), p. 82.

7 Popper, *Objective Knowledge*, p. 9.

8 W. G. Runciman, *A Treatise on Social Theory Vol. 1: The Methodology of Social Theory* (Cambridge: Cambridge University Press, 1983), p. 42.

9 J. W. Rogerson, 'The Use of Sociology in Old Testament Studies' *VTS* 36 (1985), 254–55.

10 Cf. Popper, *Objective Knowledge*, p. 193: 'Only if we require that explanations shall make use of universal statements or laws of nature (supplemented by initial conditions) can we make progress towards realizing the idea of independent, or non *ad hoc* explanations'. Note that this stricture applies precisely to historians, whose business it is to explain specific, and perhaps even 'unique', events. See *The Poverty of Historicism* (London: Routledge & Kegan Paul, 1957), pp. 120–30, 143–47. For an influential non-Marxist defence of general laws in anthropological explanation, see A. R. Radcliffe-Brown, *A Natural Science of Society* (Glencoe: Free Press, 1957).

11 N. Gottwald, *The Tribes of Yahweh* (Maryknoll: Orbis, 1979), p. 785. Here Gottwald invokes the earlier work of Marvin Harris, *The Rise of Anthropological Theory* (London: Routledge & Kegan Paul, 1968). See further K. Pike, 'Towards a Theory of the Structure of Human Behaviour' in: *Language in Culture and Society*, ed. D. Hymes (New York: Harper & Row, 1964), pp. 154–61; Harris, *Cultural Materialism* (New York: Random, 1979); R. Feleppa, 'Emics, Etics and Social Objectivity' *Curr. Anthrop.* 27 (1986), 243–55; M. G. Brett, 'Four or Five Things to do with Texts: A Taxonomy of Interpretative Interests' in: *The Bible in Three Dimensions*, ed. D. Clines, S. Fowl and S. Porter (Sheffield: Sheffield Academic Press, 1990), pp. 357–77.

Apart from the philosophical problem of translation (discussed by Feleppa), two of the key problems for emic description turn on the gender and power of informants. These problems do not, however, invalidate the distinctive goal of emics, as long as interpreters allow the possibility of cultural diversity. See further E. Ardener, 'Belief and the Problem of Women' in: *The Interpretation of Ritual*, ed. J. S. La Fontaine (London: Tavistock, 1972), pp. 135–58, and R. M. Keesing, 'Anthropology as Interpretive Quest' *Curr. Anthrop.* 28 (1987), 161–76.

12 See Runciman, *Treatise*, p. 13, here drawing on the work of M. Finley, *The Ancient Economy* (London: Chatto & Windus, 1973).

13 C. Geertz, *The Interpretation of Cultures* (New York: Basic Books, 1973), p. 14. Also p. 5: anthropology is 'not an experimental science in search of law but an interpretive one in search of meaning'. Cf. E. E. Evans-Pritchard, *Essays in Social Anthropology* (London: Faber, 1962), p. 26: anthropology 'seeks patterns and not scientific laws, and interprets rather than explains'; P. Rabinow and W. Sullivan (eds.), *Interpretive Social Science* (Berkeley: University of California Press, 1979). A. D. H. Mayes has recently also drawn attention to the work of Anthony Giddens (see bibliography), suggesting that this is superior to Runciman's in that it gives human agency a genuinely causal role in history. This, unfortunately, confuses Runciman's general and analytical account of explanation with a specific etic theory, i.e., cultural materialism. Giddens's social theory is actually etic, but it places much more stress on human agency. Mayes 'Sociology and the Old Testament' in: *The World of Ancient Israel*, ed. R. Clements (Cambridge: Cambridge University Press, 1989), pp. 58–59.

14 In *Oracles of God* (London: Darton, Longman & Todd, 1986), John Barton has shown how differing definitions of 'canon' have led to a great deal of confusion in recent debates about Hebrew scripture. Barton himself defines canon as a definitely closed list of books which is authoritative for faith and practice (pp. 30 and 56), and the element of definitive closure is reinforced by a distinction between 'scripture' (*at least* these books are authoritative) and 'canon' (*at most* these books are authoritative). But the idea of exclusive closure seems to me unworkable for historical studies. Given such definitions even Thomas Aquinas could not yet have had a biblical canon, since the authority of the Bible in his theology in no way excludes the authority of, for example, Aristotle. See M. D. Chenu, *Toward Understanding St. Thomas* (Chicago: University of Chicago Press, 1964), pp. 126–39. Indeed, Barton makes it impossible to speak of the canonization of the Torah before the Prophets and the Writings were added to it; if the Prophets and

Writings could be added to it then the Torah was not a definitively closed and *exclusive* authority. The strict distinction between scripture and canon defines the historically extended process of canonization out of existence. Barton also suggests (pp. 27 and 44) that Childs's work rests on the early dates for 'canonization' defended by Sid Leiman. Leiman's work is indeed allied to Childs's in that both place more stress on the authoritative nature of canonical literature than on its definitive and exclusive closure, but Childs does not follow Leiman uncritically (Childs 1979: 56). Although Childs leans towards early dates in his *Introduction*, and especially in a more recent study (1988), the logic of the canonical approach does not *require* them.

15 J. A. Sanders, 'Canonical Context and Canonical Criticism' *HBT* 2 (1980), 190 n. 41.

16 J. Goody and I. Watt, 'The Consequences of Literacy' in: *Literacy in Traditional Societies*, ed. J. Goody (Cambridge: Cambridge University Press, 1968), pp. 57 and 63.

17 H. Gunkel, *Schöpfung und Chaos in Urzeit und Endzeit* (Göttingen: Vandenhoeck & Ruprecht, 1985); abridged ET 'The Influence of Babylonian Mythology upon the Biblical Creation Story' in: *Creation in the Old Testament*, ed. B. W. Anderson (London: SPCK, 1984), pp. 25–52. See further, M. G. Brett, 'Motives and Intentions in Genesis 1', forthcoming in *JTS*.

18 M. Noth, *A History of Pentateuchal Traditions* (Englewood Cliffs, NJ: Prentice-Hall, 1972), p. 41.

19 J. Goody, *The Domestication of the Savage Mind* (Cambridge: Cambridge University Press, 1977), pp. 26–7.

20 In the next chapter it will become clear that Childs often does make comments on the prehistory of the final form, but I will argue that in these cases he speaks as an historical critic (usually a sceptical one) and not as an advocate of a distinctive canonical approach.

21 E. D. Hirsch, *Validity in Interpretation* (New Haven: Yale University Press 1967), p. 55. Cf. pp. 242–3. See further, Brett, 'Motives and Intentions'; Q. Skinner, 'Motives, Intentions, and the Interpretation of Texts', *NLH* 3 (1972) 393–408.

22 E. D. Hirsch, 'Meaning and Significance Reinterpreted' *Crit. Inqu.* 11 (1984), 223.

23 Hirsch, 'Meaning and Significance Reinterpreted', pp. 205–6. On face-to-face communication see the detailed linguistic work of D. Sperber and D. Wilson, *Relevance: Communication and Cognition* (Oxford: Blackwell, 1986), esp. p. 201: 'there is a continuum of cases, from implicatures which the hearer was specifically intended to recover to implicatures which were merely intended to be made manifest, and to further modifications of the mutual cognitive

environment of speaker and hearer that the speaker only intended in the sense that she intended her utterance to be relevant, and hence to have rich and *not entirely foreseeable* cognitive effects' (italics added).

24 Hirsch, 'Meaning and Significance Reinterpreted', p. 204.

25 J. L. Battersby and J. Phelan 'Meaning as Concept and Extension' *Crit. Inqu.* 12 (1986), 608.

26 See Quentin Skinner's remarks on the 'mythology of coherence' and the 'reification of doctrines' in his article 'Meaning and Understanding in the History of Ideas' *Hist. & Th.* 3 (1969), 7–12.

2 THE DEVELOPMENT OF CANONICAL EXEGESIS

1 Thus, e.g., James Barr, *Holy Scripture* (Oxford: Clarendon, 1983), p. 132: 'The effect of Childs's *Introduction* was to convince me that the programme of canonical criticism was essentially confused and self-contradictory in its *conceptual* formulation' (italics added).

2 It is unclear whether Childs means that the word functions as a proper noun to *refer* to the Babylonian monster Tiamat, whether Isa. 51: 9–10 indirectly *alludes* to a commonly known foreign narrative by means of a wordplay, or whether an early reference or allusion had already been forgotten by the editors of Isaiah.

3 In a later study, Childs says that Isa. 51: 9–10 'fuses' a victory over the sea monster with the exodus tradition of redemption at the sea (1970b: 413). This would make the text, at the very least, a hybrid of two *different* traditions.

4 Childs's meaning is quite clear in this quotation, but there is a semantic confusion: assuming that we can formulate workable notions of 'myth' and 'demythologizing' it will be narratives, ideas, or concepts which are demythologized, not individual words.

5 There is a certain irony here since the pioneering formulation of the very idea of 'phenomenological description' came from a philosopher, Edmund Husserl. Similarly, many of Childs's remarks concerning mythic 'categories' (this notion is itself highly significant) are directly or indirectly influenced by the neo-Kantian philosopher Ernst Cassirer (cited by Childs, 1960: 73, 84, 86). Cassirer's idea of mythopoeic thought was mediated to Old Testament studies primarily through the work of the Frankforts in *The Intellectual Adventure of Ancient Man* (cited by Childs, 1960: 17, 27, 28). The genealogy of the idea of mythopoeic thought has been traced by J. W. Rogerson in *Myth in Old Testament Interpretation* (Berlin: de Gruyter, 1974), ch. 7; and *Anthropology and the Old Testament* (Oxford: Blackwell, 1978), pp. 59–63.

6 The idea was first articulated by Childs (1958), but see further (1964: 438, 443–44), (1970a: 103, 112), (1974a: 295, 301–2), (1977b: 92–3), (1984a: 545).

7 See e.g. Childs (1962: 85–9), (1967a: 122), (1970a: 102, 240 n. 6), 1978a: 53), (1984a: 545). Among the authorities invoked, with certain critical qualifications, have been B. Croce, R. G. Collingwood, J. R. Lucas, P. Holmer, H. Frei and G. Lindbeck. Cf. above n. 4 to chapter 1 for Karl Barth's similar critique of 'theological historicism'.

8 See, e.g., Childs's remarks on the Book of Kings (1979: 299) where he even expresses reservations about Frei's notion of history-like narrative as applied to this particular text. Childs does, however, distinguish between *our* historical reconstruction and ancient Near Eastern historiography, stressing that exegesis turns on this ancient form of recounting experience and not on modern reconstructions.

9 A good example of this view is provided by Childs's remarks on the Jewish and Christian use of Leviticus. Both traditions have justified non-literal interpretation of the laws by drawing on their larger canons: 'in both cases the grounds for theological reinterpretation have not rested on the canonical shape of the book of Leviticus itself' (1979: 188).

10 This also applies to the 'servant songs': Childs argues that although some of the description of the servant seems to point to an historical individual 'efforts to recover the identity of a historical personage are doomed to failure. Only the biblical tradition knows of the servant, and it is silent on the issue beyond making a straightforward identification with Israel' (1979: 335).

11 Childs does not directly say that vestiges of prehistory may well become opaque, but one comment on the servant songs leads in this direction: 'in regard to this portion of the message of Second Isaiah the canonical process preserved the material in a form, the significance of which was not fully understood. The diversity within the witness could not be resolved' (1979: 336).

12 Italics added. Childs goes on to argue that older 'enemy from the north' traditions have been reused in a different way in Hab. and later apocalyptic texts. He does not, however, suggest that referential vagueness has made these later applications easier. For this latter idea, see e.g. Childs (1979: 79, 324, 510).

13 W. K. Wimsatt and M. C. Beardsley, 'The Intentional Fallacy' in: *20th Century Literary Criticism*, ed. D. Lodge (London: Longman, 1972), p. 339. This essay was first published in the *Sewanee Review* 54 (1946), pp. 468–88. Compare Childs's treatment of the 'new king over Egypt who did not know Joseph' (Exod. 1: 8). He says that it is

a mistake to sharpen this vague reference by learned discussions of Egyptian pharaohs; exegesis is not assisted by a sharper historical focus on the referent (1974a: 15, 19).

14 The problematic term 'synchronic' will be discussed below in chapter 3. For the present, I shall regard it as equivalent to 'final form' interpretation.

15 Cf. J. Barton, *Reading the Old Testament* (London: Darton, Longman & Todd, 1984), p. 105: 'The structuralist movement in literary criticism itself arose . . . in particular from the realization that there are certain kinds of text (particularly traditional, orally transmitted texts such as myths, legends and folk-tales) into which conventional criticism, with its concern for authorship . . . affords very little insight'.

16 Cf. *Pirke de Rabbi Eliezer*, ed. G. Friedlander (New York: Benjamin Bloom, 1971), p. 210, and the Targum Pseudo-Jonathan on Exod. 12: 13, cited on the same page of Friedlander.

17 It would simplify my reading if, as some have suggested, we could emend v.20 to read 'his son', but there is no textual support for this from the versions. Nevertheless, the final form has a certain logic: Gershom, introduced in 2: 22, is most relevant to this part of the story. Eliezer is not introduced until a more appropriate stage in the narrative – after the divine 'helper' had saved both Moses and the people. The explanation of Eliezer's name ('the God of my father was my helper') at this later stage (18: 4) makes more sense. Since there is no mention of divine help for Moses when he first fled to Midian, the introduction of Eliezer before the exodus events would have been out of place.

18 This kind of lexical argument would hardly be persuasive in itself, but considered together with the other arguments the connection becomes more plausible. We may also note that the verbs customarily associated with blood rituals (*zrq hzh ntn*) are not used in 12: 22. The Hiph'il usage of *ng'* in contexts like 4: 25 and 12: 22 is comparatively rare in the Hebrew Bible. Note, e.g., that the parallel command in 12:7 to apply blood to the lintels and doorposts, usually taken as priestly, uses vocabulary closer to that associated with blood rituals – *ntn* followed by the preposition *'l* (see Exod. 29: 12, 20; Lev. 8: 23, 24, 14: 14, 25).

19 T. C. Mitchell, 'The Meaning of the Noun ḤTN in the Old Testament' *VT* 19 (1969), 93–112; cf. M. Greenberg, *Understanding Exodus* (New York: Behrman, 1969), p. 114.

20 It might be objected that this suggestion is circular: one of the arguments that 4: 24–26 concerns the firstborn is the literary context of vs. 22–3, but if vs. 22–3 are themselves traditio-

historically late, then the final form reading is less plausible from a historical perspective. But the possibility remains that a story about Zipporah and Gershom was so well known that the redactor joined vs. 22–3 to vs. 24–6 because of a natural affinity in the subject matter. See further W. Beltz, 'Religionsgeschichtliche Marginale zu Ex 4, 24–26' *ZAW* 87 (1975), 209–10; H. Kosmala, 'The "Bloody Husband"' *VT* 12 (1962), 22; J. Morgenstern, 'The "Bloody Husband" (?)' *HUCA* 34 (1963), 45 and 66.

21 S. McEvenue 'The Old Testament: Scripture or Theology?' *Ex Auditu* 1 (1985), 116–17; this article first appeared in *Interpretation* 35 (1981), 229–42.

22 McEvenue, 'Scripture or Theology', p. 118 (Italics added).

23 Here I am drawing on Richard Rorty's illuminating distinction between 'rational reconstruction' and 'historical reconstruction': rational historiography, which is inevitably highly selective, treats great dead thinkers as if they were contemporaries who can contribute to our own intellectual problems; historical reconstruction treats great dead thinkers as providing answers to the questions in their own contexts, not ours. For example, 'the historian of science, who can imagine what Aristotle might have said in a dialogue in heaven with Aristarchus and Ptolemy, knows something interesting which remains unknown to the Whiggish astrophysicist who sees only how Aristotle would have been crushed by Galileo's arguments'. Rorty 'The Historiography of Philosophy: four Genres' in: *Philosophy in History*, ed. Rorty *et al.* (Cambridge: Cambridge University Press, 1984), p. 50.

24 McEvenue, 'Scripture or Theology?', p. 117.

25 See J. Wellhausen, *Die Composition des Hexateuchs* (Berlin: de Gruyter, 1963), p. 186. This is an example of the history of exegesis being used to serve 'rationalist' rather than 'historical' interests.

26 This point was put succinctly by Hugo Gressmann: 'Jeder Forscher weiss, dass die wissenschaftliche Arbeit Sisyphusarbeit ist, dass sie aber dennoch nicht vergebens geleistet wird, falls sie das rechte Wort zu ihre Zeit findet'. Undated note quoted in W. Klatt, *Herman Gunkel* (Göttingen: Vandenhoeck & Ruprecht, 1969), p. 74.

3 'INTRODUCTION' AND OLD TESTAMENT THEOLOGY

1 Barr, *Holy Scripture*, p. 152.

2 Barr, *Holy Scripture*, p. 154.

3 Thus, he says that the relation between the Testaments is a problem for 'biblical theology' rather than 'introduction'. A canonical introduction to the Hebrew Bible can be descriptive

because it 'does not assume a particular stance or faith commit-
ment on the part of the reader' (1979: 72). This means, presum-
ably, that while both Jews and Christians could participate in the
task of 'canonical introduction' a Jewish theology of the Hebrew
Bible would be 'confessional' in the same sense as Christian biblical
theology. Childs does, however, see a different relationship
between scripture and tradition in Judaism (1985: 7–8). See
further (1987a).

4 Although the earlier Childs was reluctant to neglect this larger
canonical context, his method has always contained a descriptive
focus on the Hebrew texts for their own sake. The sheer scale of the
Introduction would have restricted the range of questions it could
address; hence, it is only the 'beginning' of exegesis (1979: 83).
When Walther Zimmerli asks why the wider canonical contexts (of
synagogue and church) are only treated by Childs in the case of
Leviticus, he is asking a question about biblical theology rather
than descriptive 'introduction'. See Zimmerli's review of Childs's
Introduction in *VT* 31 (1981), 242–3.

5 Zimmerli, Review, p. 238. Note, for example, the number of times
the canonical approach is held to resolve an historical-critical
'impasse' (1979: 58, 61, 67, 68, 78, 334, 375, 426).

6 See Zimmerli, Review, p. 241. This hermeneutical belief may be
summarized as follows: the more historical particularity reconstructed behind the text, the more difficult theological appropriation becomes. In chapter 4 I shall discuss the extent to which
this belief is a legacy of the 'ugly ditch' that was introduced into
modern Old Testament studies by the pioneering work of Spinoza
and Gabler.

7 On this issue Childs stands close to the approach of Ivan Engnell.
Several scholars have pointed out that Engnell's 'tradition history'
does not demand a reconstructed *history* at all. See R. N. Whybray,
The Making of the Pentateuch (Sheffield: JSOT, 1987), p. 301; E.
Nielsen 'The Traditio-historical Study of the Pentateuch since
1945' in: *The Productions of Time*, ed. K. Jeppesen and B. Otzen
(Sheffield: Almond, 1984), p. 17.

8 For such a theory, see H. G. Gadamer, *Wahrheit und Methode*, 4th
edn (Tübingen: Mohr/Siebeck, 1975), pp. 269–75 = *Truth and
Method*, trans. of 2nd German edn, 1965 (New York: Crossroad,
1982), pp. 253–8; 'Semantik und Hermeneutik' *Kleine Schriften*, vol.
3 (Tübingen: Mohr/Siebeck, 1972), p. 256; 'Aesthetic and Religious Experience' in: *The Relevance of the Beautiful and Other Essays*
(Cambridge: Cambridge University Press, 1986), pp. 142 and 146
= 'Aesthetische und religiöse Erfahrung' *Nederlands Theologisch
Tijdschrift* 32 (1978), 219 and 223.

9 His text actually reads 'inert shreds', but I have exercised text-critical licence. Cf. Childs (1984a: 523) where he uses the same phrase, and (1987c: 245) for the same idea expressed this time in German.

10 Frank Kermode has recently argued in a similar way that although the medium in which a literary work survives is commentary, 'there is no simple and perpetual consensus as to the proper way to join the shadow of comment to the substance of the [work]. And this is what it means to call a book canonical'. Moreover, 'Permanent modernity is conferred on chosen works by arguments and persuasions that cannot, themselves, remain modern . . . Opinion, then, may act as a preservative'. *Forms of Attention* (London: University of Chicago Press, 1985), pp. 36, 62, 67, 72.

11 Childs emphasizes this point in his response to Barr (1984b: 68). An example is provided by his hypothesis of a 'canonical tradition' concerning David which 'extends in time both before and after the age of the author of Kings' (1979, 293, cf. 301).

12 Zimmerli (Review, p. 239) seems, however, to have misconstrued Childs when he infers from the *Introduction* that the Elihu speeches are a 'nachträglicher Kommentar' on the divine speeches 'und als solcher nicht Schlüssel des Verständnisses des Buches'. Childs (*qua* historical critic) does say that this section is probably a 'secondary literary development' but then goes on to say that this hypothesis is 'not particularly helpful in assessing its canonical role' (1979: 540). Thus, when he claims that the speeches 'have no independent role within the book' (e.g. reflecting the view of the final author) it is not their supposed place in the literary development of the book that lies behind this judgment. The speeches function (synchronically) 'to shape the reader's hearing of the divine speeches' (1979: 541). To call this function on the same page 'supplement and commentary' is to use a misleading diachronic metaphor. The same kind of problem arises when Childs calls II Sam. 21–4 an 'appendix' and 'theological commentary' when his real concern is to describe its 'function within the final form of the narrative' (1979: 273–5, 278–9; cf. 1985: 118–19).

13 This aspect of the canonical exegesis may be paraphrased in the following way: historical differences telescoped into the final form do not need to be reconstructed, since this has usually been done for theological reasons. Examples of this are numerous (see e.g. 1979: 75, 78, 131, 149, 151, 158, 177, 185–7, 199–200, 212, 218–19, 233–5, 250, 260–2, 278, 300, 323–7, 453–4, 460, 630). There are characteristically two assumptions behind these exegetical arguments. First, emic reconstruction is unnecessary since the canonical

process is basically a story of progressive theological refinement. Second, etic reconstruction is theologically never important. See further chapter 6 below.

14 Childs often speaks of 'the intention of the text' (see 1979: 300, 393, 486, 645), a notion which is opposed to the 'axiom' of historical criticism, namely, that a text can only be understood in the context of its original historical background and intentions (1979: 317, 337, 415, cf. 460). On the intelligibility of textual 'intentions', see D. C. Hoy, *The Critical Circle* (Berkeley: University of California Press, 1978, pp. 35–40, and below, chapter 5.

15 Childs often deals with historical particularity by speaking of a personal experience or historical figure as 'representative'. For example, some of the psalms are canonically shaped in relation to the particular history of 'David as a representative man' (1979: 522); the 'suffering of one representative man' in Lam. 3 'transcends any one fixed moment in history. The effect is that historical suffering is now understood metaphorically as in the Psalter, but its actuality is in no way diminished' (1979: 594–6, cf. 481; 1985: 102–13).

16 Zimmerli, Review, p. 239.

17 A good example of my point is Amos 1: 1. According to Childs, the temporal significance of the phrase 'two years before the earthquake' could well have been forgotten within one or two generations – a plausible inference. But then he tries to recover this vestige by connecting it metaphorically with Amos 1: 2, Yahweh's roaring from Jerusalem (1979: 401). Surely we should simply accept the fact that this definite reference ('the earthquake') assumes a kind of mutual knowledge on the part of the original audience that has been lost forever. It is an opaque residue from the past. CF. H. H. Clark and C. R. Marshall 'Definite Reference and Mutual Knowledge' in: *Linguistic Structure and Discourse Setting*, ed. I. Joshi *et al.* (Cambridge: Cambridge University Press, 1981).

18 Barr, 'Trends and Prospects in Biblical Theology' *JTS* 25 (1974), 273. Barr also observes that the final form emphasis seems to be in accord with redaction criticism, as well as with certain (unspecified) movements in literary theory and text-linguistics.

19 For example, we have archaeological evidence that Yahweh was at times worshipped along with a consort. See, among others, J. Emerton, 'New Light on Israelite Religion: The Implications of the Inscriptions from Kuntillet 'Ajrud' *ZAW* 94 (1982), 2–20; D. N. Freedman 'Yahweh of Samaria and His Asherah' *BA* 50 (1987), 241–9; P. D. Miller *et al.* (eds.) *Ancient Israelite Religion* (Philadelphia: Fortress, 1987); S. M. Olyan, *Asherah and the Cult of Yahweh in Israel* (Atlanta: Scholars Press, 1988).

20 Barr, 'Trends and Prospects', p. 277; Morgan 'Gabler's Bicentenary' *Expos. T* 98 (1987), 167.

21 See J. Z. Smith, 'Sacred Persistence: Toward a Redescription of Canon' *Imagining Religion: From Babylon to Jonestown* (Chicago: University of Chicago, 1982), pp. 36–52; W. Cantwell Smith, 'The Study of Religion and the Study of the Bible', *JAAR* 39 (1971), 131–40.

22 If A. C. Sundberg is in fact correct in his view that the LXX is a 'Christianized' text, this could be for Childs all the more reason not to use it for Old Testament theology; a Christianized text would pre-empt the independence of this pre-Christian witness. If the LXX reflects Christian selection and arrangement than it might be regarded as a kind of primitive 'Old Testament theology'. Childs, however, is in fact critical of Sundberg's proposals (1979: 665, 668) and reminds us that the LXX is a Jewish translation (1985: 7). See especially Sundberg, *The Old Testament of the Early Church* (Cambridge MA: Harvard University Press, 1964).

23 Barr, 'Trends and Prospects', p. 270.

24 Most disappointing in this respect has been Childs's failure to grapple seriously with the kind of 'intratextual' theology formulated by his colleagues at Yale, Hans Frei and, in particular, George Lindbeck. Childs agrees that the canonical approach is in many respects similar to Lindbeck's 'cultural-linguistic' model (Childs, 1984a: 541–6, yet his criticisms of Lindbeck's influential book *The Nature of Doctrine* can only be described as the criticisms of a surprisingly impatient reader. *Contra* Childs, Lindbeck's model does not exclude the use of propositions in theology, nor does it exclude the category of 'experience', nor does it deny the existence of 'external reality'. See e.g. *The Nature of Doctrine* (London: SPCK, 1984), pp. 19, 33, 64. Lindbeck's main point is that cultural-linguistic systems *shape* human experience, the use of propositions and the perception of external reality. It is not that experience, propositions and reality can be summarily disposed of. See below, chapter 6.

4 HAS CHILDS FALLEN INTO GABLER'S DITCH?

1 Anderson, 'Tradition and Scripture in the Community of Faith' *JBL* 100 (1981), 21.

2 This point is repeatedly stressed by John Barton, *Oracles of God* (London: Darton, Longman & Todd, 1986). However, Barton's argument is at several points directed against Childs, e.g. p. 150: 'in ancient times everyone assumed that the whole book of Isaiah was by that prophet, but no one read the book as a unity'.

3 McEvenue, 'The Old Testament: Scripture or Theology?' *Ex Auditu* 1 (1985), 188.

4 See Childs (1980a: 205). He speaks of the 'axiom' of original historical background in the *Introduction* (1979: 317, 337, 415; cf. also 408 and 460). One should note, however, that the issue of historical particularity is not simply identifiable with the *original* background or reference. McEvenue, for example, stresses that the successive meanings of the ark narrative, as it was redacted into larger texts, are also delimited by the successive historical contexts of editing. 'Scripture or Theology', p. 122.

5 Muilenburg, 'Form Criticism and Beyond' *JBL* 88 (1969), 5–6.

6 Wright, 'History and the Patriarchs' *Expos. T.* 71 (1960), 292–6. The logic of this last point, however, amounts to a concession that Wright's archaeological evidence cannot sustain any claims to historicity beyond those that would also apply to an historical novel. Von Rad was entirely justified in responding the way he did: 'That which is held by Wright to be authentic contains only very general and very approximate realities . . . things which were characteristic of a very large group of people'. Von Rad, 'History and the Patriarchs' *Expos. T.* 72 (1961), 214.

7 Wright, 'History and the Patriarchs', p. 293.

8 Von Rad, 'History and the Patriarchs', p. 215. This example supports Manfred Oeming's more general claim that von Rad saw the development of biblical tradition as a theological 'filtering' process. Oeming sees common ground between von Rad, Gadamer and Childs on this point. *Gesamtbiblische Theologien der Gegenwart* (Stuttgart: Kohlhammer, 1985), pp. 42, 202–3 n. 49. I have discussed this aspect of Childs's work above in terms of 'the progressive refinement of biblical tradition'. See further chapter 5 below.

9 B. C. Ollenburger, 'Biblical Theology: Situating the Discipline' in: *Understanding the Word*, ed. J. T. Butler *et al.* (Sheffield: JSOT, 1985), pp. 37–62.

10 We should note that this problem of authority was considerably intensified by the growing stress on 'literal sense' stemming from the late medieval and reformation periods. When, for example, Luther collapsed the meaning of scripture into a single sense the authority of difficult texts could no longer be easily salvaged by reference to allegorical, tropological or anagogical meanings. See K. Froehlich, 'Problems of Lutheran Hermeneutics' in: *Studies in Lutheran Hermeneutics*, ed. J. Reumann (Philadelphia: Fortress, 1974), pp. 127–41.

11 Citations of Gabler's address are from the translation by J. Sandys-Wunsch, and L. Eldredge, 'J. P. Gabler and the Distinc-

tions between Biblical and Dogmatic Theology: Translation, Commentary and Discussion of his Originality' *SJT* 33 (1980), 133–58, esp. 138, 143–4.

12 Ollenburger, 'Biblical Theology', p. 49.

13 This phrase is borrowed from Childs, *Memory and Tradition in Israel* (London: SCM, 1962), p. 83.

14 Sandys-Wunsch and Eldredge, 'J. P. Gabler', p. 144. For a detailed historical account of the theological (and political) debates that preceded Gabler, see H. G. Reventlow, *The Authority of the Bible and the Rise of the Modern World* (London: SCM, 1984).

15 See P. C. Hayner, 'The Enlightenment Concept of History and its Eighteenth Century Critics' in: *Reason and Existence: Schelling's Philosophy of History* (Leiden: E. J. Brill, 1967), pp. 1–33.

16 So H. - J. Kraus, *Geschichte der historisch-kritischen Erforschung des Alten Testaments*, 3rd edn (Neukirchen-Vluyn: Neukirchener, 1983), pp. 61–5.

17 B. Spinoza, *Tractatus theologico-politicus* in: *The Chief Works of Benedict de Spinoza*, trans. R. H. M. Elwes (1670; London: George Bell, 1909), p. 8. Subsequent references in the text are to this edition. For an illuminating account of the philosophical reactions to the religious wars, see J. Stout, *The Flight from Authority* (Notre Dame: Notre Dame University Press, 1981).

18 Spinoza, *Tractatus*, p. 191. The idea that meaning should be elicited from scripture itself may bring to mind Luther's principle 'Sacra scriptura sui ipsius interpres'. But Spinoza's idea of 'sola scriptura' diverges from Luther's in so far as it is a purely formal principle of exegesis with no relevance for the truth of scripture. Cf. E. Jüngels 'Anthropomorphismus als Grundproblem neuzeitlicher Hermenuetik' in: *Verifikationen*, ed. Jüngel *et al.* (Tübingen: Mohr/Siebeck, 1982), pp. 499–522.

19 Spinoza, *Tractatus*, p. 104; Jüngel, 'Anthropomorphismus', pp. 505–6.

20 See, e.g., Lessing, 'On the Proof of the Spirit and of Power' (1777) in: *Lessing's Theological Writings*, ed. H. Chadwick, (Stanford: Stanford UP, 1956); Kierkegaard, *Concluding Unscientific Postscript* (1846; Princeton: Princeton University Press, 1979); G. E. Michalson, 'Lessing, Kierkegaard and the Ugly Ditch' *JR* 59 (1976), 324–34; and 'Theology, Historical Knowledge, and the Contingency-Necessity Distinction' *Internat. J. Philos. Relig.* 14 (1983), 87–98.

21 Cf. R. Smend 'Universalismus und Partikularismus in der alttestamentlichen Theologie des 19. Jahrhunderts' *Ev. Th.* 22 (1962), 171: 'Bei Gabler kam zuerst die historische Darstellung, dann die philosophisch-dogmatisch-kritische Operation'.

22 Sandys-Wunsch and Eldredge, 'J. P. Gabler', pp. 137 and 144.

23 Reventlow, *The Authority of the Bible* has shown how most of the pioneering biblical critics of the seventeenth and early eighteenth centuries assumed the compatibility of historical criticism and philosophical reasoning. Spinoza seems to have had the model of Baconian science in mind (Tractatus, p. 104). Gabler, on the other hand, alluded to a doctrine of providence. He speaks of separating particularities from 'those pure notions which divine providence wished to be characteristic of all times and places'. Sandys-Wunsch and Eldridge, 'J. P. Gabler', p. 138.

24 Hayner, *Reason and Existence*, p. 11.

25 See J. W. Rogerson, *Old Testament Criticism in the 19th Century* (London: SPCK, 1984), pp. 28–49, as well as his forthcoming biography of de Wette; R. Otto, *The Philosophy of Religion based on Kant and Fries* (London: Williams & Norgate, 1931).

26 See L. Perlitt, *Vatke und Wellhausen* (Berlin: de Gruyter, 1965).

27 G. F. W. Hegel, *Lectures on the Philosophy of History* (1837), ed. H. R. Nisbet (Cambridge: Cambridge University Press, 1975), p. 148; cf. also pp. 60–1 on degenerative particularism.

28 G. Iggers, *The German Conception of History* (Middletown: Wesleyan University Press, 1968); R. A. Oden, 'Hermeneutics and Historiography' *SBL 1980 Seminar Papers*, ed. P. J. Achtemeier (Chico, Cal.: Scholars Press, 1980), pp. 135–57.

29 E. Troeltsch, *Der Historismus und seine Probleme: Gesammelte Schriften Vol.* II (Tübingen: Mohr/Siebeck, 1922), p. 737.

30 Troeltsch, 'Ueber historische und dogmatische Methode in der Theologie' in: *Gesammelte Schriften Vol.* II, p. 733. Cf. also *Der Historismus*, pp. 132–3; and 'The Dogmatics of the "Religionsgeschichtliche Schule" ' *Am. J. Theol.* 17 (1913), 1–21.

31 Troeltsch, 'Ueber historische und dogmatische Methode', p. 730.

32 Troeltsch, 'Ueber historische und dogmatische Methode', pp. 733, 739.

33 See Iggers, *The German Conception*. On Ranke's notion of intuition/Ahnung, see F. Meinecke, 'Deutung eines Ranke-wortes' *Werke* IV (Stuttgart: Koehler, 1959), pp. 117–39; and Meinecke's 'Memorial Address' on Ranke printed as an appendix to *Historism* [sic] (London: Routledge & Kegan Paul, 1972).

34 Cf. Iggers, *The German Conception*, p. 10.

35 This distinction was taken up not only by Wilhelm Dilthey but also by a long tradition of German philosophy. See Michael Ermath's comprehensive study, *Wilhelm Dilthey: The Critique of Historical Reason* (Chicago: Chicago University Press, 1978); K. -O. Apel, 'The *Erklären-Verstehen* Controversy in the Philosophy of the Natural and Human Sciences' in: *Contemporary Philosophy* II, ed. G. Floistad (The Hague: Martinus Nijhoff, 1982), pp. 19–49.

36 The review, ironically entitled 'Erhebung der Geschichte zum Rang einer Wissenschaft' is printed as an appendix to Droysen's *Historik* 5th edn (Munich: Oldenbourg, 1967), pp. 386–405. Cf. also Droysen's complaint on pp. 17–18: 'Aber kaum, daß sich unsere Wissenschaft von der philosophischen und theologischen Beherrschung freigemacht hat – das große Verdienst des 18. Jahrhunderts – so sind die Naturwissenschaften da, sich ihrer anzunehmen und sie bevormunden zu wollen'. 'Positivism' is notoriously difficult to define, but in this context its two characteristic tenets would be (1) the unity of the scientific method across both the natural and human sciences, and (2) the view that phenomena are properly explained only when they can be subsumed under general laws. Cf. G. H. von Wright, *Explanation and Understanding* (London: Routledge & Kegan Paul, 1971), p. 4. In recent philosophy of the natural sciences there is a more technical distinction between positivism and 'realism', but this is irrelevant to the nineteenth-century discussion.

37 Droysen, *Historik*, pp. 9–16.

38 Meinecke, 'Schleiermacherschen Individualitätsgedankens' *Werke*, IV (Stuttgart: K. F. Koehler, 1959), pp. 342–3. This thesis was developed at length in his major work *Die Entstehung des Historismus* (1936) = *Historism* (1972); Cf. also Schulin, E. 'Das Problem der Individualität' *Hist. Zeit.* 197 (1963), 102–33.

39 Spinoza, *Tractatus*, pp. 85–87.

40 Troeltsch, 'Ueber historische und dogmatische Methode', pp. 732–3.

41 Troeltsch, *Der Historismus*, pp. 142, 185, 381–3. Cf. Meinecke, 'Ernst Troeltsch und das Problem der Historismus' in: *Werke*, IV pp. 371–5.

42 See, e.g., the translated excerpt from Herder's 'Ideas Toward a Philosophy of History of Humanity' in: *Theories of History*, ed. P. Gardiner (London: Allen & Unwin, 1959). I am not suggesting, however, that Herder should be understood simply in the light of Ranke's achievements, a tendency of Meinecke's retrospective narrative in *Historism*. For a corrective, see H. G. Gadamer 'Herder und die geschichtliche Welt' *Kleine Schriften*, Vol. III (Tübingen: Mohr/Siebeck, 1972), pp. 101–17.

43 See F. Meinecke, 'Deutung eines Rankewortes' *Werke*, IV, pp. 117–39; C. Hinrichs, *Ranke und die Geschichtstheologie der Goethe-Zeit* (Göttingen: Musterschmidt, 1954); Iggers, *The German Conception*.

44 Gunkel, 'The "Historical Movement" in the Study of Religion' *Expos. T.* 38 (1927), 536; W. Klatt, *Hermann Gunkel* (Göttingen: Vandenhoeck & Ruprecht, 1969), p. 74.

45 Ranke, *The Theory and Practice of History*, ed. G. Iggers and K. Moltke (New York: Irvington, 1983), p. 53.
46 Troeltsch, *Der Historismus*, p. 132.
47 See Droysen, *Historik*, pp. 21, 26–7.
48 Troeltsch, *Christian Thought* (London: University of London Press, 1923), pp. 118, 44–6 = *Der Historismus und seine Ueberwindung* (Berlin: Rolf Heiser, 1924), pp. 53, 107–9.
49 Ranke, *Theory and Practice*, pp. 44, 100, 107–13, 119.
50 Meinecke, 'Deutung eines Rankewortes', p. 118.
51 Ranke, *Theory and Practice*, p. 99. Ranke's idealist theory of the state shares a good deal in common with that of Hegel discussed above. See Iggers and Moltke 'Introduction' to Ranke, *Theory and Practice*, pp. xv–lxxi.
52 Gunkel, 'The Historical Movement', pp. 533–4.
53 E.g., Gunkel, *Schöpfung und Chaos* (Göttingen: Vandenhoeck & Ruprecht, 1895), pp. vi–vii; and 'The Historical Movement', pp. 533. Cf. Klatt *Hermann Gunkel*, pp. 76, 97, 102, 209 & 205.
54 H. Gressmann, 'Die Aufgaben der alttestamentlichen Forschung' *ZAW* 42 (1924), 10.
55 Klatt, *Hermann Gunkel*, pp. 170–3, 177, 205, 240.
56 Troeltsch, 'Ueber historische und dogmatische Methode', p. 739, cf. p. 736.
57 This is one of the few points upon which Childs and Gottwald could agree. See, Gottwald's criticism of Weber: 'there remains in Weber's outlook the idealist "escape hatch" of the great personalities as the mysterious sources of religions which are later adapted into a social routine'. *The Tribes of Yahweh* (Maryknoll: Orbis, 1979), p. 630.
58 For Gunkel, the post-exilic period was marked by degeneration both in religion and literary history. See, e.g., *Reden und Aufsätze* (Göttingen: Vandenhoeck & Ruprecht, 1913), p. 36; *Die Israelitische Literatur* (1906; Darmstadt: Wissenschaftliche Buchgessellschaft, 1963), p. 45.
59 See M. J. Buss, 'The Idea of Sitz im Leben' *ZAW* 90 (1978), 159.
60 Klatt, *Hermann Gunkel*, pp. 106–16, esp. p. 110. Cf. L. L. Snyder 'Nationalistic Aspects of the Grimm Brothers' Fairy Tales' *Journal of Social Psychology* 33 (1951), 209–23.
61 Gunkel, *The Legends of Genesis* (1901; New York: Schocken, 1966), pp. 1–12; Klatt, *Hermann Gunkel*, pp. 125–6.
62 Already in 1833, Herder's English translator had stressed this point over against the tendency in Robert Lowth's influential work, *De sacra poesi Hebraeorum* (1753), to compare Hebrew poetry with Greek and Roman types. J. G. Herder *The Spirit of Hebrew*

Poetry, trans. J. Marsh (Burlington: Edward Smith, 1833), pp. 3–4.

63 F. Meinecke, 'Johann Gustav Droysen' *Hist. Zeit.* 141 (1929), 259. For Droysen's critique of narrative representation, see *Historik*, ed. R. Hübner, 5th edn (Munich: Oldenbourg, 1965), pp. 144, 149–52, 283, 297–8. Note also Gunkel's view that in the Hellenistic period 'etwas Neues beginnt' (*Die Israelitische Literatur*, p. 48). This might explain why Gunkel had a positive attitude to the apocrypha and pseudepigrapha at the same time as seeing post-exilic Israelite literature as a degeneration. See Klatt *Hermann Gunkel*, pp. 190–1, for a discussion of this issue.

64 The rise and fall of historicism are chronicled by George Iggers in *The German Conception of History*; for a brief account, see his Introduction to *The Social History of Politics* (Leamington Spa: Berg, 1985). For recent re-evaluations of the historicist tradition see H. W. Blanke and J. Rüsen, (eds.), *Von der Aufklärung zum Historismus: Zum Strukturwandel des historischen Denkens* (Paderborn: Schöningh, 1984).

65 F. S. Frick, *The City in Ancient Israel* (Missoula: Scholars Press, 1977), p. 19, here citing G. Sjoberg, *The Preindustrial City* (Glencoe: Free Press, 1960), p. 333.

66 H. White, 'Michel Foucault' in: *Structuralism and Since*, ed. J. Sturrock (Oxford: Oxford University Press, 1979), p. 113. For a strikingly similar comment on the influence of Foucault (among others) on literary critics like S. Greenblatt, see E. Pechter 'The New Historicism and Its Discontents' *PMLA* 102 (1987), 297. (I am grateful to Con Coroneos for this latter reference).

67 The recent wave of social scientific work in biblical studies is only one part of a broad movement in historical studies of this century. See e.g. the survey works of G. G. Iggers, *New Directions in European Historiography* (Middletown: Wesleyan University Press, 1975), and H. -U. Wehler, *Geschichte als Historische Sozialwissenschaft* (Frankfurt: Suhrkamp, 1973). Klatt (*Hermann Gunkel*, p. 107) notes that German folklore studies have also shifted from their early dependence on philology and broadened out into a spectrum of geographical, psychological and sociological approaches.

68 See, e.g., D. A. Knight 'Canon and the History of Tradition' *HBT* 2 (1980), 145; 'Revelation through Tradition' in: *Tradition and Theology in the Old Testament*, ed. Knight (London: SPCK, 1977), p. 177.

69 Anderson, 'Biblical Theology and Sociological Interpretation' *TT* 42 (1985–86), 299–301.

70 This description of Foucault's project comes from David Tracy, *Plurality and Ambiguity* (San Francisco: Harper & Row, 1987), p. 79. See, e.g., M. Foucault, *The History of Sexuality*, Vol. 1 (New York: Random, 1978), p. 100: 'We must not imagine a world of discourse divided between . . . the dominant discourse and the dominated one; but as a multiplicity of discursive elements that can come into play in various strategies'. For an introduction to Foucault's influential works, see H. White 'Michel Foucault'.

71 Anderson, 'Biblical Theology', pp. 303 and 306.

72 See, e.g., Norman Gottwald's attempt to delineate some of the sociological aspects of the canonical process of the Hebrew Bible. Gottwald, *The Hebrew Bible*: *A Socio-Literary Introduction* (Philadelphia: Fortress, 1985), pp. 102–14, 458–64.

73 Knight, 'Canon and the History of Tradition', p. 145.

74 J. A. Sanders, 'Canonical Context and Canonical Criticism' *HBT* 2 (1980), 190 and n.41. See above chapter 1, 'Canonical Criticism versus the Canonical Approach'.

75 Knight, 'Revelation through Tradition', pp. 149, 174–8; Anderson, 'Tradition and Scripture', p. 19.

76 Smend, 'Questions about the Importance of the Canon in Old Testament Introduction' *JSOT* 16 (1980), 48.

77 See M. Oakeshott, 'The Activity of being an Historian' in: *Rationalism and Politics* (London: Methuen, 1962), pp. 137–67; W. H. Walsh, 'The Practical and the Historical Past' in: *Politics and Experience*, ed. P. King and B. C. Parekh (Cambridge: Cambridge University Press, 1968), pp. 5–18.

78 Iggers and Moltke, 'Introduction' to Ranke, *Theory and Practice*, p. xxx; see further I. Berlin, 'Note on Alleged Relativism in Eighteenth-century European Thought' in: *Substance and Form in History*, ed. L. Pompa and W. H. Dray (Edinburgh: Edinburgh University Press, 1981), pp. 1–14, who suggests that Herder and Ranke were pluralists but not relativists.

79 Ranke, *Theory and Practice*, p. 101.

80 K. Kosík has also pointed out the irony in the fact that both historical relativism and anti-relativist theories of 'natural rights' converge at this point: both liquidate the significance of history. See his section on 'Historismus und Historizismus' in *Die Dialektik des Konkreten* (Frankfurt: Suhrkamp, 1967), pp. 132–48, esp. p. 141.

81 Klatt, *Hermann Gunkel*, p. 80.

82 Troeltsch, *Der Historismus*; Cf. T. Rendtorff and F. W. Graf, 'Ernst Troeltsch' in: *Nineteenth-century Religious Thought in the West*, vol. III, ed. N. Smart *et al.* (Cambridge: Cambridge University Press, 1985), pp. 305–28.

83 This phrase comes from R. Lapointe, 'Tradition and Language: The Importance of Oral Expression' in: *Tradition and Theology*, ed. Knight, p. 139.

84 See G. Wise, *American Historical Explanations* (Homewood, Ala.: Dorsey, 1973).

85 McEvenue ('Scripture or Theology?', p. 118) introduces this unhelpful bi-polarity.

86 See M. G. Brett, 'Motives and Intentions in Genesis 1'; N. V. Smith (ed.), *Mutual Knowledge* (London: Academic, 1982). S. C. Levinson, *Pragmatics* (Cambridge: Cambridge University Press, 1983). One should note that implicatures which are dependent upon a non-linguistic context are generally much more important in speech than they are in writing, a point made in the introduction to G. Brown and G. Yule *Discourse Analysis* (Cambridge: Cambridge University Press 1983).

87 See especially James Barr, *Comparative Philology and the Text of the Old Testament* (Oxford: Clarendon, 1968), pp. 118, 291–93. Barr refers here to W. V. O. Quine, *From a Logical Point of View* (New York: Harper and Row, 1953), pp. 9, 21f., 47. Cf. also W. G. Runciman, *A Treatise on Social Theory*, Vol. 1 (Cambridge: Cambridge University Press, 1983), p. 130.

88 I count this notorious maxim from Derrida among those 'pithy little formulae' which are 'typically right about what they implicitly deny but wrong about what they explicitly assert'. Stout, 'A. Lexicon of Postmodern Philosophy' *Relig. Stud. Rev.* 13 (1987), 19.

89 Lyons, *Semantics*, vol. 2 (Cambridge: Cambridge University Press, 1977), p. 571.

90 The most rigorous exponent of this view is once again W. V. O. Quine. For a discussion of Quine's 'indeterminacy of translation' thesis, see especially Robert Feleppa, 'Emics, Etics, and Social Objectivity' *Curr. Anthrop.* 27 (1986), 243–55; Quine, *Word and Object* (Cambridge MA: MIT, 1960), chapter 2; and 'On the Reasons for Indeterminacy of Translation' *J. Philos.* 67 (1970), 179–83.

91 Mandelbaum, *History, Man and Reason* (Baltimore: Johns Hopkins, 1971), p. 42. I am not suggesting here that Mandelbaum has captured the single correct definition of historicism. It seems, rather, that he has retrospectively pointed out the common ground between a large number of quite distinct intellectual movements. His definition suits this purpose well, but there are alternative ways of drawing the intellectual map, e.g., when Droysen and Meinecke clearly distinguish between historicism

and positivism (see above n.36). See further D. E. Lee and R. N. Beck 'The Meaning of "Historicism" ' *Am. Hist. Rev.* 59 (1954), 568–77.

92 For a discussion of survivals and cultural evolutionism in Old Testament studies, see J. W. Rogerson, *Anthropology and the Old Testament* (Oxford: Blackwell, 1978), pp. 22–45.

93 This example is taken from M. Harris, *The Rise of Anthropological Theory* (London: Routledge & Kegan Paul, 1969), p. 166. 'Retrospective sentiment' can also, of course, lead to the *invention* of tradition.

94 I should stress that there are different versions of functionalism, and even within the British schools one should distinguish between Malinowski's views and Radcliffe-Brown's 'structural-functionalism'. Cf. Harris, *Anthropological Theory*, pp. 514–67. Both, however, 'arose in opposition to the diachronic schools of the evolutionary and diffusionist traditions' (p. 546). Cf. e.g. Radcliffe-Brown's argument that evolutionary anthropologists 'considered culture and the history of culture from one standpoint only, namely, as a process of development'. *Method in Social Anthropology* (Chicago: Chicago University Press, 1958), p. 11.

95 Given, however, the paucity of evidence for ancient Hebrew linguistic systems, this principle is in practice extremely difficult to observe. Thus even Sawyer concedes that comparative philology is a 'clumsy instrument whose value in our field is mainly restricted to giving very general clues to the meaning of obscure or unknown words and phrases'. 'The "original meaning of the text" and other legitimate subjects for semantic description' *BETL* 33 (1974), 64.

96 E.g., K. Gros Louis describes work by Alter, Fishbane, Perry, Sternberg, Robertson, Ryken and himself as 'essentially ahistorical', a generalisation which at least Meir Sternberg rightly rejects. Louis, 'Some Methodological Considerations' in: *Literary Interpretations of Biblical Narratives*, vol. II, ed. Louis (Nashville: Abingdon, 1982), p. 14. See Sternberg's incisive discussion of anti-historical sentiments in *The Poetics of Biblical Narrative* (Bloomington: Indiana University Press, 1985), pp. 1–57.

97 This has recently been conceded by David Jobling, *The Sense of Biblical Narrative*, vol. II (Sheffield: JSOT, 1986), p. 90. See, e.g., Harold Bloom's essay 'From J to K, the Uncanniness of the Yahwist' in: *The Bible and the Narrative Tradition*, ed. F. McConnell (Oxford: Oxford University Press, 1986).

98 Sawyer, *Semantics in Biblical Research* (London: SCM, 1972), p. 5. Further references to this work are cited by page number in the text.

99 R. Hudson, 'Some Issues on which Linguists can Agree' *J. Ling.* 17 (1981), 2.4c. (This useful article was compiled on the basis of a survey among British linguists.)

100 A similar point is made by Barr, *Holy Scripture*, pp. 98–99. However, Barr's specific criticisms of Sawyer (p. 86) are puzzling: Sawyer explicitly argues that his method is 'arbitrary'; to object that *Semantics in Biblical Research* displays 'arbitrariness' seems to have little point. Precisely this arbitrariness makes it clear that Sawyer has not set up the Masoretic period 'as a standard', as Barr suggests.

101 Sawyer, 'A change of Emphasis in the Study of the Prophets' in: *Israel's Prophetic Tradition*, ed. R. Coggins *et al.* (Cambridge: Cambridge University Press, 1982), p. 246; 'Blessed be my people Egypt (Isaiah 19. 25)' in: *A Word in Season*, ed. J. D. Martin and P. D. Davies (Sheffield: JSOT, 1986), pp. 65–8.

102 John Emerton has, for example, argued from inscriptional comparisons that the biblical construction *jhwh sᵉbaʿôth* is not so syntactically problematic as once thought. 'New Light on Israelite Religion: the Implications of the Inscriptions from Kuntillet 'Ajrud' *ZAW* 94 (1982), 9.

103 D. Barthelemy, 'Text, Hebrew, history of' *IDB Sup* (1976), 878–84.

104 This point illustrates the tight connection between synchronic semantics and communities of *speech*, rather than *writing*. The Hebrew Bible provides an example of how textuality can in some ways undermine the 'closure' of linguistic systems, and it could therefore be used to support Derrida's attempt to subvert Saussure's distinction between synchronic and diachronic semantics. See J. Derrida, *Of Grammatology* (Baltimore: Johns Hopkins, 1977), pp. 27–73. This critique of systemic 'closure' does not in itself, however, justify the extremes of etymological playfulness found in deconstructionist criticism.

105 E.g., in justifying his study of the final form, Sawyer argues in a very similar way to Childs: reconstructing original situations 'with their inevitable particularity' works against the wide applicability of biblical texts. *Semantics*, pp. 15–16.

106 Wimsatt and Beardsley 'The Intentional Fallacy' in: *20th Century Literary Criticism*, ed. D. Lodge (London: Longman, 1972), p. 339.

107 Sternberg, *Poetics*, p. 21.

108 Wimsatt and Beardsley, 'The Intentional Fallacy', p. 345.

109 Sawyer, 'A Change of Emphasis', p. 243.

110 The recent work of Robert Morgan will, however, hopefully stimulate some fresh theological thinking about historical criticism. See R. Morgan with J. Barton, *Biblical Interpretation* (Oxford: Oxford University Press, 1988).

5 TEXTUAL INTENTIONS AND HISTORIES OF
RECEPTION

1 J. Barr, 'Childs's *Introduction*' *JSOT* 16 (1980), 13–14; M. Oeming, *Gesamtbiblische Theologien*, p. 205.

2 The formulation 'meaning without an intending subject' is derived from Popper's notion of 'epistemology without a knowing subject' developed in *Objective Knowledge* (Oxford: Oxford University Press, 1972) and discussed below.

3 H. M. Barstad 'Le canon comme principe exégétique' *Stud. Theol.* 38 (1984), 87.

4 Barr, *Holy Scripture*, pp. 76–77.

5 Barr, *Holy Scripture*, p. 1.

6 Barr, *Holy Scripture*, p. 3.

7 J. Searle, *Intentionality*, (Cambridge: Cambridge University Press, 1983), p. 99.

8 For a discussion of this notion with a useful bibliography, see W. H. Dray, 'Colligation under Appropriate Conceptions' in: *Substance and Form in History*, ed. L. Pompa and W. H. Dray (Edinburgh: Edinburgh University Press, 1981), pp. 156–70.

9 A. Danto, *Analytical Philosophy of History* (Cambridge: Cambridge University Press, 1965), p. 151.

10 Barton, *Oracles of God*, pp. 192–93; see further M. Fishbane, *Biblical Interpretation in Ancient Israel* (Oxford: Clarendon, 1985), pp. 467–74.

11 Barr, *Holy Scripture*, p. 83.

12 Barr, *Holy Scripture*, p. 84.

13 See, for example, Jonathan Z. Smith's discussion of oral and written canons in 'Sacred Persistence: Toward a Redescription of Canon' *Imagining Religion* (Chicago: Chicago University Press, 1982), pp. 37–52.

14 Childs's notion of canon becomes less perspicuous, however, when he includes the *present* action of the Holy Spirit as part of the 'canonical context' (e.g. 1984a; 40). This might suggest that the stabilized Hebrew text does not actually represent the full history of revelation after all. In this respect, Hans Barstad is right in questioning whether Childs's definition of canon can consistently include a fixed corpus of literature. See Barstad, 'Le canon comme principe exégétique', p. 89.

15 R. Eberle 'Replacing One Theory by Another Under Preservation of a Given Feature' *Philosophy of Science* 38 (1971), 495.

16 L. Danneberg and H. H. Müller 'On Justifying the Choice of Interpretive Theories' *JAAC* 43 (1984), 12.

17 This thesis is characteristic of most 'causal' theories of reference. For an unusually clear introduction to the relevant issues, see M.

Devitt, and K. Sterelny, *Language and Reality* (Oxford: Blackwell, 1987), pp. 67–88. On the use of causal theories of reference in the philosophy of science, see pp. 179–82, 203–6. For a critical response to causal theories, see J. Searle *Intentionality*, chapters 8–9.

18 Hirsch, 'Meaning and Significance Reinterpreted', p. 204.

19 Popper, *Objective Knowledge*, p. 106.

20 Popper, *Objective Knowledge*, pp. 113–14, cf. also p. 147: the idea that mental states have epistemological priority is based on the 'overrated fact that the world of objective knowledge, like the world of painting or music, is created by men'.

21 Popper, *Objective Knowledge*, pp. 74, 118–19, 148. A similar idea has been advanced by the anthropologist Jack Goody with respect to the cognitive consequences of literacy which could not have been foreseen. Goody argues that writing is not simply objectified speech, rather, it allows distinctive forms of problem-raising and problem-solving not to be found in oral cultures. See *The Domestication of the Savage Mind* (Cambridge: Cambridge University Press, 1977) and my own discussion 'Literacy and Domination' *JSOT* 37 (1987), 20–4.

22 Popper 'The Sociology of Knowledge' in: *The Sociology of Knowledge*, ed. J. E. Curtis and J. W. Petras (London: Duckworth, 1970), pp. 655–6.

23 Popper, 'The Logic of the Social Sciences' in: *The Positivist Dispute in German Sociology*, ed. T. W. Adorno *et al.* (London: Heinemann, 1976), p. 96.

24 Popper, *Objective Knowledge*, p. 146.

25 Popper, *Objective Knowledge*, p. 162.

26 J. Lyons, *Semantics*, 1, p. 231.

27 See above, pp. 53–4 and note 23 to chapter 2.

28 It should not be inferred, however, that accepting Popper's idea of world three would constrain one to reject historical reconstruction in biblical studies. A Popperian historiography would need only to reject the idea of re-enacting past mental experience and replace this with a 'logic of situations' which empties the 'second world' (mental states) of explanatory significance. See Popper, *Objective Knowledge*, pp. 183–90; 'The Logic of the Social Sciences' pp. 102–4; *The Poverty of Historicism* (London: Routledge & Kegan Paul, 1957), pp. 149–52.

29 H. J. Schmidt 'Text-adequate Concretizations' *New German Critique* 17 (1979), 158. The two English translations of Jauss's essay are taken from the second edition *Literaturgeschichte als Provokation* (Frankfurt: Suhrkamp, 1970). Citations below will be from the superior translation by Timothy Bahti in H. R. Jauss, *Toward an Aesthetic of Reception* (Brighton: Harvester, 1982), pp. 3–45.

30 G. Grimm, *Rezeptionsgeschichte* (Munich: Fink, 1977).

31 Kristeller, 'The Modern System of the Arts' *J. Hist. Ideas* 12 (1951), 496–527; and 13 (1952), 11–46.

32 M. H. Abrams, *The Mirror and the Lamp* (Oxford: Oxford University Press, 1953), pp. 14–21.

33 W. K. Wimsatt and M. C. Beardsley 'The Affective Fallacy' (1949) in: *20th Century Literary Criticism*, ed. D. Lodge, pp. 345–58. Karl Mandelkow has drawn attention to a similar view in the young Friedrich Schlegel. Mandelkow 'Probleme der Wirkungsgeschichte' in: *Sozialgeschichte und Wirkungsästhetik* (Frankfurt: Athenäum, 1974), pp. 83–4.

34 On the decline of formalism generally, see F. Lentricchia, *After the New Criticism* (Chicago: Chicago University Press, 1980). Helpful introductions to reader theory are provided by S. R. Suleiman 'Varieties of audience-oriented Criticism' in: *The Reader in the Text*, ed. S. R. Suleiman, and I. Crosman (Princeton: Princeton University Press, 1981), pp. 3–45, and R. C. Holub, *Reception Theory* (London: Methuen, 1984) who focuses more on the German scene.

35 See, Jauss, *Reception*, p. 14, where Goldmann's sociology is attacked. For an introduction to Goldmann, see J. Routh, 'A Reputation Made: Lucien Goldmann' in: *The Sociology of Literature*, ed. J. Routh and J. Wolff (Keele: Keele University Press, 1977), pp. 150–62. See further J. Leenhardt 'Toward a Sociology of Reading' in: Suleiman and Crosman (eds.), *The Reader in the Text*, pp. 205–24.

36 See also Jauss, 'The Idealist Embarrassment: Observations on Marxist Aesthetics' *New Lit. Hist.* 7 (1975), 191–208. Contrast, however, the Marxist work of Manfred Naumann, e.g., 'Literary Production and Reception, *New Lit. Hist.* 8 (1976), 107–26, as well as the more subtle Marxisms of Raymond Williams and Fredric Jameson.

37 Jauss, *Reception*, p. 28.

38 Jauss, *Reception*, pp. 40–1. An expanded account of 'horizons of expectations' appears in Jauss's *Aesthetische Erfahrung und Literarische Hermeneutik* (Frankfurt: Suhrkamp, 1984), pp. 657–703.

39 Popper, *Objective Knowledge*, p. 344–5.

40 Jauss, *Reception*, p. 41 (italics added). Cf. Shklovsky 'Art as Technique' in: *Russian Formalist Critics*, ed. L. T. Lemon and M. J. Reis (Lincoln: University of Nebraska Press, 1965), pp. 3–25.

41 Jauss, *Aesthetische Erfahrung*, pp. 750–1.

42 Jauss, *Reception*, pp. 26–8, 42–5.

43 Jauss, *Reception*, p. 45. Cf. also Jauss 'Die Partialität der rezeptionsästhetischen Methode' in: *Rezeptionsästhetik*, ed. R. Warning (Munich: Fink, 1975), pp. 392–3.

44 I should note here that there are even a number of Marxist critics who agree that art can have socially transformative effects. See Ernst Bloch *et al.*, *Aesthetics and Politics* (London: NLB, 1977), and R. Wolin, *Walter Benjamin: An Aesthetic of Redemption* (New York: Columbia, 1982).

45 Jauss, *Reception*, p. 146.

46 Jauss, *Reception*, p. 32.

47 Here one could draw on Jack Goody's account of orality and literacy which I have discussed in 'Literacy and Domination' *JSOT* 37 (1987), pp. 20–4.

48 See the quotation from Goody, above pp. 20–21.

49 A. MacIntyre, *After Virtue*, 2nd edn (Notre Dame: Notre Dame University Press, 1984), p. 222.

50 This kind of objection has been raised against Childs by, among others, R. P. Carroll, 'Canonical Criticism' *Expos. T.* 92 (1980), 73–8, and N. K. Gottwald, 'Social Matrix and Canonical Shape' *TT* 42 (1986), pp. 307–21. Cf. also David Tracy, *Plurality and Ambiguity* (London: Harper & Row, 1987), pp. 77–9: 'The critique of ideologies insists that all interpretations of every classic should include an analysis of the material conditions that underlie both its production and its reception . . . We can trust ourselves to a conversation with the classics with this proviso . . . Retrieval now demands both critique and suspicion'.

51 Jauss, *Reception*, pp. 30–32.

52 H. G. Gadamer, *Truth and Method* (New York: Crossroad, 1982) = *Wahrheit und Methode*, 2nd edn (Tübingen: Mohr/Siebeck, 1965). Subsequent citations in the text will refer by page number first to this English translation, and then to the 4th German edition (1975) using the German abbreviation 'S'. I have at some points emended the translation.

53 Gadamer, *Truth and Method*, pp. 255–6, S. 271–2. On Droysen, see above pp. 88–9 and 93.

54 Gadamer, *Truth and Method*, p. xxv, S. xxv. For examples, see H. G. Stobbe, *Hermeneutik: Ein Ökumenisches Problem* (Zürich: Benziger, 1981), pp. 160, 166, 186.

55 Cf. H. Putnam, *Realism and Reason: Philosophical Papers Vol. 3* (Cambridge: Cambridge University Press, 1983), pp. 302–3. For an elegant exposition of the historical situation within which Descartes' argument for the freedom of reason was formulated, see J. Stout, *The Flight from Authority* (Notre Dame: Notre Dame University Press, 1981), pp. 37–61.

56 Gadamer, *Truth and Method*, pp. 248–9, S. 363–4. For a similar view, see H. Arendt, 'What is Authority?' *Between Past and Future* (Harmondsworth: Penguin, 1977), p. 93.

57 I am not suggesting that Gadamer's work marks the *origin* of a new hermeneutical movement. Theologians, for example, will see the emphasis on the truth of the subject matter as, in some respects, a recapitulation of 'kerygmatic' theology. For a perceptive analysis of Gadamer's theological dispositions, see W. N. Gray, 'Gadamer on Theology' *Encounter* 46 (1985), 327–37.

58 See Hirsch's comment in 'Meaning and Significance Reinterpreted', p. 223: 'Kripke could be considered the ultimate Gadamerian. It is this proximity which made Hirsch rethink his earlier criticism of Gadamer.

59 Surprisingly enough, Gadamer does not draw on any social theory to defend this point. Rather, he turns to more 'humanistic' sources like Johann Huizinga's *Homo Ludens* (London: Routledge & Kegan Paul, 1949). See *Truth and Method*, pp. 93ff., S. 99ff.

60 Gadamer, 'The Problem of Language in Schleiermacher's Hermeneutics' *JTC* 7 (1970), 81.

61 For a comparison of Danto and Gadamer, see Jürgen Habermas, 'A Review of Gadamer's *Truth and Method*' in: *Understanding and Social Inquiry*, ed. F. R. Dallmayr and T. A. McCarthy (Notre Dame: Notre Dame University Press, 1977), pp. 346–50.

62 Gadamer, 'Schleiermacher's Hermeneutics', p. 93.

63 Gadamer, *Truth and Method*, p. 272, S. 288. Cf. p. 341: 'To reach an understanding with one's partner in a dialogue is not merely a matter of total self-expression and the successful assertion of one's own point of view, but a transformation into a communion, in which we do not remain what we were'.

64 There are, of course, considerable differences between Popper and Gadamer, but it remains a puzzle how the author of *Wahrheit und Methode* (1960) could have overlooked Popper's *Logik der Forschung* (1935). See further Joel Weinsheimer's important essay, 'Hermeneutics and the Natural Sciences' *Gadamer's Hermeneutics* (London: Yale University Press, 1985), pp. 1–59.

65 Gadamer, *The Relevance of the Beautiful and Other Essays* (Cambridge: Cambridge University Press, 1986), p. 42.

66 Gadamer, *Relevance*, p. 146.

67 Cf. F. Kermode, *Forms of Attention* (Chicago: Chicago University Press, 1985), pp. 67 and 92: 'the preservation of canonical works is achieved by means of argument that may not be truly worthy of that name . . . Permanent modernity is conferred on chosen works by arguments and persuasions that cannot, themselves, remain modern'.

68 Barton, *Reading the Old Testament* (London: Darton, Longman & Todd, 1984), p. 97.

69 F. W. Farrar *History of Interpretation* (London: Macmillan, 1886), p. 210.

70 Gadamer, *Truth and Method*, pp. 253 and 430, S. 269 and 448; cf. Weinsheimer, *Gadamer's Hermeneutics*, p. 254. One might question how Gadamer can both dispose of 'the progressive approximation to the truth' and at the same time argue that classical traditions 'filter' out bad prejudices. However, one does not need an ideal end of inquiry in order to evaluate the relative values of different traditions. For a clear defence of a similar kind of non-relativist 'historicism', see Stout, *The Flight from Authority*, chapter 12.

71 For an exemplary neo-Aristotelian work that does just this, see MacIntyre, *After Virtue*. For a brief, theological argument for 'productive' exegesis, see R. D. Williams 'Postmodern Theology and the Judgment of the World', in: *Postmodern Theology*, ed. F. B. Burnham (London: Harper & Row, 1989), pp. 92–112.

6 THE FUTURE OF THE CANONICAL APPROACH

1 Here one should stress that the truth value of the Old Testament has never, for Childs, been a matter simply of historicity. See, e.g., his remark in the *Introduction*: 'whether myth, history, or saga – the canonical shape of Genesis serves the community of faith and practice as a truthful witness to God's activity' (1979: 158). For Childs's view of 'theological' (as opposed to 'scientific') reality see above, pp. 31–33.

2 Childs resists 'the corollary of most redactional criticism that the key to a text's shape lies in some force outside the text requiring a reconstruction of the hidden indices' (1979: 300).

3 Note that there are at least two ways of formulating this question, one concerned with emics and the other with etics. An emic inquiry would seek out suppressed voices by looking for the *conscious recognition* of domination. An etic enquiry could, on the other hand, search out ideological mystification which would not have been recognized as such by native informants.

4 Gottwald, 'Social Matrix and Canonical Shape' *TT* 42 (1986), 313.

5 Gottwald, 'Social Matrix', p. 319.

6 For an analytical discussion of the views which construe 'ideology' in this pejorative sense, see R. Geuss, *The Idea of a Critical Theory: Habermas and the Frankfurt School* (Cambridge: Cambridge University Press, 1981), pp. 12–22.

7 Gottwald, 'Social Matrix', p. 321. Gottwald is here focusing on the *motives* of the canonizers. See above, p. 23, for the distinction

between motives and communicative intentions; Brett, 'Motives and Intentions in Gen. 1', *JTS* (forthcoming).

8 Habermas, 'A Review of Gadamer's *Truth and Method*' in: *Understanding and Social Inquiry*, ed. F. R. Dallmayr and T. A. McCarthy (Notre Dame: Notre Dame University Press, 1977), pp. 335–63.

9 Gadamer, 'Rhetoric, Hermeneutics, and the Critique of Ideology: Metacritical Comments on *Truth and Method*' in: *The Hermeneutics Reader*, ed. K. Mueller-Vollmer (New York: Continuum, 1985), p. 284. This essay will be cited hereafter as *RHCI*.

10 Gadamer, *RHCI*, p. 286. The comment in square brackets is Gadamer's.

11 Gadamer, *RHCI*, p. 283. For Habermas's attempt to do this, see his 'Review', p. 361.

12 Gadamer, *RHCI*, p. 286. For a similar thesis, see A. MacIntyre, 'Epistemological Crises, Dramatic Narrative and the Philosophy of Science' *Monist* 60 (1977), 453–72.

13 Lindbeck, *The Nature of Doctrine* London: SPCK, 1984), p. 118; cf. H. Frei, 'The "Literal Reading" of Biblical Narrative' in: *The Bible and the Narrative Tradition*, ed. F. McConnell (Oxford: Oxford University Press, 1986), p. 72.

14 R. Thiemann, *Revelation and Theology: The Gospel as Narrated Promise* (Notre Dame: Notre Dame University Press, 1985), p. 187. This attitude toward pluralism may be contrasted with the attempts of Descartes and Spinoza to overcome the theological and philosophical conflict of their day by making recourse to a supposedly presuppositionless reason. See above, pp. 82–84.

15 See D. Tracy, 'Lindbeck's New Program for Theology: A Reflection' *Thomist* 49 (1985), pp. 460–72; G. Comstock, 'Truth or Meaning: Ricoeur versus Frei on Biblical Narrative' *J. Relig.* 66 (1986), 117–40. T. Tilley has argued that intratextuality is only vulnerable to the charge of fideism if it is understood in *purely* biblical terms. See further below, Tilley, 'Incommensurability, Intratextuality, and Fideism' *Mod. Theol.* 5 (1989), 87–111.

16 J. Stout 'A Lexicon of Postmodern Philosophy' *Relig. Stud. Rev.* 13 (1987), 18–22. Stout describes the work of Frei, Lindbeck and Thiemann as 'postmodern theology' (p. 22). See further Stout, *Ethics after Babel* (Boston: Beacon, 1988). J. W. McClendon, 'Distinguishing Modern and Postmodern Theologies' *Mod. Theol.* 5 (1989), 191–214.

17 See especially Jean-Francois Lyotard, *The Postmodern Condition: A Report on Knowledge* (Minneapolis: University of Minnesota Press, 1984); R. Rorty 'Habermas and Lyotard on Postmodernity' in: *Habermas and Modernity*, ed. R. J. Bernstein (Cambridge: Polity, 1985), pp. 161–75. Cf. also T. McCarthy, 'Rationality and

Relativism: Habermas's "Overcoming" of Hermeneutics' in: *Habermas: Critical Debates*, ed. J. B. Thompson and D. Held (London: Macmillan, 1982), pp. 57–78.

18 Williams, *Ethics and the Limits of Philosophy* (Cambridge MA: Harvard University Press, 1985), p. 84.

19 Frei, 'Literal Reading', p. 65.

20 See also Lyotard, *Postmodern Condition*, pp. 8, 23, 27, who opposes narrative knowledge to totalizing 'metanarratives'.

21 Thiemann, *Revelation*, pp. 72, 172 n. 3.; Lindbeck, *Doctrine*, p. 20. On Geertz, see above, pp. 17–18 and n. 13 to chapter 1.

22 Thiemann, *Revelation*, p. 72; cf. Lindbeck, *Doctrine*, pp. 63–73.

23 Lindbeck, *Doctrine*, pp. 64–65.

24 Thiemann, *Revelation*, p. 93. Here one could compare the similar view of Donald Davidson who maintains a realist view of truth while arguing that only 'coherence' (intrasystematic truth) can yield correspondence to reality. His slogan is therefore 'correspondence without confrontation'. See 'A Coherence Theory of Truth and Knowledge' in: *Truth and Interpretation*, ed. E. Le Pore (Oxford: Blackwell, 1986), pp. 307–19, and Davidson's earlier essays in *Inquiries into Truth and Interpretation* (Oxford: Clarendon, 1984).

25 Lash, *Theology on the Way to Emmaus* (London: SCM, 1986), p. 116.

26 It is not at all clear whether this strain of Marxist epistemology is compatible with the kind of reflective, scientific Marxism practised by Norman Gottwald and Marvin Harris.

27 Tracy, *The Analogical Imagination* (London: SCM, 1981), p. 108.

28 Lindbeck, *Doctrine*, p. 136 n. 4; cf. Frei, 'Literal Reading', pp. 67–8, who attacks the same passage from Tracy's work.

29 These quotations come from Wittgenstein, *On Certainty* (Oxford: Blackwell, 1969): sects. 87, 152, 211, 88. See Anthony Thiselton's discussion of Wittgenstein and biblical authority in *The Two Horizons* (Grand Rapids: Eerdmans, 1980), pp. 432–8.

30 W. Meeks, 'A Hermeneutics of Social Embodiment' *HTR* 79 (1986), 176–86. Meeks would now have to reformulate his argument, however, in the light of Lindbeck's recent essay on ecclesiology which takes as its starting point the fact that early Christians possessed only the Hebrew canon. See Lindbeck 'The Church' in: *Keeping the Faith*, ed. G. Wainright (London: SPCK, 1989), pp. 179 ff.

31 Thiemann, *Revelation*, p. 1.

32 Barr, *The Bible in the Modern World*, p. 121; Thiemann, *Revelation*, p. 79.

33 Thiemann, *Revelation*, pp. 80, 174 n. 14. cf. above pp. 1–2, 9–10.

34 Thiemann, *Revelation*, pp. 80–1 (italics added).
35 See, P. R. Ackroyd, 'Original Text and Canonical Text' *USQR* 32 (1977), 171.
36 Thiemann, *Revelation*, p. 81.
37 See Fiorenza, *In Memory of Her* (New York: Crossroad, 1983). For a similar argument concerning the canon's distortion of early Israelite experience, see C. Meyers, *Discovering Eve* (Oxford: Oxford University Press 1988), esp. pp. 176, 195–96.
38 Lindbeck, 'The Church', p. 182. This qualification of intratextuality brings it in line with the more general cultural-linguistic model of religion. Cf. *Doctrine*, p. 39: 'Religious traditions are not transformed, abandoned, or replaced because of an upwelling of new or different ways of feeling about the self, world or God, but because a religious interpretive scheme (embodied, as it always is, in religious practice and belief) develops anomalies in its application in new contexts'.
39 See, e.g., J. Piper, 'The Authority and Meaning of the Christian Canon: A Response to Gerald Sheppard on Canon Criticism' *Journal of the Evangelical Theological Society* 19 (1976), 87–96.
40 Lindbeck is careful to point out that the category of 'realistic' or history-like narrative, which is opposed to 'historical or scientific descriptions', was 'unavailable before the development of modern science and historical studies'. *Doctrine*, p. 122.
41 See, e.g., Mikhail Bakhtin, *Problems of Dostoevsky's Poetics* (Minneapolis: University of Minnesota Press, 1984) and the introductory essay by Wayne Booth; D. Bialostosky 'Dialogic Criticism' in: *Contemporary Literary Theory*, ed. G. D. Atkins and L. Morrow (London: Macmillan, 1989), pp. 214–28.
42 Internal contradiction is, for example, a key theme in deconstructive criticism. For a readable introduction, see J. Culler, *On Deconstruction* (Ithaca: Cornell University Press, 1982). For an application of these insights to the study of the Synoptic Gospels, see further A. P. Winton, *The Proverbs of Jesus*: *Issues of History and Rhetoric* (Sheffield: Sheffield Academic Press, 1990), chapter 4.
43 R. Barthes, 'The Death of the Author' in: *Image, Music, Text* (New York: Hill & Wang, 1977), p. 146.
44 See, e.g., P. Trible, *Texts of Terror* (Philadelphia: Fortress, 1984).
45 This issue is worthy of an independent study, but for a sense of the diverse theological opinions which converge on this point see e.g., Ernesto Cardenal 'Preface: Revolution and Theology' in: H. Assmann, *Practical Theology of Liberation* (London: Search, 1975), p. 3; A. T. Pearson 'Antagonism to the Bible' *Our Hope* 15 (1909), 475; K. Barth *Church Dogmatics* 1/2 (Edinburgh: T&T

Clark, 1956), pp. 693 and 714 ff.; M. Kähler *The So-Called Historical Jesus and the Historic, Biblical Christ* (Philadelphia; Fortress, 1965), p. 102.

46 Sanders, *Canon and Community: A Guide to Canonical Criticism* (Philadelphia: Fortress, 1984), pp. 40–1.

47 Sanders, *Canon and Community*, e.g., p. 61. For a clear recognition of this kind of problem, see G. O. West, 'Reading "the Text" and Reading "Behind-the-Text": The Cain and Abel Story in a Context of Liberation' in: *The Bible in Three Dimensions*, ed. D. Clines, S. Fowl, S. Porter (Sheffield: Sheffield Academic Press, 1990), pp. 316–17.

48 See, e.g., R. B. Crotty's sociological remarks on the decline of diachronic methods in 'Changing Fashions in Biblical Interpretation' *Aust. Bib. Rev.* 33 (1985), 15–30.

49 Cf. T. Tilley, 'Incommensurability', p. 100. See also the conclusion to G. Warnke, *Gadamer: Hermeneutics, Tradition, and Reason* (Oxford: Polity, 1987), pp. 167–74.

50 This is also the conclusion drawn by John Barton, *Reading the Old Testament* (London: Darton, Longman & Todd, 1984), p. 211. One wonders, however, whether some of the arguments in this book are really consistent with its pluralist conclusion. See, e.g., the key theses on pp. 156 and 188.

51 See Stephen Fowl's article, 'The Ethics of Interpretation' in: *The Bible in Three Dimensions*, pp. 379–98; Robert Morgan has also argued that the diverse interpretative interests of biblical scholars need to be theologically evaluated. See Morgan, *Biblical Interpretation* (Oxford: Oxford University Press, 1988).

52 Kermode, *Forms of Attention* (Chicago: Chicago University Press, 1985), p. 62.

Bibliography

Abercrombie, N., Hill, S., and Turner, B. S., *The Dominant Ideology Thesis* (London: Allen & Unwin, 1980).

Abercrombie, N. and Turner, B. S. 'The Dominant Ideology Thesis' in: *Classes, Power and Conflict*, ed. Giddens, A. and Held, D. (London: Macmillan, 1982), pp. 396–414.

Abrams, M. H. *The Mirror and the Lamp* (New York: Oxford University Press, 1953).

'The Deconstructive Angel' *Crit. Inqu.* 3 (1977), 425–38.

Ackroyd, P. R. 'The Open Canon' *Colloqu.* 3 (1970), 279–91. Reprinted in Ackroyd (1987).

'An Authoritative Version of the Bible?' *Expos. T.* 85 (1973–4), 374–7.

'Original Text and Canonical Text' *USQR* 32 (1977), 166–73. Reprinted in Ackroyd (1987).

'Continuity and Discontinuity: Rehabilitation and Authentication', in Knight (1977), pp. 215–34. Reprinted in Ackroyd (1987).

Studies in the Religious Tradition of the Old Testament (London: SCM, 1987).

Adorno, T. W. *et al.*, *The Positivist Dispute in German Sociology* (London: Heinemann, 1976).

Albright, W. F. *et al.* 'The Development of Culture in the National States' in: *City Invincible*, ed. Kraeling, C. H. and Adams, R. M. (Chicago: Chicago University Press, 1960), pp. 102–23.

Albright, W. F. 'New Light on Early Recensions of the Hebrew Bible' *BASOR* 140 (1955); reprinted in Leiman (1974), pp. 327–33.

'Introduction' to Gunkel, H. *The Legends of Genesis* (New York: Schocken, 1964), pp. vii–xii.

History, Archaeology and Christian Humanism (London: Adam & Charles Black, 1965).

Anderson, B. W. 'Introduction' to Noth, M. *A History of Pentateuchal Traditions* (Englewood Cliffs NJ: Prentice-Hall, 1972), pp. xii–xxxii.

Review of Childs' *Introduction to the Old Testament as Scripture* *TT* 37 (1980), 100–105.

'Tradition and Scripture in the Community of Faith' *JBL* 100 (1981), 5–21.

'Biblical Theology and Sociological Interpretation' *TT* 42–43 (1985), 292–306.

Antoni, C. *From History to Sociology* (Detroit: Wayne State University Press, 1959).

Apel, K. O. 'The *Erklären-Verstehen* Controversy in the Philosophy of the Natural and Human Sciences' in: *Contemporary Philosophy* II, ed. Floistad, G. (The Hague: Martinus Nijhof, 1982), pp. 19–49.

Ardener, E. 'Belief and the Problem of Women' in: *The Interpretation of Ritual*, ed. J. S. La Fontaine (London: Tavistock, 1972), pp. 135–58.

Arendt, H. 'What is Authority?' *Between Past and Future* (Harmondsworth: Penguin, 1977).

Arthur, C. E. 'Gadamer and Hirsch: The Canonical Work and the Interpreter's Intention' *Cult. Herm.* 4 (1977) 183–97.

Assmann, A. and J. 'Nachwort' in *Schrift und Gedächtnis*, ed. Assmann, A. and J. and Hardmeier, C. (Munich: Fink, 1983), pp. 265–84.

Assmann, H. *Practical Theology of Liberation* (London: Search, 1975).

Barnes, B. 'On Authority and its Relationship to Power' in: *Power, Action and Belief*, ed. Law, J. (London: Routledge & Kegan Paul, 1986), pp. 180–95.

Barnes, H. E. *A History of Historical Writing* (New York: Dover, 1962).

Barr, J. *The Semantics of Biblical Language* (Oxford: Oxford University Press, 1961).

'Revelation through History' *Interp.* 17 (1963), 193–205.

Comparative Philology and the Text of the Old Testament (Oxford: Clarendon, 1968).

The Bible in the Modern World (London: SCM, 1973).

'Trends and Prospects in Biblical Theology' *JTS* 25 (1974), 265–82.

'Childs' *Introduction to the Old Testament as Scripture*' *JSOT* 16 (1980), 12–23.

The Scope and Authority of the Bible (London: SCM, 1980).

'Jowett and the "Original Meaning" of Scripture' *Relig. Stud.* 18 (1982), 433–7.

Old and New in Interpretation, 2nd edn (London: SCM, 1982).

Holy Scripture: Canon, Authority, Criticism (Oxford: Oxford University Press, 1983).

'The Theological Case against Biblical Theology' in: *Canon, Theology, and Old Testament Interpretation*, ed. Tucker, G. M., Petersen, D. L., and Wilson, R. R. (Philadelphia: Fortress, 1988), pp. 3–19.

Barstad, H. M. 'Le canon comme principe exégétique' *Studia Theologica* 38 (1984), 77–91.

Barth, H. and Steck, O. H. *Exegese des Alten Testaments*, 10th edn (Neukirchen-Vluyn: Neukirchener, 1984).

Barth, K. *Church Dogmatics* 1/2 (Edinburgh: T&T Clark, 1956).

Barthelemy, D. 'Text, Hebrew, History of' *IDB Sup* (1976), pp. 878–84.

Barthes, R. 'The Death of the Author' *Image, Music, Text* (New York: Hill & Wang, 1977), pp. 142–8.

'The Discourse of History' in: *Rhetoric and History* Comparative Criticism Yearbook, ed. Shaffer, E. (Cambridge: Cambridge University Press, 1981), pp. 3–20.

Barton, J. *Reading the Old Testament* (London: Darton, Longman & Todd, 1984).

Oracles of God: Perceptions of Ancient Prophecy in Israel after the Exile (London: Darton, Longman & Todd, 1986).

Bascom, W. 'The Forms of Folklore' in: *Sacred Narrative* (Berkeley: University of California Press, 1984), pp. 5–25.

Battersby, J. L. and Phelan, J. 'Meaning as Concept and Extension' *Crit. Inqu.* 12 (1986), pp. 605–15.

Baumgartner, H. M. *Kontinuität und Geschichte* (Frankfurt: Suhrkamp, 1972).

Bellah, R. N. 'Social Science as Practical Reason' *The Hastings Center Report* 12 (1982), pp. 32–9.

'The Ethical Aims of Social Inquiry' in: *Social Science as Moral Inquiry*, ed. Haan, N. *et al.* (New York: Columbia, 1983), pp. 360–81.

Beltz, W. 'Religionsgeschichtliche Marginale zu Ex 4, 24–26' *ZAW* 87 (1975), 209–10.

Benjamin, W. 'Theses on the Philosophy of History' (1936) in: *Illuminations* (London: Jonathan Cape, 1968), pp. 255–66.

'The Work of Art in the Age of Mechanical Reproduction' (1950) in: *Illuminations* (London: Jonathan Cape, 1968), pp. 219–53.

Benoit, P., Milik, J. T., de Vaux, R. *Les Grottes de Murabba'ât* Discoveries in the Judaean Desert II (Oxford: Clarendon, 1961).

Berger, P. L. 'Charisma and Religious Innovation: the Social Location of Israelite Prophecy' *Am. Soc. Rev.* 28 (1963), 940–50.

'Identity as a Problem in the Sociology of Knowledge' In: *The Sociology of Knowledge*, ed. Curtis, J. E. and Petras, J. W. (London: Duckworth, 1970), pp. 373–84.

Berger, P. L. and Luckmann, T. *The Social Construction of Reality* (Harmondsworth: Penguin, 1967).

Berlin, I. 'Introduction' to Meinecke, F. *Historism* (London: Routledge & Kegan Paul, 1972).

'Note on Alleged Relativism in Eighteenth-Century European Thought' in: *Substance and Form in History*, ed. Pompa, L. and Dray, W. H. (Edinburgh: Edinburgh University Press, 1981), pp. 1–14.

Bernstein, J. M. *The Philosophy of the Novel* (Brighton: Harvester, 1984).

Bernstein, R. J. *Beyond Objectivism and Relativism* (Oxford: Blackwell, 1983).

Betti, E. 'Problematik einer allgemeinen Auslegungslehre als Methodik der Geisteswissenschaften' in: *Hermeneutik als Weg heutiger Wissenschaft* (Salzburg: Anton Pustet, 1971), pp. 13–30.

'Hermeneutics as the General Methodology of the Geisteswissenschaften' in: *Contemporary Hermeneutics*, ed. Bleicher, J. (London: Routledge & Kegan Paul, 1980), pp. 51–94.

'The Epistemological Problem of Understanding as an Aspect of the General Problem of Knowing' in: *Hermeneutics*, ed. Shapiro, G. and Sica, A. (Amherst: University of Massachusetts Press, 1984), pp. 25–53.

Betz, H. D. ed. *The Bible as a Document of the University* (Chicago: Scholars, 1981).

Birch, B. C. 'Tradition, Canon and Biblical Theology' *HBT* 2 (1980), 113–25.

Black, M. 'Meaning and Intention' *New Lit. Hist.* 4 (1973), 257–79.

Blanke, H. W. and Rüsen, J. eds. *Von der Aufklärung zum Historismus: Zum Stukturwandel des historischen Denkens* (Paderborn: Ferdinand Schöningh, 1984).

Bleicher, J. *Contemporary Hermeneutics* (London: Routledge & Kegan Paul, 1980).

The Hermeneutic Imagination: Outline of a Positive Critique of Scientism and Sociology (London: Routledge & Kegan Paul, 1982).

Blenkinsopp, J. *Prophecy and Canon* (London: Notre Dame University Press, 1977).

'A New Kind of Introduction: Professor Childs' *Introduction to the Old Testament as Scripture*' *JSOT* 16 (1980), 24–7.

Bloch, E. *et al. Aesthetics and Politics* London NLB, 1977).

Bloch, J., 'Outside Books', in Leiman (1974), pp. 202–23.

Booth, W. C. *The Rhetoric of Fiction* (Chicago: Chicago University Press, 1961).

"Preserving the Exemplar': 'Or, How not to dig our own graves' *Crit Inqu.* 3 (1977), 407–24.

Critical Understanding: The Powers and Limits of Pluralism (Chicago: Chicago University Press, 1979).

Brett, M. G. 'Literacy and Domination: G. A. Herion's Sociology of History Writing' *JSOT* 37 (1987), 15–40.

'Four or Five Things to do with Texts: A Taxonomy of Interpretative Interests' in: *The Bible in Three Dimensions*, ed. Clines, D., Fowl, S. and Porter, S. (Sheffield: Sheffield Academic Press, 1990), 357–77.

'Intratextuality' in: *A Dictionary of Biblical Interpretation*, ed. Coggins, R. J. and Houlden, L. (London: SCM, 1990).

'Motives and Intentions in Genesis 1', forthcoming in *JTS*.

Bright, J. *A History of Israel*, 3rd edn (London: SCM, 1981).

Brueggemann, W. and Wolff, H. W. *The Vitality of Old Testament Traditions* (Atlanta: John Knox, 1975).

Brueggemann, W. 'Trajectories in Old Testament Literature and the Sociology of Ancient Israel' *JBL* 98 (1979), 161–85.

'A Shape for Old Testament Theology II: Embrace of Pain' *CBQ* 47 (1985), 395–415.

Budde, K. 'Poetry (Hebrew)' in: *A Dictionary of the Bible* IV, ed. Hastings, J. (Edinburgh: T&T Clark, 1902), pp. 2–13.

Bürger, P. *Aktualität und Geschichtlichkeit* (Frankfurt: Suhrkamp, 1977).

Burling, R. 'Linguistics and Ethnographic Description' *Am. Anthrop.* 71 (1969), 817–27.

Buss, M. J. 'The Idea of Sitz im Leben' *ZAW* 90 (1978), 157–70.

'The Social Psychology of Prophecy' *BZAW* 150 (1980), 1–11.

Butterfield, H. *Man on his Past* (Cambridge: Cambridge University Press, 1955).

Butler, T. C. 'An Anti-Moses Tradition in Exodus' *JSOT* 12 (1979), 9–15.

Campbell, A. F. 'Yahweh and the Ark: A Case Study in Narrative' *JBL* 98 (1979), 31–43.

Canary, R. H. and Kozicki, H. eds. *The Writing of History: Literary Form and Historical Understanding* (Madison: University of Wisconsin Press, 1978).

Cantwell Smith, W. 'The Study of Religion and the Study of the Bible', *JAAR* 39 (1971), 131–40.

Carroll, R. P. 'Canonical Criticism: A Recent Trend in Biblical Studies?' *Expos. T.* 92 (1980), 73–8.

Review of Childs' *Introduction to the Old Testament as Scripture* *SJT* 33 (1980), 285–91.

'Prophecy and Dissonance' *ZAW* (1980), 108–99.

Cazelles, H. 'The Canonical Approach to Torah and Prophets' *JSOT* 16 (1980), 28–31.

Chaney, M. L. 'Ancient Palestinian Peasant Movements and the Formation of Premonarchic Israel' in: *Palestine in Transition*, ed. Freedman, D. N. and Graf, D. F. (Sheffield: Almond Press, 1983), pp. 39–90.

Chenu, M. D. *Toward Understanding St. Thomas* (Chicago: Chicago University Press, 1964).

Childs, B. S. (See bibliographical appendix)

Cioffi, F. 'Intention and Interpretation in Criticism' in: *Proceedings of the Aristotelian Society* 64 (1963–64), 85–106.

Clark, H. H. and Carlson, T. B. 'Context for Comprehension' in: *Attention and Performance* IX, ed. Long, J. and Baddeley, A. (Hillsdale: Erlbaum, 1981), pp. 313–30.

Clark, H. H. and Carlson, T. B. 'Speech Acts and Hearers' Beliefs' in: *Mutual Knowledge*, ed. Smith, N. V. (London: Academic, 1982), pp. 1–36.

Clark, S. 'The Annales Historians' in: *The Return of Grand Theory to the Human Sciences*, ed. Skinner, Q. (Cambridge: Cambridge University Press, 1985), pp. 179–98.

Clements, R. E. *A Century of Old Testament Study* (London: SCM, 1976).
'Patterns in the Prophetic Canon', in Coats and Long (1977), pp. 42–55.

Clements, R. E. ed. *The World of Ancient Israel: Sociological, Anthropological and Political Perspectives* (Cambridge: Cambridge University Press, 1989).

Clines, D. J. A. 'Theme in Gen. 1–11' *CBQ* 38 (1976), 483–507.

Coats, G. W. and Long, B. O. eds. *Canon and Authority* (Philadelphia: Fortress, 1977).

Cohen, A. P. *The Symbolic Construction of Community* (London: Tavistock, 1985).

Cohen, R. *New Directions in Literary Theory* (London: Routledge & Kegan Paul, 1974).
'History and Genre' *NLH* 17 (1986), 203–18.

Connolly, J. M. 'Gadamer and the Author's Authority: A Language-game Approach' *JAAC* 44 (1986), 271–77.

Copleston, F. C. 'Pantheism in Spinoza and the German Idealists' *Philos.* 21 (1946), 42–56.

Coward, D. 'The Sociology of Literary Response' in: *The Sociology of Literature*, ed. Routh, J. and Wolff, J. (Keele: University of Keele Press, 1977), pp. 8–17.

Craig, C. T. 'Biblical Theology and the Rise of Historicism' *JBL* 62 (1943), 281–94.

Crosman, R. 'Do Readers Make Meaning?', in Suleiman and Crosman (1981), pp. 149–64.

Cross, F. M. 'Yahweh and the God of the Patriarchs' *HTR* 55 (1962), 225–59.
'The History of the Biblical Text in the Light of Discoveries in the Judaean Desert' *HTR* 57 (1964), 281–99.

'The Contribution of the Qumran Discoveries to the Study of the Biblical Text' *Israel Exploration Journal* 16 (1966), 81–95; reprinted in Leiman (1974), pp. 334–48.

Canaanite Myth and Hebrew Epic (Cambridge MA: Harvard University Press, 1973).

Crüsemann, F. 'Alttestamentliche Exegese und Archäologie: Erwägungen angesichts des gegenwärtigen Methodenstreits in der Archäologie Palästinas' *ZAW* 91 (1979), 177–93.

Culler, J. 'Presupposition and Intertextuality' *MLN* 91 (1976), 1,380–96.

On Deconstruction (Ithaca: Cornell University Press, 1982).

Culley, R. C. 'Oral Tradition and Historicity' in: *Studies on the Ancient Palestinian World*, ed. Wevers J. W. and Redford, D. B. (Toronto: Toronto University Press, 1972), pp. 102–16.

Curtis, J. E. and Petras, J. W. *The Sociology of Knowledge: A Reader* (London: Duckworth, 1970).

Dallymayr, F. R. 'Comments on Giddens' in: *Hermeneutics*, ed. Shapiro, G. and Sica, A. (Amherst: University of Massachusetts Press, 1984), pp. 231–38.

Dallmayr, F. R. and McCarthy, D. eds. *Understanding and Social Science* (London: University of Notre Dame Press, 1977).

Dannenberg, L. and Müller, H. H. 'Wissenschaftstheorie, Hermeneutik, Literaturwissenschaft' *Deutsche Vierteljahrschrift für Literaturwissenschaft und Geistesgeschichte* 2 (1984), 177–237.

'On Justifying the Choice of Interpretive Theories: A Critical Examination of E. D. Hirsch's Arguments in Favor of an Intentionalist Theory of Interpretation' *JAAC* 43 (1984), 7–16.

Danto, A. *Analytical Philosophy of History* (Cambridge: Cambridge University Press, 1965).

Davidson, D. *Inquiries into Truth and Interpretation* (Oxford: Clarendon, 1984).

'A Coherence Theory of Truth and Knowledge' in: *Truth and Interpretation* (Oxford: Blackwell, 1986), pp. 307–19.

Davis, L. J. 'A Social History of Fact and Fiction' in: *Literature and Society*, ed. Said, E. W. (London: Johns Hopkins University Press, 1979), pp. 120–47.

Davis, W. A. 'The Fisher King: Wille zur Macht in Baltimore' *Crit. Inqu.* 10 (1984), 668–94, 706–18.

de Certeau, M. 'History: Ethics, Science and Fiction' in: *Social Science as Moral Inquiry*, ed. Haan, N. *et al.* (New York: Columbia, 1983), pp. 125–52.

de Saussure, F. *Course in General Linguistics*, trans. Baskin, W. 3rd edn (Glasgow: Collins, 1974) = *Cours de linguistique générale*, ed. Bally, C. and Sechehaye (Paris: Payot, 1916).

Deetz, S. 'Conceptualizing Human Understanding: Gadamer's Hermeneutics and American Communication Studies' *Communication Quarterly* 26 (1978), 12–23.

Derrida, J. 'The Law of Genre' *Crit. Inqu.* 7 (1980–81), 55–81.
  Of Grammatology, trans. Spivak, G. C. (Baltimore: Johns Hopkins, 1977) = *De la grammatologie* ((Paris: Les Editions de Minuit, 1967).

Devitt, M. and Sterelny, K. *Language and Reality* (Oxford: Blackwell, 1987).

Dilthey, W. 'The Rise of Hermeneutics' (1900) *New Lit. Hist.* 3 (1972), 229–45.
  Descriptive Psychology and Historical Understanding (The Hague: Martinus Nijhof, 1977).

Dostal, R. J. 'Kantian Aesthetics and E. D. Hirsch' *JAAC* 38 (1980), 299–305.

Douglas, M. 'The Social Preconditions of Radical Scepticism' in: *Power, Action and Belief*, ed. Law, J. (London: Routledge & Kegan Paul, 1986), pp. 68–87.

Downes, W. *Language and Society* (London: Fontana, 1984).

Dray, W. H. 'On the Nature and Role of Narrative in Historiography' *Hist. & Th.* 10 (1974), 153–71.
  'Colligation under Appropriate Conceptions' in: *Substance and Form in History*, ed. Pompa, L. and Dray, W. H. (Edinburgh: Edinburgh University Press, 1981), pp. 156–70.
  'Conflicting Interpretations in History: The Case of the English Civil War' in: *Hermeneutics*, ed. Shapiro, G. and Sica, A. (Amherst: University of Massachusetts Press, 1984), pp. 239–57.

Droysen, J. G. *Outline of the Principles of History* (Boston: Ginn & Co., 1893) = *Grundriss der Historik* 3rd edn (1881).
  Historik, ed. Hübner, R. (1857; Munich: Oldenbourg 5th edn, 1967).

Dundes, A. *Sacred Narrative* (Berkeley: University of California Press, 1984).

Eagleton, T. 'Marxist Literary Criticism' in: *The Sociology of Literature*, ed. Routh, J. and Wolff, J. (Keele: University of Keele Press, 1977), pp. 85–91.

Eaton, M. M. 'Good and Correct Interpretations of Literature' *JAAC* 29 (1970–1), 227–33.

Egan, K. 'Thucydides, Tragedian' in: *The Writing of History*, ed. Canary, R. H. and Kozicki, H. (Madison: University of Wisconsin Press, 1978), pp. 63–92.

Eliade, M. 'Cosmogonic Myth and Sacred History' in: *Sacred Narrative*, ed. Dundes, A. (Berkeley: University of California Press, 1984), pp. 137–51.

Eliot, T. S. 'Tradition and the Individual Talent' (1919) in: *20th Century Literary Criticism: A Reader*, ed. Lodge, D. (London: Longman's, 1972), pp. 71–7.

Emerton, J. A. 'New Light on Israelite Religion: the Implications of the Inscriptions from Kuntillet 'Ajrud' *ZAW* 94 (1982), 2–20.

Ermath, M. *Wilhelm Dilthey: The Critique of Historical Reason* (Chicago: Chicago University Press, 1978).

Feenberg, A. 'Lukács and the Critique of "Orthodox" Marxism' *The Philosophical Forum* 3 (1972), 422–67.

Feleppa, R. 'Emics, Etics, and Social Objectivity' *Curr. Anthrop.* 27 (1986), 243–55.

Fiorenza, E. *In Memory of Her* (New York: Crossroad, 1983).

Firth, J. R. 'On Sociological Linguistics' in: *Language in Culture and Society*, ed. Hymes, D. (New York: Harper & Row, 1964), pp. 66–70.

Firth, R. 'The Plasticity of Myth' in: *Sacred Narrative*, ed. Dundes, A. (Berkeley: University of California Press, 1984), pp. 207–16.

Fish, S. *Is there a Text in this Class?* (Cambridge MA: Harvard University Press, 1980).

'With the Compliments of the Author: Reflections on Austin and Derrida' *Crit. Inqu.* 8 (1982), 693–721.

Fishbane, M. 'Torah and Tradition', in Knight (1977), pp. 275–300.
Biblical Interpretation in Ancient Israel (Oxford: Clarendon, 1985).

Fisher, L. E. and Werner, D. 'Explaining Explanation: Tension in American Anthropology' *Journal of Anthropological Research* 34 (1978), 194–218.

Ford, D. F. 'Barth's Interpretation of the Bible' in: *Karl Barth – Studies of his Theological Methods*, ed. Sykes, S. W. (Oxford: Clarendon, 1979), pp. 55–87.

Foucault, M. 'What is an Author?' in: *Textual Strategies*, ed. Harari, J. V. (Ithaca: Cornell University Press, 1979), pp. 141–60.

Fowl, S. 'The Canonical Approach of Brevard Childs' *Expos. T.* 96 (1985), 173–76.

'The Ethics of Interpretation, or, What's Left Over After the Elimination of Meaning' in: *The Bible in Three Dimensions*, ed. Clines, D., Fowl, S., and Porter, S. (Sheffield: Sheffield Academic Press, 1990), pp. 379–98.

Freedman, D. N. 'The Law and the Prophets' *SVT* 9 (1962), 250–65; reprinted in Leiman (1974), pp. 5–20.

'Son of Man, Can these Bones Live?' *Interp.* 29 (1975), 171–86.

'Early Israelite History in the Light of Early Israelite Poetry' in: *Unity and Diversity*, ed. Goedicke, H. and Roberts, J. J. M. (London: Johns Hopkins, 1975), pp. 3–35.

Frei, H. *The Eclipse of Biblical Narrative* (New Haven: Yale University Press, 1974).

'The "Literal Reading" of Biblical Narrative in the Christian Tradition: Does it Stretch or Will it Break?' in: *The Bible and the Narrative Tradition* (Oxford: Oxford University Press, 1986), pp. 36–77.

Frick, F. S. *The City in Ancient Israel* (Missoula: Scholars Press, 1977). *The Formation of the State in Ancient Israel* (Sheffield: Almond, 1985).

Froehlich, K. 'Problems in Lutheran Hermeneutics' in: *Studies in Lutheran Hermeneutics*, ed. Reumann, J. (Philadelphia: Fortress, 1979), pp. 127–41.

'Biblical Hermeneutics on the Move' *Word and World* 1 (1981), 140–52; reprinted in *Ex Auditu* 1 (1985), 3–13.

Gadamer, H. G. *Truth and Method* (New York: Crossroad, 1982) = *Wahrheit und Methode*, 2nd edn (1965).

'Rhetoric, Hermeneutics and the Critique of Ideology' in: *The Hermeneutics Reader*, ed. Mueller-Vollmer, K. (New York Continuum, 1985), pp. 274–92 = 'Rhetorik, Hermeneutik und Ideologiekritik' *Kleine Schriften* 1 (Tübingen: Mohr/Siebeck, 1967), pp. 113–30.

'The Problem of Language in Schleiermacher's Hermeneutic' *JTC* 7 (1970), 68–95 = 'Das Problem der Sprache in Schleiermachers Hermeneutik' *Kleine Schriften* III (Tügingen: Mohr/Siebeck, 1972).

'Herder und die geschichtliche Welt' *Kleine Schriften* III, pp. 101–17.

Wahrheit und Methode, 4th edn Tübingen: Mohr/Siebeck, 1975).

Philosophical Hermeneutics (London University of California Press, 1976).

'Aesthetische und Religiöse Erfahrung' *Nederlands Teologisk Tidsskrift* 32 (1978), 218–30.

Reason in an Age of Science (Cambridge MA: MIT, 1981).

'Unterwegs zur Schrift?' in: *Schrift und Gedächtnis*, ed. Assmann, A. and J. and Hardmeier, C. (Munich: Fink, 1983).

The Relevance of the Beautiful and other Essays (Cambridge: Cambridge University Press, 1986).

Gadamer, H. G. and Strauss, L. 'Correspondence Concerning Wahrheit und Methode' *Unabhängige Zeitschrift für Philosophie* 2 (1978), 5–12.

Gallie, W. B. 'Art as an Essentially Contested Concept' *Philosophical Quarterly* 6 (1956), 97–114.

Gardiner, P. *Theories of History* (London: Allen & Unwin, 1959).

Gay, P. *Freud for Historians* (Oxford: Oxford University Press, 1985).

Geertz, C. *The Interpretation of Cultures* (New York: Basic Books, 1973).

'From the Native's Point of View' in: *Culture Theory* ed. Shweder, R. A. and Le Vine, R. A. (Cambridge: Cambridge University Press, 1984), pp. 123–36.

Gese, H. 'The Idea of History in the Ancient Near East and the Old Testament' *Journal for Theology and the Church* 1 (1965), 49–64.

'Tradition and Biblical Theology', in Knight (1977), pp. 301–26.

Geuss, R. *The Idea of a Critical Theory: Habermas and the Frankfurt School* (Cambridge: Cambridge University Press, 1981).

Giddens, A. *New Rules of Sociological Method* (London: Hutchinson, 1976).

'Habermas's Critique of Hermeneutics' in *Studies in Social and Political Theory* (London: Hutchinson, 1977).

'Hermeneutics and Social Theory' in: *Hermeneutics*, ed. Shapiro, G. and Sica, A. (Amherst: University of Massachusetts Press, 1984), pp. 215–30.

The Constitution of Society (Cambridge: Polity, 1984).

Social Theory and Modern Sociology (Oxford: Blackwell, 1987).

Gilkey, L. 'Cosmology, Ontology, and the Travail of Biblical Language' *JR* 41 (1961), 194–205.

Goodenough, W. 'Cultural Anthropology and Linguistics' in: *Language in Culture and Society*, ed. Hymes, D. (New York: Harper & Row, 1964).

Goody, J. *The Domestication of the Savage Mind* (Cambridge: Cambridge University Press, 1977).

Goody, J. and Watt, I. 'The Consequences of Literacy' in: *Literacy in Traditional Societies*, ed. Goody, J. R. (Cambridge: Cambridge University Press, 1968), pp. 27–68.

Gottwald, N. K. *The Tribes of Yahweh* (Maryknoll: Orbis, 1979).

The Hebrew Bible: A Socio-literary Introduction (Philadelphia: Fortress, 1985).

'Social Matrix and Canonical Shape' *TT* 42 (1986), 307–21.

Gottwald, N. K. ed. *The Bible and Liberation* (Maryknoll: Orbis, 1983).

Gray, W. N. 'Gadamer on Theology' *Encounter* 46 (1985), 327–37.

Greenberg, M. *Understanding Exodus* (New York: Behrman, 1969).

'The Stabilization of the Text of the Hebrew Bible' in: Leiman (ed.) (1974), pp. 298–326.

Grice, H. P. 'Meaning' *The Philosophical Review* 66 (1957), 377–88.

'Logic and Conversation' in: *Syntax and Semantics* III, ed. Cole, P. and Morgan, J. (London: Academic, 1975).

Grimm, G. *Rezeptionsgeschichte* (Munich: Fink. 1977).

Grove, R. 'Canon and Community: Authority in the History of Religions', PhD thesis, University of California, Santa Barbara, 1983.

Gumbrecht, H. U. 'Soziologie und Rezeptionsästhetik' in: *Neue Ansichten einer künftigen Germanistik*, ed. Kolbe, J. (Munich: Fink, 1973), pp. 49–74.

Gumperz, J. J. 'The Speech Community' in: *Language and Social Context*, ed. Giglioli, P. (Harmondsworth: Penguin, 1972), pp. 219–31.

'Sociocultural Knowledge in Conversational Inference' in: *Linguistics and Anthropology*, ed. Saville-Troike, M. (Washington: Georgetown University Press, 1977), pp. 191–211.

Gunkel, H. *Schöpfung und Chaos in Urzeit und Endzeit* (Göttingen: Vandenhoeck & Ruprecht, 1985).

The Legends of Genesis (1901; New York: Schocken, 1966).

Die Israelitische Literatur (1906; Darmstadt: Wissenschaftliche Buchgesellschaft, 1963).

'Ziele und Methoden der Erklärung des Alten Testaments.' *Reden und Aufsätze* (Göttingen: Vandenhoeck & Ruprecht, 1913).

'The "Historical Movement" in the Study of Religion' *Expos. T.* 38 (1926–27), 532–36.

Gunn, D. *The Story of King David* (Sheffield: JSOT, 1982).

Habermas, J. *Knowledge and Human Interests* (Boston: Beacon, 1971).

'A Review of Gadamer's *Truth and Method*' in: *Understanding and Social Inquiry*, ed. Dallmayr, F. R. and McCarthy, T. A., (London: Notre Dame University Press, 1977), pp. 335–63 = *Zur Logik der Socialwissenschaften* (Frankfurt: Suhrkamp, 1970), pp. 251–90.

'On Hermeneutics' Claim to Universality' in: *The Hermeneutics Reader*, ed. Mueller-Vollmer, K. (New York: Continuum, 1985), pp. 294–319.

'The Entwinement of Myth and Enlightenment' *New German Critique* 26 (1982), 13–30.

'H. G. Gadamer: Urbanizing the Heideggerian Province' in: *Philosophical-Political Profiles* (Baskerville: MIT, 1983), pp. 189–97.

Hacking, I. 'Five Parables', in Rorty *et al.* (1984), pp. 103–24.

Hallo, W. W. 'Biblical History in its Near Eastern Setting' in: *Scripture in Context*, ed. Evans, C. D. *et al.* (Pittsburgh: Pickwick, 1980), pp. 1–26.

Handelman, S. S. *The Slayers of Moses: The Emergence of Rabbinic Interpretation in Modern Literary Theory* (Albany: State University of New York Press, 1982).

Hanson, P. D. 'The Theological Significance of Contradiction within the Book of the Covenant' in Coats and Long (1977), pp. 110–31.

'The Responsibility of Biblical Theology to Communities of Faith' *TT* 37 (1980), 39–50.

The Diversity of Scripture (Philadelphia: Fortress, 1982).

Hardmeier, C. 'Verkündigung und Schrift bei Jesaja' *Theologie und Glaube* 73 (1983), 119–34.

Harris, M. *The Rise of Anthropological Theory* (London: Routledge & Kegan Paul, 1969).

'History and Significance of the Emic-Etic Distinction' *Annual Review of Anthropology* 5 (1976), 329–50.

Cultural Materialism (New York: Random, 1979).

Hayner, P. C. *Reason and Existence: Schelling's Philosophy of History* (Leiden: Brill, 1967).

Hegel, G. F. W. *Lectures on the Philosophy of History* (1837), ed. Nisbet, H. R. (Cambridge: Cambridge University Press, 1975).

Held, D. *et al. States and Societies* (Oxford: Martin Robertson, 1983).

Helm, P. 'Revealed Propositions and Timeless Truths' *Relig. Stud.* 8 (1972), 126–36.

Hennen, M. and Prigge, W. U. *Autorität und Herrschaft* (Darmstadt: Wissenschaftliche Buchgesellschaft, 1977).

Herder, J. G. *The Spirit of Hebrew Poetry*, trans. Marsh, J. (Burlington: Edward Smith, 1883).

Herion, G. A. 'The Impact of Modern and Social Science Assumptions on the Reconstruction of Israelite History' *JSOT* 34 (1986), 3–33.

Hirsch, E. D. *Validity in Interpretation* (New Haven: Yale University Press, 1967).

Aims of Interpretation (Chicago: Chicago University Press, 1976).

'Beyond Convention?' *New. Lit. Hist.* 14 (1983), 389–97.

'Meaning and Significance Reinterpreted' *Crit. Inqu.* 2 (1986), 627–30.

Hohendahl, P. U. 'Introduction to Reception Aesthetics' *New German Critique* 10 (1977), 29–63.

'Literary Sociology in West Germany' *New German Critique* 17 (1979), 170–75.

The Institution of Criticism (Ithaca: Cornell University Press, 1982).

'Beyond Reception Aesthetics' 28 (1983), 108–46.

Holland, N. 'Unity Identity Text Self' in Tompkins (1980), pp. 118–33.

Hollis, M. 'Reason and Ritual' *Philosophy* 43 (1968), 231–47.

Holub, R. C. *Reception Theory* (London: Methuen, 1984).

Houtman, C. 'Exodus 4: 24–26 and its Interpretation' *Journal of Northwest Semitic Languages* 11 (1983), 81–105.

Hoy, D. 'Literary History: Paradox or Paradigm?' *Yale French Studies* 52 (1975) 268–86.

The Critical Circle (Berkeley: University of California Press, 1978).

'Hermeneutic Circularity, Indeterminacy and Incommensurability' *New Lit. Hist.* 10 (1978), 161–73.

'Taking History Seriously: Foucault, Gadamer and Habermas' *USQR* 24 (1979), 85–95.

'Jacques Derrida', in Skinner (1985), pp. 43–64.

Hudson, R. 'Some Issues on which Linguists can Agree' *Journal of Linguistics* 17 (1981), 333–343.

Huizinga, J. 'A Definition of the Concept of History' in: *Philosophy and History*, ed. Klibansky, R. and Paton H. J. (Oxford: Clarendon, 1936).

Homo Ludens (London: Paladin, 1970).

Hyatt, J. P. 'Were there an Ancient Historical Credo in Israel and an Independent Sinai Tradition?' in: *Translating and Understanding the Old Testament*, ed. Frank, H. T. and Reed, W. L. (Nashville: Abingdon, 1970), pp. 152–70.

Iggers, G. G. *The German Conception of History* (Middletown: Wesleyan University Press, 1968).

New Directions in European Historiography (Middletown: Wesleyan University Press, 1975).

'Introduction' to *The Social History of Politics* (Leamington Spa: Berg, 1985).

Iggers, G. G. and Moltke, K. 'Introduction' to von Ranke, L. *The Theory and Practice of History* (New York: Irvington, 1983), pp. xv–lxxi.

Jacob, E. 'Principe canonique et formation de l'Ancien Testament' *VTS* 28 (1975), 101–22.

Jaffee, M. S. 'Oral Torah in Theory and Practice' *Religion* 15 (1985), 387–440.

Jameson, F. *The Political Unconscious* (Ithaca: Cornell University Press, 1981).

'The Alterity and Modernity of Medieval Literature' *NLH* 10 (1979, 181–229.

Jauss, H. R. *Toward an Aesthetic of Reception* (Brighton: Harvester, 1982).

'Die Partialität der rezeptionsästhetischen Methode' in: *Rezeptionsäesthetik* (Munich: Fink, 1975), pp. 380–400.

'The Idealist Embarrassment: Observations on Marxist Aesthetics' *New Lit. Hist.* 7 (1975), 191–208.

Jay, M. *Adorno* (London: Fontana, 1984).

Jeanrond, W. G. 'The Theological Understanding of Texts and Linguistic Explication' *Modern Theology* 1 (1984), 55–66.

Text and Interpretation as Categories of Theological Thinking (Dublin: Gill & Macmillan, 1988).

Jobling, D. *The Sense of Biblical Narrative II* (Sheffield: JSOT, 1986).

Jones, D. 'The Traditio of the Oracles of Isaiah of Jerusalem' *ZAW* 67 (1955), 226–46.

Juhl, P. D. *Interpretation* (Princeton: Princeton University Press, 1980).

Jüngel, E. 'Anthropomorphismus als Grundproblem neuzeitlicher Hermeneutik' in: *Verifikationen* eds. Jüngel, E. *et al.* (Tübingen: Mohr/Siebeck, 1982), pp. 499–522.

Kant, I. *Kritik der Urteilskraft*, ed. Weischedel, W. (1790; Frankfurt: Suhrkamp, 1974).

Keesing, R. M. 'Paradigms Lost: The New Ethnography and the New Linguistics' *Southwestern Journal of Anthropology* 28 (1972), 299–332.

'Simple Models of Complexity: The Lure of Kinship' in: *Kinship Studies in the Morgan Centennial Year*, ed. Reining,P. (Washington DC: Anthropological Society of Washington, 1972), pp. 17–31.

'Anthropology as Interpretive Quest' *Curr. Anthrop.* 28 (1987), 161–76.

Kermode, F. 'Institutional Control of Interpretation' *Salmagundi* 43 (1979). pp. 72–86.

Forms of Attention (London: Chicago University Press, 1985).

'The Argument about Canons' in: *The Bible and the Narrative Tradition* (Oxford: Oxford University Press, 1986), pp. 78–96.

Kimmerle, H. 'Hermeneutical Theory or Ontological Hermeneutics' *Journal for Theology and the Church* 4 (1976), pp. 107–21.

Kincaid, J. R. 'Coherent Readers, Incoherent Texts' *Crit. Inqu.* 3 (1977), 781–802.

Klatt, W. *Hermann Gunkel: zu seiner Theologie der Religionsgeschichte und zur Entstehung der formgeschichtlichen Methode* (Göttingen: Vandenhoeck & Ruprecht, 1969).

Klein, R. W., Stansell, G. and Brueggemann, W. 'The Childs Proposal' *Word and World* 1 (1981), 105–15.

Kinkenborg, V. L. 'Canon and Literary Criticism' PhD thesis, Princeton University, 1982.

Knight, D. A. ed. *Tradition and Theology in the Old Testament* (London: SPCK, 1977).

'Canon and the History of Tradition: A Critique of Brevard Childs' *HBT* 2 (1980), 127–49.

Kortian, G. *Metacritique: The Philosophical Argument of Jürgen Habermas* (Cambridge: Cambridge University Press, 1980).

Kosík, K. *Die Dialektik des Konkreten* (Frankfurt: Suhrkamp, 1967).

Kosmala, 'The "Bloody Husband" ' *VT* 12 (1972) 14–28.

Kraus, H. J. 'Zur Geschichte des Ueberlieferungsbegriffe in der alttestamentlichen Wissenschaft' *Biblisch-theologische Aufsätze* (Neukirchen-Vluyn: Neukirchener, 1972), pp. 278–95.

'Theologie als Traditionsbildung' *Ev. Th.* 36 (1976), 498–507.

Geschichte der historisch-kritischen Erforschung des Alten Testaments, 3rd edn (Neukirchen-Vluyn: Neukirchener, 1983).

Krecher, J. and Müller, H. P. 'Vergangenheitsinteresse in Meso-
    potamien und Israel' *Saeculum* 26 (1975), 13–44.
Kripke, S. 'Speaker's Reference and Semantic Reference' in: *Con-
    temporary Perspectives in the Philosophy of Language*, ed. French, P. A.
    et al. (Minneapolis: Minnesota University Press, 1977), pp. 6–27.
    Naming and Necessity (Oxford: Blackwell, 1980).
Kristeller, P. O. 'The Modern System of the Arts: A Study in the
    History of Aesthetics' *Journal of the History of Ideas* 12 (1951),
    496–527, and 13 (1952), 17–46.
Kuhn, T. S. *The Structure of Scientific Revolutions*, 2nd edn (London:
    Chicago University Press, 1970).
    'Logic of Discovery or Psychology of Research?', in Lakatos and
    Musgrave (1970), pp. 1–23.
    'Reflections on my Critics', in Lakatos and Musgrave (1970), pp.
    231–78.
Lakatos, I. 'Falsification and the Methodology of Scientific Research
    Programmes', in Lakatos and Musgrave (1970), pp. 91–196.
Lakatos, I. and Musgrave, A. *Criticism and the Growth of Knowledge*
    (Cambridge: Cambridge University Press, 1970).
Lang, P. C. *Hermeneutik Ideologiekritik Aesthetik* (Königstein/Ts.: Forum
    Academicum, 1981).
Laurin, R. B. 'Tradition and Canon', in Knight (1977), pp. 261–74.
Lee, D. E. and Beck, R. N. 'The Meaning of "Historicism" '
    Am. Hist. Rev. 59 (1954), 568–77.
Leach, E. 'Anthropological Approaches to the Study of the Bible
    during the Twentieth Century' in: *Humanizing America's Iconic
    Book*, ed. Tucker, G. and Knight, D. (Chico: Scholars Press,
    1982), pp. 73–94.
Leech, G. N. *Principles of Pragmatics* (London: Longman, 1983).
Leenhardt, J. 'Towards a Sociology of Reading', in Suleiman and
    Crosman (1981), pp. 205–24.
Leiman, S. Z. ed. *The Canon and Masorah of the Hebrew Bible: An
    Introductory Reader* (New York: KTAV, 1974).
    *The Canonization of Hebrew Scripture: The Talmudic and Midrashic
    Evidence* (Hamden: Archon, 1976).
Levin, D. *History as Romantic Art* (Stanford: Stanford University Press,
    1959).
    'The Literary Criticism of History' in *In Defence of Historical Literature*
    (New York: Hill & Wang, 1967), pp. 1–33.
Levinson, S. *Pragmatics* (Cambridge: Cambridge University Press,
    1983).
Lewis, J. P. 'What do We Mean by Jabneh?' *JBR* 32 (1964), 125–32;
    reprinted in Leiman (1974), pp. 254–61.

Lindbeck, G. A. *The Nature of Doctrine: Religion and Theology in a Postliberal Age* (London: SPCK, 1984).

'Scripture, Consensus, and Community' *This World* 23 (1988), 5–24.

'The Church' in: *Keeping the Faith*, ed. Wainright, G. (London: SPCK, 1989).

Long, B. O. 'Recent Field Studies in Oral Literature and their Bearing on Old Testament Criticism' *VT* 26 (1976), 186–98.

'Prophetic Authority as Social Reality' in Coats and Long (1977), pp. 3–20.

'The Social World of Ancient Israel' *Interp.* 36 (1982), 243–55.

Luke, J. T. 'Abraham and the Iron Age: Reflections on the New Patriarchal Studies' *JSOT* 4 (1977), 35–47.

Lyons, J. *Semantics*, 2 vols. (Cambridge: Cambridge University Press, 1977).

Language and Linguistics (Cambridge: Cambridge University Press, 1981).

Lyotard, J. F. *The Postmodern Condition* (Minneapolis: Minnesota University Press, 1984).

McCann, D. P. 'Habermas and the Theologians' *Relig. Stud. Rev.* 7 (1981), 15–21.

McCarthy, T. 'Rationality and Relativism: Habermas's "Overcoming" of Hermeneutics' in: *Habermas: Critical Debates*, ed. Thompson, J. B. and Held, D. (London: Macmillan, 1982), pp. 57–78.

McEvenue, S. E. 'The Old Testament, Scripture or Theology?' *Interp.* 35 (1981), pp. 229–42; reprinted *Ex Auditu* 1 (1985), 115–24.

MacIntyre, A. 'Contents of Interpretation: Reflections on Hans-Georg Gadamer's Truth and Method' *Boston University Journal* 24 (1976), 41–6.

'Epistemological Crises, Dramatic Narrative and the Philosophy of Science' *Monist* 60 (1977), 453–72.

After Virtue (Notre Dame: Notre Dame University Press, 1981).

McKane, W. *Studies in the Patriarchal Narratives* (Edinburgh: Handsel, 1979).

McKenzie, J. L. 'Myth and the Old Testament' *Myths and Realities* (London: Chapman, 1963), pp. 182–200.

MacLean, I. 'Reading and Interpretation' in *Modern Literary Theory*, ed. Jefferson, A. and Robey, D. (London: Batsford, 1986), pp. 122–44.

Mailloux, S. 'Reader-Response Criticism?' *Genre* 10 (1977), 413–31.

Malinowski, B. 'The Role of Myth in Life' in: *Sacred Narrative*, ed. Dundes, A. (Berkeley: University of California Press, 1984), pp. 193–205.

Mandelbaum, M. *History, Man and Reason* (Baltimore: Johns Hopkins, 1971).

Mandelkow, K. R. 'Probleme der Wirkungsgeschichte' in: *Sozialgeschichte und Wirkungsästhetik*, ed. Hohendahl, P. U. (Frankfurt: Athenäum, 1974), pp. 82–96.

Maranda, P. 'The Dialectic of Metaphor: An Anthropological Essay on Hermeneutics', in Suleiman and Crosman (1981), pp. 183–204.

Marrou, H. I. *The Meaning of History* (Dublin: Helicon, 1966) = *De la connaissance historique*, 4th edn (Paris: Editions du Seuil, 1959).

Mayes, A. D. H. 'Sociology and the Old Testament' in: *The World of Ancient Israel*, ed. R. Clements (Cambridge: Cambridge University Press, 1989), pp. 39–63.

Mays, J. L. 'Historical and Canonical' *Magnalia Dei*, ed. Cross, F. M. *et al.* (Garden City: Doubleday, 1976), pp. 510–28.
'What is Written' *HBT* 2 (1980), 151–63.

Medick, H. ' "Missionare im Ruderboot"? Ethnologische Erkenntnisweisen als Herausforderung an die Sozialgeschichte' *Geschichte und Gesellschaft* 10 (1984), 295–319.

Meeks, W. A. 'A Hermeneutics of Social Embodiment' *HTR* 79 (1986), 176–86.

Meinecke, F. 'Johann Gustav Droysen' *Hist.Zeit.* 141 (1929), 249–87. *Werke* IV (Stuttgart: K. F. Koehler, 1959).
Historism: The Rise of a New Historical Outlook, trans. Anderson, J. E. (London: Routledge & Kegan Paul, 1972).

Mendenhall, G. E. *The Tenth Generation* (Baltimore: Johns Hopkins, 1973).
'Ancient Israel's Hyphenated History' in: *Palestine in Transition*, ed. Freedman, D. N. and Graff, G. (Sheffield, Almond, 1983), pp. 91–103.

Meyers, C. *Discovering Eve: Ancient Israelite Women in Context* (Oxford: Oxford University Press, 1988).

Michalson, G. E. 'Lessing, Kierkegaard and the Ugly Ditch' *JR* 59 (1979), 324–34.
'Theology, Historical Knowledge, and the Contingency-Necessity Distinction' *Internat. Journ. for the Philos. of Relig.* 14 (1983), 87–98.

Middleton, J. and Tait, D. *Tribes Without Rulers* (London: Routledge & Kegan Paul, 1958).

Miller, J. Hillis 'Tradition and Difference' *Diacritics* 2 (1972) 6–13.
'The Critic as Host' *Crit.Inqu.* 3 (1977), 439–47.

Miller, P. D. 'Faith and Ideology in the Old Testament' in: *Magnalia Dei*, ed. Cross, F. M. *et al.* (Garden City: Doubleday, 1976), pp. 464–79.

Miller, P. D. *et al.* eds. *Ancient Israelite Religion* (Philadelphia: Fortress, 1987).

Miller, W. B. 'Two Concepts of Authority' *Am. Anthrop.* 57 (1955), 271–89.

Mink, L. O. 'History and Fiction as Modes of Comprehension' in: *New Directions in Literary History*, ed. Cohen, R. (London: Routledge & Kegan Paul, 1974), pp. 107–24.

'Narrative Form as a Cognitive Instrument' in Canary and Kozicki (1978), pp. 129–49.

Mitchell, T. C. 'The Meaning of the Noun ḤTN in the Old Testament' *VT* 19 (1969), 93–112.

Momigliano, A. 'Historiography on Written Tradition and Historiography on Oral Tradition' *Studies in Historiography* (London: Weidenfeld & Nicholson, 1966), pp. 211–20.

Morgan, R. 'Gabler's Bicentenary' *Expos.T.* 98 (1987), 164–8.

Morgan, R. with Barton, J. *Biblical Interpretation* (Oxford: Oxford University Press, 1988).

Morgenstern, J. 'The "Bloody Husband"(?) (Exodus 4: 24–26) Once Again' *HUCA* 34 (1963), 35–70.

Morris, T. V. *Understanding Identity Statements* (Aberdeen: Aberdeen University Press, 1984).

Mowinckel, S. 'Israelite Historiography' *Annual of the Swedish Theological Institute* 2 (1963), 4–26.

Muilenburg, J. 'Form Criticism and Beyond' *JBL* 89 (1969), 1–18.

Munson, H. 'Geertz on Religion: the Theory and the Practice' *Religion* 16 (1986), 19–32.

Munz, P. 'History and Myth' *Philos. Quart.* 6 (1956), 1–16.

Murphy, N. and McClendon, J. W. 'Distinguishing Modern and Postmodern Theologies' *Mod. Theol* 5 (1989), 191–214.

Murray, M. 'The New Hermeneutic and the Interpretation of Poetry' *Univ. of Ottawa Quart.* 50 (1980), 374–94.

Naumann, M. 'Literary Production and Reception' *New Lit. Hist.* 8 (1976), 107–26.

Nicholson, E. W. 'Israelite Religion in the Pre-Exilic Period: A Debate Renewed' in: *A Word in Season*, ed. Martin, J. D. and Davies, P. R. (Sheffield: JSOT, 1986), pp. 3–34.

Nielsen, E. 'The Traditio-historical Study of the Pentateuch since 1945, with Special Emphasis on Scandinavia' in: *The Productions of Time*, ed. Jeppesen, K. and Otzen, B. (Sheffield: Almond, 1984), pp. 11–28.

Noth, M. *A History of Pentateuchal Traditions* (Englewood Cliffs NJ: Prentice-Hall, 1972).

'Geschichtsschreibung, Im AT' *Die Religion in Geschichte und Gegenwart* (Tübingen: Mohr/Siebeck, 1958), cols. 1,498–501.

Oakeshott, M. 'The Activity of Being an Historian' *Rationalism in Politics and other Essays* (London: Methuen, 1962), pp. 37–67.

Oden, R. A. 'Hermeneutics and Historiography: Germany and America' in: *SBL 1980 Seminar Papers*, ed. Achtemeier, P. J. (Chico: Scholars Press, 1980), pp. 135–57.

Oeming, M. 'Bedeutung und Funktionen von Fiktionen in der alttestamentlichen Geschichtsschreibung' *Ev.Th.* 44 (1984), 254–66.

    Gesamtbiblische Theologien der Gegenwart (Stuttgart: Kohlhammer, 1985).

    'Text-Kontext-Kanon' *JBT* 3 (1988), 241–51.

Ohmann, R. 'Speech Acts and the Definition of Literature' *Philosophy and Rhetoric* 4, 9 (1971), 1–19.

Ollenburger, B. C. 'Biblical Theology: Situating the Discipline' in: *Understanding the Word*, ed. Butler, J. T. et al. (Sheffield: JSOT, 1985), pp. 37–62.

Olrik, A. 'Epic Laws of Folk Narrative' in: *The Study of Folklore* (Englewood Cliffs NH: Prentice-Hall, 1965), pp. 131–41.

Olyan, S. M. *Asherah and the Cult of Yahweh in Israel* (Atlanta: Scholars Press, 1988).

Ommen, T. B. 'Bultmann and Gadamer' *Thought* 59 (1984), 348–59.

Oppenheim, A. L. *Ancient Mesopotamia* (Chicago: Chicago University Press, 1964).

Otto, R. *The Philosophy of Religion based on Kant and Fries* (London: Williams & Norgate, 1931).

Outhwaite, W. *Understanding Social Life* (London: Allen & Unwin, 1975).

    'Hans-Georg Gadamer' in Skinner (1985), pp. 23–39.

Pannenberg, W. 'Hermeneutics and Universal History' *History and Hermeneutic* (New York: Harper & Row, 1967), pp. 122–52 = 'Hermeneutik und Universalgeschichte' *ZTK* 60 (1963), 90–121.

Pecher, E. 'The New Historicism and its Discontents' *PMLA* 102 (1987), 292–303.

Pike, K. 'Towards a Theory of the Structure of Human Behaviour' in: *Language in Culture and Society*, ed. Hymes, D. (New York: Harper & Row, 1964), pp. 154–61.

Plantinga, A. and Wolterstorff, N. eds. *Faith and Rationality* (Notre Dame: Notre Dame University Press, 1983).

Polzin, R. *Moses and the Deuteronomist* (New York: Seabury, 1980).

Popper, K. *The Poverty of Historicism* (London: Routledge & Kegan Paul, 1957).

    'The Sociology of Knowledge' in: *The Sociology of Knowledge: A Reader*, ed. Curtis, J. E. and Petras, J. W. (London: Duckworth, 1970), pp. 649–67.

'Normal Science and Its Dangers' in Lakatos and Musgrave (1970), pp. 51–58.

Objective Knowledge (Oxford: Oxford University Press, 1972).

Pospisil, L. 'Law and Order' in: *Introduction to Cultural Anthropology*, ed. Clifton, J. A. (Boston: Houghton Mifflin, 1968), pp. 201–22.

Priest, J. F. 'Canon and Criticism' *JAAR* 48 (1980), 259–71.

Prince, H. 'Fernand Braudel and Total History' *Journal of Historical Geography* 1 (1975), 103–6.

Quine, W. V. O. *Word and Object* (Cambridge MA: MIT, 1960).

From a Logical Point of View (New York: Harper & Row, 1963).

Rabinowitz, P. 'Truth in Fiction: A Reexamination of Audiences' *Crit. Inqu.* 4 (1977), 121–42.

Rabinow, P. 'Humanism as Nihilism' in: *Social Science as Moral Inquiry*, ed. Haan, N. *et al.* (New York: Columbia University Press, 1983), pp. 52–75.

Rabinow, P. and Sullivan W. M. eds. *Interpretive Social Science* (Berkeley: University of California Press, 1979).

Ravenhill, P. L. 'Religious Utterances and the Theory of Speech Acts' in: *Language in Religious Practice*, ed. Samarin, W. J. (Rowley: Newbury, 1976), pp. 26–39.

Ray, W. *Literary Meaning: From Phenomenology to Deconstruction* (Oxford: Blackwell, 1984).

Rendtorff, R. *Gesammelte Studien zum Alten Testament* (Munich: Kaiser, 1975).

'Zur Bedeutung des Kanons für eine Theologie des Alten Testaments' in: *'Wenn nicht jetzt, wann dann?' Aufsätze für J. J. Kraus* eds. Geyer, H. G. *et al.* (Neukirchen-Vluyn: Neukirchener, 1983), pp. 3–11.

'Between Historical Criticism and Holistic Interpretation: New Trends in Old Testament Exegesis' *VTS* 40 (1988), 298–303.

'Jesaja 6 im Rahmen der Composition des Jesajabuches' *BETL* 81 (1989), 73–82.

Rendtorff, O. and Graf, F. W. 'Ernst Troeltsch' in: *Nineteenth-Century Religious Thought in the West Vol.* III, ed. Smart, N. *et al.* (Cambridge: Cambridge University Press, 1985), pp. 305–28.

Reventlow, H. G. 'Basic Problems in Old Testament Theology' *JSOT* 11 (1979), 2–22.

The Authority of the Bible and the Rise of the Modern World (London: SCM, 1984).

Richter, W. *Exegese als Literaturwissenschaft* (Göttingen: Vandenhoeck & Ruprecht, 1971).

Ricoeur, P. *The Contribution of French Historiography to the Theory of History*, Zaharoff Lectures 1978–9 (Oxford: Clarendon, 1980).

Hermeneutics and the Human Sciences, ed. Thompson, J. B. (Cambridge: Cambridge University Press, 1981).

Roberts, J. J. M. 'Myth versus History' *CBQ* 38 (1976), 1–13.

Rogerson, J. W. 'Recent Structuralist Approaches to Biblical Interpretation' *The Churchman* 90 (1976), 165–77.

Anthropology and the Old Testament (Oxford: Blackwell, 1978).

Old Testament Criticism in the Nineteenth Century: England and Germany (London: SPCK, 1984).

'The Use of Sociology in Old Testament Studies' *SVT* 36 (1985), 245–56.

Rohrbaugh, R. L. ' "Social Location of Thought" as a Heuristic Construct in New Testament Study' *JSNT* 30 (1987), 103–19.

Rooney, E. Review of W. C. Booth's *Critical Understanding: The Powers and Limits of Pluralism*, *MLN* 97 (1982), 1,232–4.

Rorty, R. *Philosophy and the Mirror of Nature* (Princeton: Princeton University Press, 1979).

'Deconstruction and Circumvention' *Crit. Inqu.* 11 (1984), 1–23.

'Historiography of Philosophy: Four Genres' in: *Philosophy in History*, ed. Rorty, R. *et al.* (Cambridge: Cambridge University Press, 1984), pp. 49–75.

'Habermas and Lyotard on Postmodernity' in: *Habermas and Modernity*, ed. Bernstein, R. J. (Cambridge: Polity, 1985), pp. 161–75.

Routh, J. 'A Reputation Made: Lucien Goldmann' in Routh and Wolff (1977), pp. 150–62.

Routh, J. and Wolff, J. *The Sociology of Literature* (Keele: University of Keele Press, 1977).

Rumscheidt, H. M. *Revelation and Theology: An Analysis of the Barth-Harnack Correspondence of 1923* (Cambridge: Cambridge University Press, 1972).

Runciman, W. G. *A Treatise on Social Theory Vol* I: *The Methodology of Social Theory* (Cambridge: Cambridge University Press, 1983).

Saebø, M. 'Johann Philipp Gablers Bedeutung für die Biblische Theologie' *ZAW* 99 (1987), 1–16.

'Vom Zusammendenken zum Kanon. Aspekte der traditionsgeschichtlichen Endstadien des Alten Testaments' *JBT* 3 (1988), 115–33.

Said, E. W. 'The Text, The World, the Critic' in: *Textual Strategies*, ed. Harari, J. V. (Ithaca: Cornell University Press, 1979), pp. 161–88.

Sanders, J. A. 'Cave 11 Surprises and the Question of Canon' *McCormick Quarterly* 21 (1968), pp. 284–98; reprinted in Leiman (1974), pp. 37–51.

'Models of God's Government' *Interp.* 24 (1970), pp. 359–68.

Torah and Canon (Philadelphia: Fortress, 1972).

'Adaptable for Life: The Nature and Function of Canon' in: *Magnalia Dei*, ed. Cross, F. M. *et al.* (Garden City: Doubleday, 1976), pp. 531–59.

'Text and Canon: Concepts and Method' *JBL* 98 (1979), 5–29.

'Canonical Context and Canonical Criticism' *HBT* 2 (1980), 173–97.

Canon and Community: A Guide to Canonical Criticism (Philadelphia: Fortress, 1984).

From Sacred Story to Sacred Text (Philadelphia: Fortress, 1987).

Sandys-Wunsch, J. and Eldridge, L. 'J. P. Gabler and the Distinction between Biblical and Dogmatic Theology: Translation, Commentary, and Discussion of his Originality' *SJT* 33 (1980), 135–58.

Sawyer, J. F. A. *Semantics in Biblical Research* (London: SCM, 1972).

'The "Original Meaning" of the Text and Other Legitimate Subjects for Semantic Description' *BETL* 33 (1974), 63–70.

'A Change of Emphasis in the Study of the Prophets' in: *Israel's Prophetic Tradition*, ed. Coggins, R. J. *et al.* (Cambridge: Cambridge University Press, 1982), pp. 233–49.

'The Role of Jewish Studies in Biblical Semantics' in: *Scripta Signa Vocis*, Festschrift for Hans Hospers (Groningen: Forsten, 1986), pp. 201–7.

'Blessed be my People Egypt' in: *A Word in Season*, ed. Martin, J. D. and Davies, P. D. (Sheffield: JSOT, 1986), pp. 57–71.

Schleiermacher, F. D. E. 'The Hermeneutics: Outline of the 1819 Lectures' *NLH* 10 (1978), pp. 1–16.

Schmidt, H. J. 'Text-adequate Concretizations' *New German Critique* 17 (1979), pp. 157–69.

Schnädelbach, H. *Geschichtsphilosophie nach Hegel: Die Probleme des Historismus* (Freiburg: Karl Alber, 1974).

Schneiders, S. M. 'Faith, Hermeneutics and the Literal Sense of Scripture' *Theological Studies* 39 (1978), 719–36.

Schott, R. 'Das Geschichtsbewusstsein schriftloser Völker' *Archiv für Begriffsgeschichte* 12 (1968), pp. 166–205.

Schulin, E. 'Das Problem der Individualität' *Historische Zeitschrift* 197 (1963), pp. 102–33.

Searle, J. *Speech Acts* (Cambridge: Cambridge University Press, 1969).

Intentionality (Cambridge: Cambridge University Press, 1983).

Shapiro, G. and Sica, A. eds. *Hermeneutics* (Amherst: University of Massachusetts Press, 1984).

Sheppard, G. 'Canon Criticism: The Proposal of Brevard Childs and an Assessment for Evangelical Hermeneutics' *Studia Biblica et Theologica* 4 (1974), 3–17.

Wisdom as a Hermeneutical Construct (Berlin: de Gruyter, 1980).

'Canonization: Hearing the Voice of the Same God through Historically Dissimilar Traditions' *Interp.* 36 (1982), 21–33; reprinted in *Ex Auditu* 1 (1985), 106–14.

'Barr on Canon and Childs: Can One Read the Bible as Scripture?' *TSF Bulletin* Nov.-Dec. 1983, 2–4.

Shils, E. 'The Concept and Function of Ideology' in: *International Encyclopedia of the Social Sciences* VII, ed. Sills, D. (London: Macmillan, 1968), pp. 66–76.

'Tradition' *Comparative Studies in Society and History* 13 (1971), 122–59.

Shklovsky, V. 'Art as Technique' in: *Russian Formalist Critics* (Lincoln: University of Nebraska Press, 1965), pp. 3–24.

Shweder, R. A. 'Anthropology's Romantic Rebellion against the Enlightenment' in: *Culture Theory*, ed. Shweder, R. A. and Le Vine, R. A. (Cambridge: Cambridge University Press, 1984), pp. 27–66.

Skinner, Q. 'Meaning and Understanding in the History of Ideas' *History and Theory* 8 (1969), 3–53.

'Motives, Intentions, and the Interpretation of Texts' *NLH* 3 (1972), 393–408.

'Hermeneutics and the Role of History' *NLH* 7 (1975), 209–32.

Skinner, Q. ed. *The Return of Grand Theory in the Human Sciences* (Cambridge: Cambridge University Press, 1985).

Smend, R. 'Universalismus und Partikularismus in der alttestamentlichen Theologie des 19, Jahrhunderts' *Ev. Th.* 22 (1962), 169–79.

'Johann Philipp Gablers Begründung der biblischen Theologie' *Ev. Th.* 2 (1962), pp. 345–57.

'Nachkritische Schriftauslegung' in: *Parrhesia: Karl Barth zum achtzigsten Geburtstag* (Zürich: EVZ, 1966), pp. 215–37.

'Questions about the Importance of the Canon in the Old Testament Introduction' *JSOT* 16 (1980), 45–51.

Smith, J. Z. 'Sacred Persistence: Toward a Redescription of Canon' *Imagining Religion: From Babylon to Jonestown* (Chicago: Chicago University Press, 1982), pp. 36–52.

Smith, M. 'The Common Theology of the Ancient Near East' *JBL* 71 (1952), 135–47.

Palestinian Parties and Politics that Shaped the Old Testament (New York: Columbia University Press, 1971).

Snyder, L. L. 'Nationalistic Aspects of the Grimm Brothers' Fairy Tales' *Journal of Social Psychology* 33 (1951), 209–23.

Soggin, J. A. *Introduction to the Old Testament* (Philadelphia: Westminster, 1980).

Sperber, D. 'Interpretive Ethnography and Theoretical Anthropology' *On Anthropological Knowledge* (Cambridge: Cambridge University Press, 1982), pp. 9–34.

Sperber, D. and Wilson, D. 'Mutual Knowledge and Relevance in Theories of Comprehension' in: *Mutual Knowledge*, ed. Smith, N. V. (London: Academic, 1982).

Relevance: Communication and Cognition (Oxford: Blackwell, 1986).

Spina, F. 'Canonical Criticism: Childs versus Sanders' in: *Interpreting God's Word for Today*, ed. McCown, W. and Massey, J. E. (Anderson: Warner, 1982), pp. 165–94.

Spinoza, B. *Tractatus Theologico-Politicus: The Chief Works of Benedict de Spinoza* I, trans. Elwes, R. H. M. (London: George Bell, 1909).

Steiger, L. 'Revelation-History and Theological Reason' *Journal for Theology and the Church* 4 (1967), 82–106.

Sternberg, M. *The Poetics of Biblical Narrative* (Bloomington: Indiana University Press, 1985).

Stierle, K. H. 'Story as Exemplum – Exemplum as Story' in: *New Perspectives in German Literary Criticism*, ed. Amacher, R. E. and Lange, V. (Princeton: Princeton University Press, 1979), pp. 389–417.

'The Reading of Fictional Texts' in Suleiman and Crosman (1981), pp. 83–105.

Stobbe, H. G. *Hermeneutik: Ein Oekumenisches Problem* (Zurich: Benziger, 1981).

Stock, B. 'Literary Discourse and the Social Historian' *New Lit. Hist.* 8 (1977), 183–94.

Stocking, G. W. 'Introduction: The Basic Assumptions of Boasian Anthropology' in: *The Shaping of American Anthropology 1883–1911: A Franz Boaz Reader*, ed. Stocking, G. W. (New York: Basic Books, 1974), pp. 1–20.

Stone, L. 'The Revival of Narrative: Reflections on a New Old History' *Past & Present* 85 (1979), 3–24.

Stout, J. *The Flight from Authority: Religion, Morality and the Quest for Autonomy* (Notre Dame: Notre Dame University Press, 1981).

'What is the Meaning of a Text?' *New Lit. Hist.* 19 (1982), 1–12.

'A Lexicon of Postmodern Philosophy' *Rel. Stud. Rev.* 13 (1987), 18–22.

Struever, N. S. 'The Study of Language and the Study of History' *Journal of Interdisciplinary History* 4 (1974), 401–15.

Suleiman, S. R. 'Varieties of Audience-Oriented Criticism', in Suleiman and Crosman (1981), pp. 3–45.

Suleiman, S. R. and Crosman, I. eds. *The Reader in the Text* (Princeton: Princeton University Press, 1981).

Sundberg, A. C. *The Old Testament of the Early Church* (Cambridge: Harvard University Press, 1964).

'The "Old Testament": A Christian Canon' *CBQ* 30 (1968), 143–55; reprinted in Leiman (1974), pp. 99–111.

Sykes, S. *The Identity of Christianity* (London: SPCK, 1984).

Tarski, A. 'The Semantic Conception of Truth' *Philosophy and Phenomenological Research* 4 (1944), 341–76.

Taylor, M. K. 'Symbolic Dimensions in Cultural Anthropology' *Curr. Anthrop.* 26 (1985), 167–85.

Thiemann, R. F. *Revelation and Theology* (Notre Dame: Notre Dame University Press, 1985).

Thompson, T. L. *The Historicity of the Patriarchal Narratives* BZAW 133 (Berlin: de Gruyter, 1974).

Tilly, T. W. 'Incommensurability, Intratextuality, and Fideism' *Mod. Theol.* 5 (1989), 87–111.

Tomashevski, B. 'Literature and Biography' in: *Readings in Russian Poetics* ed. Matejka, L. and Pomorska, K. (Cambridge MA: MIT, 1971), pp. 47–55.

Tompkins, J. P. ed. *Reader-Response Criticism* (Baltimore: Johns Hopkins, 1980).

Tracy, D. *The Analogical Imagination* (London: SCM, 1981).

'Lindbeck's New Program for Theology: A Reflection' *Thomist* 49 (1985) 46–72.

Plurality and Ambiguity (London: Harper & Row, 1987).

Trigg, R. *Understanding Social Science* (Oxford: Blackwell, 1985).

Troeltsch, E. 'The Dogmatics of the "religionsgeschichtliche Schule" ' *The American Journal of Theology* 17 (1913), 1–21.

'Ueber historische und dogmatische Methode in der Theologie' *Gesammelte Schriften* II (1922), reprinted (Aalen: Scientia, 1962), pp. 729–52.

Christian Thought (London: University of London Press, 1923) = *Der Historismus und seine Ueberwindung* (Berlin: Rolf Heise, 1924).

Turner, V. 'Social Dramas and Stories about Them' *Crit. Inqu.* 7 (1980–1, pp. 141–68.

van Dijk, T. A. *Pragmatics of Language and Literature* (Amsterdam: North Holland, 1976).

van Seters, J. *Abraham in History and Tradition* (New Haven: Yale, 1975).

'The Religion of the Patriarchs in Genesis' *Biblica* 61 (1980), 220–33.

In Search of History (New Haven: Yale, 1983).

Vermes, G. 'Baptism and Jewish Exegesis: New Light from Ancient Sources' *NTS* 4 (1957–58), 308–19.

'Biblical Studies and the Dead Sea Scrolls 1947–1987: Retrospects and Prospects' *JSOT* 39 (1987), 113–28.
von Campenhausen, H. *The Formation of the Christian Bible* (Philadelphia: Fortress, 1972).
von Rad, G. 'Die falschen Propheten' *ZAW* (1933), pp. 109–20.
'History and the Patriarchs' *Expos.T.* 72 (1961), pp. 213–16.
The Problem of the Hexateuch and Other Essays (Edinburgh: Oliver & Boyd, 1966).
God at Work in History (Nashville: Abingdon, 1980).
von Ranke, L. *The Theory and Practice of History*, ed. Iggers, G. G. and Moltke, K. (New York: Irvington, 1983).
von Wright, G. H. *Explanation and Understanding* (London: Routledge & Kegan Paul, 1971).
Waldman, M. R. *Toward a Theory of Historical Narrative: A Case Study in Perso-Islamicate Historiography* (Columbus: Ohio State University Press, 1980).
Walsh, W. H. 'The Practical and the Historical Past' in: *Politics and Experience*, ed. King, P. and Parekh, B. C. (Cambridge: Cambridge University Press, 1968), pp. 5–18.
Warner, S. M. 'Primitive Saga Men' *VT* 29 (1979), 325–35.
Warning, R. 'Rezeptionsästhetik als literaturwissenschaftliche Pragmatik' in: *Rezeptionsästhetik*, ed. Warning, R. (Munich: Fink, 1975), pp. 9–41.
Weder, H. 'Zum Problem einer 'Christlichen Exegese'' *NTS* 27 (1980–1), 64–82.
Wehler, H. U. *Geschichte als Historische Sozialwissenschaft* (Frankfurt: Suhrkamp, 1973).
Weigert, A. J., Teitge, J. and D. W. *Society and Identity* (Cambridge: Cambridge University Press, 1986).
Weinsheimer, J. C. *Gadamer's Hermeneutics: A Reading of Truth and Method* (New Haven: Yale University Press, 1985).
Weiser, A. *Introduction to the Old Testament* (London: Darton, Longman & Todd, 1961).
Weippert, M. 'Fragen des israelitischen Geschichtsbewusstseins' *VT* 23 (1973), 415–42.
West, G. D. 'Reading "The Text" and Reading "Behind the Text": The Cain and Abel Story in a Context of Liberation' in: *The Bible in Three Dimensions* ed. Clines, D., Fowl, S. and Porter, S. (Sheffield: Sheffield Academic Press, 1990), pp. 299–320.
Westermann, C. 'Zur Auslegung des Alten Testaments' in: *Hermeneutik als Weg heutiger Wissenschaft*, ed. Warnach, V. (Salzburg: Anton Pustet, 1971), pp. 197–230.
'The Old Testament's View of History in Relation to that of the

Enlightenment' in: *Understanding the Word*, ed. Butler, J. T. *et al.* (Sheffield: JSOT, 1985), pp. 207–19.

Wharton, J. A. 'Splendid Failure or Flawed Success?' *Interp.* 29 (1975), 266–76.

White, H. *Metahistory: The Historical Imagination in Nineteenth Century Europe* (Baltimore: Johns Hopkins, 1973).

'Historical Text as Literary Artifact' in Canary and Kozicki (1978), pp. 41–62.

'Michel Foucault' in: *Structuralism and Since*, ed. Sturrock, J. (Oxford: Oxford University Press, 1979), pp. 81–115.

'The Question of Narrative in Contemporary Historical Theory' *History and Theory* 23 (1984), 1–33.

Whitelam, K. W. 'Recreating the History of Israel' *JSOT* 35 (1986), 45–70.

Whybray, N. 'Reflections on Canonical Criticism' *Theology* 84 (1981), 29–35.

The Making of the Pentateuch (Sheffield: JSOT, 1987).

Williams, R. *Marxism and Literature* (Oxford: Oxford University Press, 1977).

Williams, R. D. 'Postmodern Theology and the Judgment of the World' in: *Postmodern Theology*, ed. F. B. Burnham (London: Harper & Row, 1989), pp. 92–11.

Wimsatt, W. K. and Beardsley, M. C. 'The Intentional Fallacy' (1946) in: *20th Century Literary Criticism*, ed. Lodge, D. (London: Longman, 1972), pp. 334–45.

Winton, A. P. *The Proverbs of Jesus: Issues of History and Rhetoric* (Sheffield: Sheffield Academic Press, 1990).

Wise, G. *American Historical Explanations* (Homewood: Dorsey, 1973).

Wolff, J. *Hermeneutic Philosophy and the Sociology of Art* (London: Routledge & Kegan Paul, 1975).

'The Interpretation of Literature in Society: The Hermeneutic Approach', in Routh & Wolff (1977), pp. 18–31.

Wolin, R. *Walter Benjamin: An Aesthetic of Redemption* (New York: Columbia University Press, 1982).

Wright, G. E. 'Archaeology and Old Testament Studies' *JBL* 77 (1958), 39–51.

'History and the Patriarchs' *Expos. T.* 71 (1960), 292–6.

Ziff, P. 'On H. P. Grice's Account of Meaning' *Analysis* 28 (1967), 1–8.

Zimmerli, W. Review of Childs's *Introduction to the Old Testament as Scripture VT* 31 (1981), 235–44.

Bibliographical key to the works of Brevard S. Childs

1958a 'Jonah: A Study in Old Testament Hermeneutics' *SJT* 11: 53–61.
1958b 'Prophecy and Fulfilment' *Interp.* 12: 259–71.
1959 'The Enemy from the North and the Chaos Tradition' *JBL* 78: 187–98.
1960 *Myth and Reality in the Old Testament* (London: SCM).
1962 *Memory and Tradition in Israel* (London: SCM).
1963 'A Study of the Formula 'Until this Day'' *JBL* 82: 279–92.
1964 'Interpretation in Faith' *Interp* 18: 432–49.
1965 'The Birth of Moses' *JBL* 84: 109–22.
1967a *Isaiah and the Assyrian Crisis* (London: SCM).
1967b 'Deuteronomic Formulae of the Exodus Traditions' *SVT* 16: 30–9.
1969a 'Psalm 8 in the Context of the Christian Canon' *Interp.* 23: 20–31.
1969b 'Karl Barth as Interpreter of Scripture' in: *Karl Barth and The Future of Theology Memorial Colloquium*, Yale Divinity School, Jan. 1969, ed. D. L. Dickerman (New Haven: Yale Divinity School Assoc.): 30–9.
1970a *Biblical Theology in Crisis* (Philadelphia: Westminster).
1970b 'A Traditio-historical Study of the Reed Sea Tradition' *VT* 20: 406–18.
1971 'Psalm Titles and Midrashic Exegesis' *JSS* 16: 137–50.
1972a 'The Old Testament as Scripture of the Church' *Concordia Theological Monthly* 43: 709–22
1972b 'Midrash and the Old Testament' in: *Understanding the Sacred Text*, ed. J. Reumann (Valley Forge: Judson): 47–59.
1972c Sprunt Lectures (unpublished).
1972d 'A Tale of Two Testaments' *Interp.* 26: 20–9.
1973 Review of Sanders, *Torah and Canon, Interp.* 27: 88–91.
1974a *Exodus* (London: SCM).
1974b 'The Etiological Tale Re-examined' *VT* 24: 387–97.

1976a 'Reflections on the Modern Study of the Psalms' in: *Magnalia Dei*, ed. F. M. Cross *et al.* (Garden City: Doubleday): 377–88.
1976b 'The Search for Biblical Authority Today' *Andover Newton Quarterly* 16: 199–206.
1977a 'The Exegetical Significance of Canon' *VTS* 29: 66–88.
1977b 'The Sensus Literalis of Scripture: An Ancient and Modern Problem' in: *Beiträge zur Alttestamentlichen Theologie Festschrift Zimmerli*, ed. H. Donner *et al.* (Göttingen: Vandenhoeck & Ruprecht): 80–93.
1977c 'Symposium on Biblical Criticism' *TT* 33: 358–9.
1978a 'The Canonical Shape of the Prophetic Literature' *Interp.* 32: 46–68.
1978b 'Canonical Shape of the Book of Jonah' in: *Biblical and Near Eastern Studies*, ed. G. A. Tuttle (Grand Rapids: Eerdmans, 1978), 122–8.
1979 *Introduction to the Old Testament as Scripture* (London: SCM).
1980a 'A Response' *HBT* 2: 199–211.
1980b 'Response to Reviewers' *JSOT* 16: 52–60.
1980c 'On Reading the Elijah Narratives' *Interp.* 34: 128–37.
1982a 'Some Reflections on the Search for a Biblical Theology' *HBT* 4: 1–12.
1982b 'Wellhausen in English' *Semeia* 25: 83–8.
1984a *The New Testament as Canon: An Introduction* (London: SCM).
1984b Review of Barr, *Holy Scripture,*' *Interp.* 38: 66–70.
1985 *Old Testament Theology in a Canonical Context* (London: SCM).
1986 'Gerhard von Rad in American Dress' in: *The Hermeneutical Quest*, ed. D. G. Miller (Allison Park: Pickwick): 77–86.
1987a 'Die Bedeutung des jüdischen Kanons in der alttestamentlichen Theologie' in: *Mitte der Schrift? Ein jüdisch-christliches Gespräch* ed. M. Klopfenstein *et al.* (Bern): 269–81.
1987b 'Death and Dying in Old Testament Theology' in: *Love and Death in the Ancient Near East*, ed. J. H. Marks and R. M. Good (Guildford: Four Quarters Publishing Co.): 89–91.
1987c 'Die theologische Bedeutung der Endform eines biblischen Textes' *Theologische Quartalschrift* : 242–51.
1988 'Biblische Theologie und der christliche Kanon' *Jahrbuch für biblische Theologie* 3: 13–27.
1990 'Critical Reflections on James Barr's Understanding of the Literal and the Allegorical' *JSOT* 46: 3–9.

Index of Old Testament references

231

Subject index

233

Author index

235